THE LOGIC OF SOCIETY

THE LOGIC OF SOCIETY

A

Philosophical

Study

by

LAIRD ADDIS

UNIVERSITY OF MINNESOTA PRESS, MINNEAPOLIS

Printed in the United States of America
at North Central Publishing Co., St. Paul, Minnesota.
Published in Canada by Burns & MacEachern Limited, Don Mills, Ontario

Library of Congress Catalog Card Number: 74-83131

ISBN 0-8166-0733-8

Acknowledgments

The first draft of the essay that follows was written during my tenure as a Senior Fulbright Lecturer at the State University of Groningen during the academic year 1970–71. My family and I were shown the warmest of hospitality by the Dutch community and especially by the members of the Philosophical Institute of the university and its director, Prof. Dr. Bernard Delfgaauw. I was provided with a virtually ideal atmosphere for scholarly writing. Conversations with three members of the Institute, Prof. Dr. H. G. Hubbeling, Prof. Dr. L. W. Nauta, and Dr. G. M. A. Corver, were especially helpful to me, particularly in regard to the third chapter.

Those who know the work of my friend, colleague, and former teacher Gustav Bergmann would be able to tell, even without benefit of the frequent references to him, how great my debt is to him. Almost the same can be said of what I owe to May Brodbeck, one of the foremost of contemporary philosophers of the social sciences. Those who know their work well may also recognize my differences with each of them even when they are not explicit in the text.

Materials in the third and fifth chapters were delivered as lectures at the University of Kent at Canterbury, England; the University College of Swansea, Wales; and the University of Bergen, Norway. I have benefited from comments received at all three universities.

The chapters on reduction, the fourth and the fifth, were considerably influenced by discussions with Carol O. Copeland, presently of the Department of Psychology at the University of Pittsburgh.

My wife, Patricia Addis, and my father, Laird Addis, Sr., both were involved in the typing of the manuscript and in making useful suggestions on many points.

The Graduate College of my home institution, the University of Iowa, facilitated the publication of this book by providing me with generous financial assistance, partly in the form of an Old Gold Summer Faculty Research Fellowship.

The material of the seventh chapter is taken substantially from my "Historicism and Historical Laws of Development" which appeared in *Inquiry*, 11, 1968. Permission to use it has been received from the journal and its publisher, Universitetsforlaget, Oslo.

L. A.

January 1975

Contents

THE LOGIC OF SOCIETY

I Introduction

In recent years there have arisen from several quarters, even within analytic philosophy itself, various challenges to the "positivist" conception of science, especially in its application to history and the social sciences. With several qualifications, the present essay may be described as a positivist's attempt to meet some of those challenges. Some of my reservations will be indicated in the first section of this chapter, *general frame of reference*. Then I shall outline in a few paragraphs the *themes of the essay*. This introductory chapter is, finally, the appropriate place to take care of *some matters of ontology*.

General Frame of Reference

One recent challenge to the positivist view of social science, albeit of a form less extreme than many others, is to be found in von Wright's book *Explanation and Understanding*. In it he characterizes the positivist position as follows:

> One of the tenets of positivism is *methodological monism*, or the idea of the unity of scientific method amidst the diversity of subject matter of scientific investigation. A second tenet is the view that the exact natural sciences, in particular mathematical physics, set a methodological ideal or standard which measures the degree of development and perfection of all the other sciences, including the humanities. A third tenet, finally, is a characteristic view of scientific explanation. Such explanation is, in a broad sense, "causal." It consists, more specifically, in the subsumption of individual cases under hypothetically assumed general laws of nature, including "human nature." The attitude towards finalistic explanations, *i.e.* towards attempts to account for facts in terms of intentions, goals, purposes, is either to reject them as unscientific or to try to show that they can, when duly purified of "animist" or "vitalist" remains, be transformed into causal explanations.[1]

With respect to von Wright's first tenet I shall maintain that while the methods of generating hypotheses may very well differ in some degree from science to science and especially between the natural sciences and the social sciences, the tasks of confirmation and falsification as well as the kinds of facts (lawful connections) that are discovered are essentially the same in all the sciences. One might agree with Abel, for example, that although the method of *verstehen* may be of some use in suggesting hypotheses in the human sciences, it cannot also provide the confirmation or falsification of those same hypotheses.[2] The latter tasks can only be done by the "usual" methods of observation, experimentation when possible, and the like. As for the second tenet, it will be one of the major contentions of this book that no human science, at least as their limits of investigation are usually conceived, can reasonably expect ever to approximate physics-chemistry in its "degree of development and perfection." Yet I also shall maintain that the world is such that in principle all phenomena could be accounted for in a science of the scope and reliability of the most highly "developed" sciences. This obviously is in need of further explanation and it will come. But it connects closely with what is expressed in von Wright's third tenet, for here it will be argued analogously — perhaps it really comes down to the same thing — that while every event that occurs in the world is in principle capable of the sort of explanation that is envisioned on the hypothetico-deductive model, it *may* not be a reasonable scientific procedure for the social scientist actually to seek such explanations. Yet the social scientist looking in these pages for any *prescription* of how to go about his business will be disappointed. What he will find, especially in the sixth chapter, is a *description* of the kinds of lawful connections he may in the course of his investigations expect to discover. If he isn't looking for lawful connections ultimately, then, as I conceive the activity, he isn't doing science at all.

As for "finalistic" explanations, the reader will encounter no detailed argument whether or not they are a distinct or even a legitimate species of explanation. What he will find is the assumption, and refutations of some arguments to the contrary, that, whatever be the case with finalistic explanations, every event can be given (again, in principle) a "complete" causal explanation. Questions about the "real" kind(s) of explanation have always perplexed me. Expressed differently, this book embraces a view according to which the world is, in certain crucial respects, the way in which the positivists typically conceived it to be, and so the kinds of explanations they recommended for everything that happens in it are in principle possible; but it does not follow that this approach to the world, even within science, is the only possible or even always the best one. This is not because the world *is* many ways (whatever that might mean), but rather because one and the same event in the one and only world there is may be explainable in quite different senses, according to the purposes at hand.

This essay then is not one in the methodology of the social sciences or even in the philosophy of the social sciences, for I am more concerned with what social phenomena are and the kinds of lawful connections they may have to one another and to other kinds of phenomena than with how social scientists do or ought or might make the kinds of discoveries they do or ought or might. I am in no case interested here in problems of theory construction, axiomatization, measurement, and the like — what we might call the pure methodology of the social sciences. Hence this study might more properly be called one in the philosophy of history.

As the final section of this introductory chapter will show in practice as it were, my acceptance of certain major aspects of the positivist philosophy of science must not be taken as indicating any belief on my part in the impossibility or nonsensicality of metaphysics. Quite the contrary! But I do believe that the philosophy of society, as I conceive it, requires one to take a stand on only a few, relatively superficial questions in ontology. The most important of these is whether there is a real and not merely a linguistic distinction between simple and complex properties. Using the words loosely, then, one could say that the general frame of reference of this essay is one of positivism and its frequent concomitants — determinism and naturalism.

Themes of the Essay

With that brief statement of the point of view from which this book is written in mind, I may proceed to indicate in a few paragraphs the themes of the essay. In the last section of this chapter, I shall try to indicate the extent to which one must settle certain issues of general ontology in order to answer satisfactorily some of the questions of the philosophy of society.

The second and third chapters are still broadly introductory to what I regard as the major chapters. In the first of the two, based on the conviction that a good philosophy of society or history requires an adequate if necessarily (in this context) somewhat sketchy philosophy of science, I indicate with some defense my conceptions of causation and lawfulness as well as characterize some related notions such as those of process and interaction. The other chapter is concerned with outlining a philosophical account of the natures of and connections between conscious states, bodily states, and behavior. In the course of that, I examine briefly the distinction, which some presently make so much of, between behavior and action with a view not to obliterating the distinction but rather of deemphasizing its importance for the philosophy of society. In the final part of that chapter, by way of an examination of MacIntyre's ideas about the relation of belief to action in the social sciences, I am able to indicate in yet more detail my metaphysics of causation and its relation to the nature of mind.

The fourth and fifth chapters deal with what many would consider to be the central questions in the philosophy of society: the nature of social "objects" or facts and the possibilities of sociological explanations being "reduced" to psychological explanations. The resolution of these issues may be described as determining the theoretical — as opposed to the institutional — autonomy (or its lack) of the social sciences. The sixth chapter begins by considering an issue argued very much in recent years: the nature of historical explanation and its relation to the hypothetico-deductive model of explanation. But I shall use this issue as a springboard to considerations of a more general nature: what the world and particularly the social "world" is like with respect to the possibility of explanation and, more importantly, the kinds of lawful connections that may reasonably be supposed to exist among social phenomena.

The main question faced in the seventh chapter is whether or not there are "laws of historical development" and if so what their status might be. Popper devoted a whole book to this question and its relation to historicism, so both historicism and his conception of it are treated, especially his criticism of the idea of prophecy as the "function" of the social sciences. The eighth chapter is devoted to a topic of singular neglect, namely, the logical analysis of monistic theories of society. A monistic theory holds that a certain "factor" or set of "factors" is the only or crucially determining one in the explanation of social phenomena. While monistic theories themselves abound, few philosophers have found it necessary or worth their while to understand the possible logical structures of such theories. Two who have, although in widely differing ways and degrees, Hook and Plamenatz, both undergo some critical examination in this chapter.

The last three chapters are concerned with some traditional issues and problems in the philosophy of society that arose primarily though not exclusively in the context of Marxism. Although the *idéologues* and the Hegelians were both in their ways interested in the role of ideas in society and history, Marx and his successors seriously raised for the first time the *scientific* question of how ideas "function" in society. Unfortunately, the Marxists in large measure also succeeded in confusing this scientific question with the *philosophical* one of idealism and materialism. The ninth chapter is in part an attempt to sort out the questions in a way that avoids this confusion. But it is also concerned with the more general issue of how, in what way, and to what extent intentions are realized in society. This question is picked up from another direction in the main section of the next chapter through a discussion of the role of the individual in history. A related question, that of the freedom of the individual in history, is also taken up, particularly with respect to some distinctions and some possibilities referred to in the chapters on reduction. The tenth chapter also offers the most convenient place to say a few words about purpose in history and society.

The final chapter, on the other hand, besides involving some rather detailed analyses of aspects of Marx's social theory, also provides in its subject matter a convenient way to summarize many of the issues and topics discussed in the preceding chapters. For the social theory of historical materialism is exactly the sort of theory about which one can raise the issues of reductionism, holism, monism, determinism, and so on. Perhaps needless to say, no attempt is made to assess the approximation to empirical truth of the many empirical claims found in the full-blown version of Marx's social theory.

Some Matters of Ontology

If ontological questions are those which, in the manner peculiar to philosophy, are concerned with what exists and the nature of those existents, then the philosophy of society inevitably touches here and there on, and for its success depends on, previous answers to certain questions of ontology. The very issue of what a social object is, is itself an ontological question in its nontrivial sense and for its formulation requires a certain answer to a certain ontological question. That the question what a social object is necessitates both an exhaustive and a correct answer for an adequate philosophy of society is obvious. In the fourth chapter I hope to give it. But some other questions, reasonably called ontological, while relevant to our investigations and needing some sort of answers, do not require anything like a thorough treatment. Two of the most important of these I shall take up in the third chapter: What is a person? and What is an action? Here I wish to show only that they need answers but that the answers need not be exhaustive.

It is clear, I suppose, that whatever else social phenomena may be they consist in part of people acting in certain ways. Thus it should also be clear that it is necessary to have some philosophical understanding of what a person is and what acting is. We need to know, for example, what the connection is between intentions and behavior or more generally between mind and body. How shall we face the question of the role of ideas in the social process, for example, unless we already have some conception of how an idea gets "translated" into behavior to begin with? At the same time it is evident, I think, that we do not need an absolutely general theory, if there be such a thing, of human beings. For example, we do not need a general epistemological theory or a theory of perception. It is of no relevance to the questions I shall be asking whether we accept some form of naive realism or instead some form of representative realism as an account of perception and knowledge. I shall adopt a general empiricism in the questions where it is relevant, but this is only at a level where it means, roughly, that we generally come to know how the world is by our senses and does not require a more detailed theory of perception.

It will probably be widely agreed that most of the issues of general ontology are irrelevant to the philosophy of society. Whether, for example, an ordinary object such as a chair is a substance or a series of classes of momentary individuals or just a "bundle" of properties or something else would seem to matter not at all to the questions that constitute the philosophy of society. Nor would the question whether or not there are universals in either major sense — as Platonic entities or as the literally common entity in a ball and a tomato of the same shade of red. But there is one question of general ontology which has a bearing on several questions that will be raised subsequently and to which therefore I must now devote a few words. This is the question whether there is a real distinction among properties between those that are "simple" and those that are "complex." Roughly, a simple property is one which has no other properties as "parts" and any property which is not simple is complex. Linguistically there is a distinction, more apparent usually in formal than in natural languages, between "primitive" or undefined predicate expressions and "nonprimitive" or defined predicate expressions. Is this distinction, as so many now maintain, *only* one of language or does it after all reflect, if somewhat imperfectly in any natural language, a real distinction between two kinds of properties? Before I give what I believe to be the answer and my reasons for it, let us see the relevance of the distinction for our purposes.

In the first place there is the traditional mind/body issue. In the contemporary literature this is often discussed as the question of the "identity" or "nonidentity" of mental states and certain bodily states. This question in turn is frequently posed as one of the "reducibility" or "definability" of mental predicates to or in terms of physical predicates. The very possibility of such a "reduction," I would suggest, can be coherently raised only if one has previously settled the question of whether or not mental properties are all complex. If there are simple mental properties, it makes no sense to speak of defining them (or, rather, their names) in terms of (the names of) other properties — mental or physical — in the only sense of 'definition' relevant here. In the second place the issue of the relation of belief to action and some connected matters such as the nature of dispositions and external and internal relations also seem to presuppose a prior distinction of simple and complex properties. For the interesting theses about internal relations and the "externality" of causation always presume it is simple properties only that one is talking about. Finally, the question I mentioned earlier of what a social object is can be raised only in light of an assumption that there is a real distinction between simple and complex properties. For the issue whether *there are* social objects "above and beyond" individual people, their properties, and relations in the end can only be the question whether there are simple properties of social wholes. This claim will be argued for only in the relevant chapter.

A full defense of the *de re* distinction between simple and complex properties would require an exposition and defense of philosophical method. Here a few comments must suffice, even though it is virtually received doctrine these days that the distinction is one that can only be made relative to some language. Since I believe that the distinction is phenomenological and not merely linguistic, an example may help. When I see something which is a particular shade of red, the shade is given to me as having no other properties as "constituents." On the other hand when I see an apple, the property of being an apple is at least sometimes given to me as having other properties as "constituents" — a certain shape, a certain color, and so on. The phrase 'at least sometimes' alludes to a fact I have no wish to deny: that complex properties are sometimes presented as having a kind of unity; indeed that they may possibly on occasion be given as phenomenologically simple. My argument requires only that genuine simples never be presented as complex. In the case at hand one must be careful not to suppose that a *property* of the shade, such as its intensity, is a *constituent* of it, or, even more absurdly, to attempt to identify the shade with a wavelength. The simplicity of shades of color is reflected in the linguistic circumstance that no definitions can be given of their names. Certainly the dictionary does not define 'red' in the sense in which it defines 'bachelor', that is, by telling us the constituent properties, in stating that it is a color or that it lies next to orange on the spectrum.

To this we may add that unlike complex properties a simple property is one with which I must be acquainted — by perceiving something with the property — in order to be able to imagine it or an object with it. Thus, for example, I can imagine a mermaid, even though I have never seen one, because being a mermaid is a complex property (the name of) which is definable in terms of (the names of) properties which I have seen exemplified. On the other hand I cannot imagine what, say, those "colors" outside the range of human perception look like to those animals who can perceive them or would look like to me if my sensory apparatus were different. Finally, simple properties cannot be "pictured" except by themselves or by another property of the same "sort." So, for example, a picture of a horse is not a horse or any other animal, but a picture of a red ball while neither a ball nor any other similar object is itself either red or some other color. But with this I must conclude this brief defense of the view that there is a real and not merely a linguistic distinction between those properties which are simple and those which are complex.

II Philosophy of Science

An adequate philosophy of society presupposes an adequate philosophy of science. Yet it does not require a treatise on the subject or anything like an exhaustive treatment of it, whatever that would be. Some of the subject's most common themes, such as axiomatization, the "theoretical" entities of quantum physics, and the so-called problem of induction, can be ignored altogether. Other matters, such as the notion of statistical laws, the nature of dispositions, and the structure of scientific theories, require some consideration but not of the sort one might expect to find in a book on the philosophy of science. These and some other related ideas are given the treatment they require for our main themes in different parts of this essay. In this chapter we shall deal with those topics in the philosophy of science which are of central importance to those main themes and which necessitate therefore a somewhat longer, individual treatment. They are as follows: the notions of *lawfulness and causation*; those of *process, determinism, and interaction*; and that of a *law of coexistence*.

Lawfulness and Causation

In what follows I shall not bother systematically to distinguish the statement of a law of nature — a linguistic entity — from the thought or "concept" of a law of nature — a mental or partly mental entity — from the nature of lawful connections in the world. It is only the last mentioned which is of any philosophical significance and is of interest to me here, but it is convenient to be able to express one's view in terms of what laws (as linguistic entities) assert or are about. Finally, although I shall spend a paragraph on the distinction between laws of nature on the one hand and accidental generalities and contrary-to-fact conditionals on the other, and although I am inclined to agree with Bergmann,[1] Nagel,[2] and others that in the end what distinguishes laws of nature are their relations to other propositions, our main interest is in the intrinsic nature of the lawful connection itself and its relation with the nature of causation.

Laws assert a logically contingent and "hypothetically" constant conjunction between or among two or more properties as exemplified by particular things.[3] The last phrase makes it clear that laws are about properties as actually instanced rather than relations that may hold among the properties themselves, as it were. 'Scarlet is darker than pink' is a truth, but it is not, on my view, a law. Nor, of course, is it an accidental generality, for it isn't a generality at all. But in saying that laws are about properties as actually instanced, I do not mean that there must be instances in order for the law to be true. The law of inertial motion tells us what happens to a material body when there are no net external forces acting upon it, yet by the law of universal gravitation and what we know about the actual distribution of mass in the universe, we have reason to believe that no body actually ever has absolutely no net external forces acting upon it. The law, nevertheless, is both true and important. For this reason the phrase 'constant conjunction' by itself can be and in fact has been misleading. I would not presume to guess what Hume actually had in mind by it — whether, for example, he believed that no law can be true, or perhaps can be known to be true, unless there are actual instances of it or actual *and* observed instances of it. But in the first place, I am not here interested in how we come to know that certain laws of nature are true, either in general or in particular cases (I have not, for example, described laws as inductive generalizations, a description that carries with it their alleged mode of discovery); and secondly, the fact that the law of inertial motion is both true and important, quite independent of whether it has instances or not, is something for a philosophical theory of laws of nature, or of lawfulness, to account for and not to dispute.

The constant conjunction of lawfully conjoined properties then is "hypothetical" in two related senses. First, laws of nature do not themselves assert that they have instances or, to speak with the logicians, laws of nature are best treated as universal conditionals ("hypotheticals") without existential import. Secondly, even if there are, as in the typical case, actual instances of the conjunction, the law is not about them alone, but also about "hypothetical" cases. This idea is captured in the logical fact that from a genuine law of nature one may infer subjunctive ("hypothetical") conditionals about particular cases whereas from nonlaw "universals" one cannot. Thus from the law that water when heated to 100°C at sea level boils, one may infer of a particular sample of water never to be so heated that if it were heated to 100°C at sea level it would boil. But one may not infer from the nonlaw ''universal'' that all the coins in my pocket are pennies that if this quarter were in my pocket it would be a penny.

It is at this point that some would press certain questions designed to cast doubt on this ''Humean'' theory of lawfulness. On the one hand it will be queried whether expressing the difference between laws of nature and accidental generalities in terms of hypothetical as opposed to simple constant conjunction does not show that there is more to the lawful connection than is captured by the logical connective of material implication. On the other hand, but in the same vein, some will wonder whether all contrary-to-fact generalities will not also, on this theory, qualify as laws of nature if the lawful connection is captured by material implication. Since I cannot here mount a meaningful defense of my view and since in any case there is little or nothing I can add to what already exists in the literature, I shall make only one observation. If establishing that a (universal) lawful connection is mere (possibly ''hypothetical'') constant conjunction shows that the linguistic expression in a (formal) language will satisfy (by its instantiations) the truth table for material implication, then it must be admitted that it passes the test. It is the accidental generality which fails that test if, for example, 'If Joseph Stalin had sat on bench A, he would have been an Irishman' is taken as an instantiation of the accidental generality 'All who sat on bench A were Irishmen', for presumably the former is false while the latter, by assumption, is true. And that all contrary-to-fact conditionals should pass the test as a result of vacuous antecedents surely does not imply that genuine laws of nature do not. Nor finally does the circumstance that some genuine laws of nature, such as the law of inertial motion, have vacuous antecedents show either that they fail the truth-table test (obviously!) or that they cannot be distinguished in some way from nonlaw contrary-to-fact conditionals.

The phrase 'logically contingent' in my characterization of the lawful connection calls attention to the fact that it is never contradictory to deny of any two or more properties that are asserted to be lawfully connected in some given way that they are connected in that way or indeed that they have any lawful connection at all. The two or more properties involved in a given lawful connection may be properties of the same object or of different objects. Furthermore, the law may assert that the instances of the properties occur at the same time or that they occur at different times. If they occur at different times according to the law, that is, if one succeeds the other, the law then may be referred to as a *law of succession*. Most laws are of this type though there are many logical subtypes of it. If the law asserts a connection of a simultaneous kind, then it may be referred to as a *law of coexistence*. They are of fundamental importance for the discussion of certain issues, and I shall devote the section after next to them. About statistical laws, let us say here only that when they are interpreted as being about the properties of collectives rather than about those of members of collectives, they too have the characteristics of laws as so far characterized.

Metaphysically speaking, causation is nothing beyond lawful connection. There are only the lawful connections of properties (as exemplified by particular things) or, as we may also speak, the lawful connections of events or states of affairs (facts). Some of these lawful connections we pick out for various practical and theoretical reasons, and differently in different contexts, and call them causal connections. This well-known theory is not intended, at least as held by me, to be an account of how people use the words 'cause', 'causal', or 'causation' but is intended to be an account of what is or is not in the world. In different contexts the ordinary as well as the scientific uses of these words carry many "implications," for example, of temporal order, of moral or legal responsibility, of manipulable conditions, or of relatively changing in contrast to relatively permanent conditions. I have no desire, for foolish it would be, to deny any of these or any other connotations of the "cause"-words in English or in any other natural language. I do wish to deny that there are in the world such things as "necessary connections" or metaphysical "activities" or "powers" and the like. More specifically yet, I wish to deny by this theory (a) that there is anything of metaphysical interest that intrinsically distinguishes what, in some ordinary context, may nevertheless be distinguished as "cause" and "effect," and (b) that there is any additional entity, the causal connection or whatever, in addition to the properties or events said to be causally connected. The "connection" in the particular case is nothing — nothing, that is, but the lawful connection of which it is an instance. But this leads us directly to my other point which, trivial as it may seem, will prove to be of importance later in this essay.

The thesis that causation is but lawful connection does not imply, some critics to the contrary notwithstanding,[4] that whenever, in an ordinary context, a statement of the form '*A* caused *B*' is true, there must therefore be a true law of the form 'If *A* then (always) *B*'. Nor does it imply that there must be a true law of the form 'If *A*, then usually *B*' (if any laws really have that form) or indeed that there must be any law that assigns a definite probability to *B* given only *A*. What is implied is only that there must be some law, whether known or not, which mentions, in a nontrivial way, both *A* and *B*. It might, to take the simplest case, have the form 'If *A* and *C*, then *B*'. For example, if *C* is the presence of oxygen, *A* the striking of a match of a certain composition against a surface of a certain sort with a certain force, and *B* the lighting of the match, then we have a true law of that form. Yet in a particular case we might reasonably and truly say, as the words are used, that the striking of the match caused it to light. Here, as in many contexts, we call attention to the relatively transient condition(s) — the striking of the match — as opposed to the relatively permanent condition(s) — the presence of oxygen — in speaking of *the* cause of the event in question. This example makes it clear what I mean in saying that *A* and *B* may be lawfully connected even though there is no true law of the form 'If *A* then *B*' or 'If *B* then *A*'. It also shows how little significance I attach to such distinctions as that between, say, "causes" and "conditions" or "conditions" and "grounds" on the one hand and to such notions as those of "necessary and sufficient conditions" on the other for the purposes of the philosophical analyses of lawfulness and causation.

Russell once said that we could in principle do without the notion of causation altogether, at least in science and philosophy.[5] I agree, but not with his prescription that we actually try to do so. Hence, I too shall continue to use the language of causation along with that of lawful connection.

Process, Determinism, and Interaction

Consider a temporal universe in which there are three material objects, *a, b,* and *c*, each with a mass, a position, and a velocity. Since each object may at any given moment have any one of many different masses, one of many different positions, and one of many different velocities, let us refer to mass, position, and velocity as *variables* which can take various *values*. Thus having a mass of four units (whatever the unit of measurement may be) will be a value of the variable mass. And having a velocity of six kilometers an hour relative to some given object will be a value of the variable velocity. Let us also refer to our little universe, considered as something which exists through time, as a *system*. Let us further say that a temporal cross section of the system is a *state of the system*. Call a description of a state of the system a *state description*. Thus a state description for our system will tell us the mass (*M*), position (*P*), and velocity (*V*) for each object at some given moment, that is, the value of each variable for each object at that time. A state description then might look like this, assuming that each value of each variable can be coordinated to a number, that is, that the property is measurable:

	M	*P*	*V*
a . . .	4	0	8
b . . .	7	9	3
c . . .	2	6	7

Let us further suppose that, to speak roughly for the moment, there are no other properties which make any difference to the values of *M, P,* and *V*. This supposition we may also express more technically by saying that *M, P,* and *V* constitute a *complete set of relevant variables*, relevant, that is, to their own values. Suppose finally that there is a law, or set of laws, such that it, in conjunction with any given state description of the system, allows one to compute accurately the state description for any other given moment, earlier or later. If the system is such that such a law, or set of laws, holds for it, we shall say that the system has *process*.[6] And the law or set of laws, a species of laws of succession, which permits such computations, we shall call a *process law*. Such a system may reasonably also be called a *deterministic system*. And *determinism* we may characterize as the thesis that every value of every variable, whether quantifiable or not, as actually exemplified in the world is in a system which has process. Thus determinism is true if no property of any object falls outside a system which has process, in short, if the whole universe is a system which has process or is wholly constituted of any number of systems each of which has process. In a later chapter we shall loosen this characterization of determinism for certain analytic purposes, but for now it will be adequate.

A given system, then, is picked out, first, by indicating the cardinality of the objects in it and, second, by specifying their properties (variables). (The properties may, of course, include relations. In our example, position, for one, is actually a relational, not a monadic, property.) Any such system may not have process (be deterministic) for one of three reasons: (1) It may not include all the objects which, again to speak loosely, make a difference to what happens to the given set of objects. Thus, for example, the system constituted by the sun and the planets and their satellites and the properties of mass, position, and velocity does not have process because other objects such as comets also affect the motions of the planets. A system which does not have process for this reason lacks *closure*.

(2) It may not include all the variables which, once more to speak loosely,

make a difference to the values of those variables which have already been specified. So, for example, the system of the sun, the planets and their satellites, and the comets considered only with the properties of velocity and position does not have process because the variable mass has not been taken into account. Such a system does not contain a complete set of relevant variables, or, briefly, fails to achieve *completeness*. Using the language of causality and treating causality as a relation between and among variables, we may say that such a system is not *causally closed*. A causally closed system, one in which we might know all the relevant variables, may yet not have closure, as I am using the words. Systems which are not causally closed may reflect a lack of lawful knowledge, whereas systems which do not have closure may reflect a lack of knowledge of what objects are to be considered. To take the best historical example: Until Newton we did not know the *laws* of the system which is the solar system considered with the usual properties, but even then we did not yet (and still do not) know all the objects which constitute the system. Indeed it was those very laws (combined with information about the masses, positions, and velocities of known objects) which enabled astronomers to find other objects — Uranus, Neptune, and Pluto most notably. Technically then the process laws either will state the cardinalities of the systems to which they apply or will implicitly apply to systems of all (finite) cardinalities.[7] Obviously completeness or its lack is theoretically more interesting than closure or its lack. Hence the greatness of Newton.

(3) Determinism may be false. This possibility implies that for some system, even if we know all the values of all the relevant variables and are acquainted with all the objects which "make a difference," there is no law or set of laws which enables us to make calculations of the sort indicated above. When I say there is no law, I mean of course that there is none to be discovered and not simply that we don't know it. Thus when we come across a system which is not deterministic, that is, a system which does not have process, we may conclude that either it is part of a larger system, in terms of objects or properties or both, which is deterministic; or else determinism is false. Generally I shall assume in this book that determinism is true as I believe it to be, but I shall not argue for it except negatively and indirectly by way of refuting certain arguments for indeterminism, mainly some of those for "free will."

Several times I have used an expression such as 'makes a difference' accompanied by an expression such as 'to speak loosely'. I now wish to give a precise characterization of *interaction*.

Suppose that we have two systems which both have process, each of them containing again three individuals and the properties of mass, position, and velocity. Suppose further that the following are accurate state descriptions for each system at some given moment, t_1:

	M	P	V		M	P	V
a . . .	6	2	5	a' . . .	6	2	4
b . . .	1	0	4	b' . . .	1	0	7
c . . .	3	5	8	c' . . .	3	5	8

Notice that the only difference in the two systems at t_1 is in the values of V for a and a', b and b'. We now observe the values of M, P, and V for all our objects at some other, earlier or later, time, say, t_2. We discover, let us suppose, a difference in the values of P for b and b'. Since we have assumed that each system has closure and contains a complete set of relevant variables, we must conclude that the differing values of V at t_1 made the difference, that is, that V *interacts* with P. Let us generalize this idea of interaction. We shall say that one variable interacts with another, or, better, two variables are interacting variables, if *some* difference in the value of the one variable makes a difference in the value(s) of the other variable, at some earlier or later time.

Several points need further emphasis. (1) My way of expressing this idea may perhaps violate the ordinary-language sensibilities of some in using the expressions 'interacts' and 'makes a difference' so that a later value of some variable, as instanced by some particular object, can have an effect on the value(s) of some variable at some earlier time. Adjust the language as you will; I am talking only of a lawful connection which of logical necessity goes both ways. (2) More importantly, it must be clearly seen that as I have characterized interaction not every difference of a value in some variable must make a difference in the value(s) of the other variable in order for them to be said to interact. Thus, for example, as I sit here and write, it makes no difference to my activity whether it is 10°C or 20°C outside. But it would certainly make a difference if it were, say, 2000°C rather than 10°C. Hence temperature interacts with that very complex property which as exemplified constitutes my activity at the moment. (It might not, by the way, interact with all the simple properties which make up that complex property.) If every different value had to make a difference in the value of the other variable, then so defined there might very well be no interacting properties in the world. (3) Two properties which do interact may be in one object or in two distinct objects (to take the simplest case). When they are in two, we often speak of the objects themselves interacting. No harm comes from that, even for our purposes, if it is clearly realized that that is a shorthand way of saying that the two objects have some properties the value(s) of which in the one object make a difference to the value(s) of which in the other. We may also speak of the objects rather than their properties as interacting when it is the values of the same property in the two or more objects which affect each other. Thus the velocity of one object may affect the velocity of another, for example.

(4) Every variable, we may suppose, interacts with itself. The value of a variable at a given moment makes a difference to its value(s) at some other time. And its value for some object at a given time may make a difference in its value for some other object at some time, the same or not. Still, without presupposing that there actually are any, it will be useful to speak of a variable whose values make a difference at most to values of itself as an *absolutely noninteracting variable*. (5) Finally, as I first defined 'interaction' I spoke of making a difference at some earlier or later time. Interaction is primarily a notion of making a difference through time. But I now wish to add the idea of making a difference at the same time. This addition will not pick out any pair of properties as interacting not already picked out in the more restricted characterization unless some kind of radical indeterminism were true. This is so because if some value of a given variable makes a difference to the value(s) of some other variable at the same time, it will also make a difference to the latter's value(s) at some later (or earlier) time. But this notion of making a difference at the same time leads to a discussion of the last business of this chapter.

Laws of Coexistence

Here my task is to make clear the notion of what is variously called a functional law or a parallelistic law or a cross-sectional law, but what I shall call a *law of coexistence*. Let us speak abstractly and consider first the simplest kind of case. Suppose we have a system that has process and three properties, f_1, f_2, and f_3. By assumption these three variables constitute a complete set of relevant variables. But there may still be another property, f_4, such that whenever any object has f_3 at a value of 2, it has f_4 at a value of 6; whenever it has f_3 at a value of 7, it has f_4 at a value of 3; and so on. In short whenever an object has f_3 at a certain value, it also has at the same time f_4 at some lawfully corresponding value. A law which asserts a connection of this sort between f_3 and f_4 we shall call a law of coexistence. (Calling it a functional law is often either prejudging or misleading; for one, this terminology often contrasts such laws with "causal" laws presupposing certain views about causation, and, for another, every law states a functional connection in the good sense of that word — that of mapping something onto something else.)

A series of comments will make the notion of such a connection clearer. (1) If *every* different value of f_3 has a lawfully corresponding different value in f_4, and vice versa, and if f_1, f_2, and f_3 constitute a complete set of relevant variables, that is, a set such that only their values need be known in order to calculate earlier and later values of the same set, it follows that f_1, f_2, and f_4 constitute such a set. For whenever we need the value of f_3 among other values in order to calculate, say, a later value of f_1, we could just as well use the lawfully corresponding value of f_4 (and vice versa). Thus if f_3 interacts with f_1 and/or f_2, so does f_4 (and vice versa), for a different value of f_4 means, by the law of coexistence, a different value of f_3 and hence a difference that may make a difference in the values of f_1 and f_2. In a given context, f_4 might be said to be a *merely parallel* property with respect to f_3 in particular and the system of which f_1, f_2, and f_3 are the properties in general. But in terms only of the lawful connections involved in the system as I have described it, f_4 is no more and no less merely parallel to the system containing f_1, f_2, and f_3 than f_3 is to a (logically, not lawfully) corresponding system containing f_1, f_2, and f_4.

(2) Having stated the idea with respect to a system with process and where there is a different value of f_4 for every different value of f_3 and vice versa, it will now be useful to loosen up the notion somewhat. Consider once more the situation in which f_1, f_2, and f_3 are all the properties in a system with process. But this time, although for every different value of f_4 there is a different value of f_3, the converse is not true. In other words, many different values of f_3 yield the same value for f_4. In this case, from all the laws of coexistence that would hold, one could, given the law(s) and any value of f_3, calculate the value of f_4 in every instance; but given the same law(s) and a value of f_4 one might or might not, depending on the case, be able to calculate the value of f_3. We already assumed that f_1, f_2, and f_3 are all the properties of a causally closed system, so it is useful to observe that in these circumstances where no law permits the calculation of the value of f_3 from some values of f_4, and on the assumption that the different values of f_3 make a difference to the values of f_1 and f_2, we would not have a causally closed system consisting of f_1, f_2, and f_4. For this reason, one would have a basis for saying that in such a universe f_4 is a merely parallel property in a sense in which f_3 is not. Still, of course, the values of f_4 make a difference to the values of the other variables (certainly to f_3 by assumption and therefore to f_1 and f_2 if and only if f_3 makes a difference to

f_1 and f_2) and so is, as I characterized the notion, an interacting variable. To anticipate a bit, if we assume for the moment that f_1, f_2, and f_3 constitute the physical world, with the values of f_3 being particular brain or neurophysiological states and those of f_4 particular conscious states, we see that the terminology of interactionism *versus* parallelism can be quite misleading.

(3) To return to the more extreme case in order to make a point more clearly, let us again suppose that every different value of f_4 has a lawfully corresponding different value in f_3 and vice versa. Or to take an even simpler case, let us suppose that the world were such that everything in it which is red is also round and vice versa. Then, whether such a correspondence were lawful or only an accidental generality, the properties in question would be *extensionally equivalent*. According to the so-called "axiom" of extensionality, any two properties which are extensionally equivalent are "identical." Some would conclude that in such a case the "two" properties are really one.[8] Some such idea, for example, seems to be behind some of the cruder arguments for materialism with respect to mind, as if the discovery, falsification, or confirmation of certain putative laws could make materialism more or less likely. (Such discoveries, falsifications, and confirmations are of course quite relevant to *historical* materialism; it is the thesis of, or more precisely a certain argument for, so-called mind-brain "identity" that I am here obliquely attacking.)

But let us look at this more closely. In the first place, one may deny the relevance of the "axiom" of extensionality, for it would seem that it really is not a universally valid formula anyway if we allow unrestricted substitution for its predicate variables. But assume it is universally valid. There is still no basis for saying that the two properties are really one, for such an "identity" is not sameness. Russellian or, more generally, logical identity is just what it is defined to be and nothing more. And it is so defined that two identical properties are that if and only if (a) they determine all and only the same classes and (b) they are members of all and only the same classes. It does not follow that they are the same property any more than it follows from the fact that two individuals have all and only the same properties that they are really one. Leibniz's principle of the identity of indiscernibles (or, in my language, the sameness of identicals), for the assertion of which he had primarily theological reasons, is by no means a logical truth. Thus, to repeat, the mere extensional equivalence of two properties is no ground whatsoever for saying that they really are one property after all. To suppose that it is a reason is to confuse the contexts of *description* or the specification of what properties there are on the one hand and of *explanation* or the account of what lawful connections there are on the other. How many properties there are in the world and of what ''kinds'' in no way depends on what connections there may be among them, whether lawful or not. The many philosophers who believe to the contrary are, I believe, victims of the scientism of our day.

We are now in possession of what I hope are tolerably clear notions of process and process laws, of interaction, and of parallel properties and laws of coexistence. In addition, I have sketched a reasonably orthodox theory of lawfulness and causation. This orthodoxy extends also in some measure to my view of what constitutes an adequate scientific explanation. But this hint should be enough for the moment.[9]

III Minds, Beliefs, and Actions

In the next chapter it will be argued that all social objects including society itself are nothing but certain properties of and relations between and among individual human beings (and perhaps other "individual" objects). Even for one who disagrees it may still be maintained that a philosophical theory of certain aspects of human beings, primarily those deriving from the fact that we have minds, is both a constituent of and in part preliminary to an adequate philosophy of society. I need only mention the issues of the extent to which we can shape our destinies and of the nature of a social action in order to justify that claim. Thus this chapter deals at some length with the following areas: *mind and body*; *behavior and action*; and *belief and action*.

Mind and Body

Before we inquire what the relation of mind to body is (and hence to the world) we must first ask what a mind is. A few sketchy comments will do for our purposes. Minds consist of (a) states of consciousness and (b) dispositions. Examples of the latter are knowing that two and two make four, believing that the earth is flat, and hoping to marry a wealthy woman. Examples of the former are suddenly remembering an appointment, feeling a pain in one's leg, perceiving a tree, and thinking that two and two make four. Dispositions I put aside for the moment, remarking simply that they are dispositions either to exhibit a certain kind of behavior or to have certain states of consciousness, or both.[1] A state of consciousness has two crucial features. In the first place it is always *of* something. When I suddenly remember my appointment with the dentist, it is just "that I have an appointment with the dentist" that my remembering is *of*. This is usually called the *intentional* feature of consciousness. Secondly, a state of consciousness is distinguished by whether it is a remembering or a perceiving or a thinking or a something else. Thinking about the tree in front of my house is different from perceiving the tree even though what is intended is the same. This characteristic of consciousness, what identifies the kind of mental state it is, is what some call its *species*.

According to the analysis of mind for which I have argued in more detail elsewhere,[2] a state of consciousness is (at least) an individual which exemplifies two properties, one a species property such as *being-a-remembering* and the other an intentional property such as *that-I-have-an-appointment-with-the-dentist*. An intentional property must not be confused with the fact which it intends or with the sentence which in a particular case may be used to assert the fact and to express the thought. At this point one could raise a question which, fortunately, we need not answer concerning the nature of the connection between an intentional property and the fact which it intends. Bergmann, following up an earlier suggestion of Moore's, argues that it is a sui generis "relation" of the sort he calls *meaning*.[3] The intentional property *means* the fact it is about. But for our purposes we can concentrate only on the two kinds of crucial properties since, according to Bergmann and any view like his I can imagine, the meaning connection exists when and only when some intentional property is exemplified.

Thus, in the relevant sense, a mind consists of properties among properties. Hence, too, a mind is not a metaphysical "activity" or the "form" of the body or, as on the views of existentialists such as Sartre and Ortega y Gasset, something ontologically so radically different from material objects that to allow even the possibility that minds enter the causal realm is absurd. But before I turn to the question of the causal connection between minds and bodies, a final point is appropriate.

When I remember that my first trip to the dentist was in New York, I know directly and with (psychological) certainty both that I am remembering and not doubting and that it is the trip to the dentist I am remembering and not my first day at school. My emphasis here is not once more on the two crucial kinds of properties themselves but on the fact that these properties of these kinds are, in the typical situation, given to me as phenomenologically simple. Whether or not these properties are exemplified by the same individuals which exemplify the properties of the brain, whether those individuals are momentary or continuant, I am not certain. But of this I am confident: the attempts to establish materialism by showing either that mental properties do not exist or that they are really the "same" as certain publicly observable properties since they are (or may be) extensionally equivalent to certain physical properties are doomed to failure. Materialism *is* absurd, as Bergmann once wrote, for it is committed to maintaining either that certain simple properties with which I am directly acquainted (as I might be with a certain shade of red or a certain shape) are not really there at all, are exemplified by nothing, or that those properties are the same as some other properties, which is a contradiction. Where does philosophy, not to mention science and everyday experience, begin if not with the properties with which we are directly acquainted either by the senses or by introspection?

Ontology, as I understand it, rules out no lawful connections which would be otherwise possible. Thus on the view of mind I have sketched, the properties which make states of consciousness the particular states of consciousness they are might, so far at any rate, enter into any lawful connections whatsoever, including the limiting case of none at all, with the properties of the physical world. I have spelled out all the possibilities I could think of elsewhere[4] and there is no need to do that here anyway. Some ontologies and some views of causation have ''prohibited,'' or have placed nearly insuperable difficulties in supposing, a ''causal'' connection between mind and body. It is these views which Ryle attacked in *The Concept of Mind*, unfortunately mistaking them for all forms of dualism. It is clear at any rate that my views of causation and the nature of mind in no way imply that ''a cause must be like its effect'' or ''there must be spatial contiguity for causal interaction'' or ''mind and body are ontologically too unlike each other for any causal connection.''

Let us suppose that determinism is true. That will make it easier to state the two realistic possibilities for the connection of mind and body, though both can be stated and either could be true without that suppposition. If determinism is true, then either the variables that are all those of the physical world constitute a causally closed system (or a set of such systems) or they do not. If they do not, then one must add the mental variables in order to get such a system (or set of such systems). Let me spell out each possibility in more detail.

On the second possibility some events which occur in the physical world can be fully explained (lawfully) only by appealing to mental variables as well as physical ones. That is, some physical variables belong to no set of physical variables which, in themselves, constitute a causally closed set. Presumably, these physical variables would be those which are, most importantly, properties of human bodies and, secondarily, the properties of those things with which human bodies interact. On this view, which some call *interactionism*, the values of the mental variables certainly "make a difference" to the values of the physical ones; what a person believes and chooses presumably affects the physical variables that are his body and through them the world "outside." But it is impossible on such a view for there to be (strict) laws of coexistence connecting the mental variables to any physical ones; otherwise the physical variables would constitute a causally closed set, assuming that there is such a set at all. This has an untoward and, I believe, fatal consequence for the interactionist view. Knowledge of the contents of minds other than one's own would be impossible. Since there would be no simple, lawful correspondence between bodily or behavioral states on the one hand and mental states on the other, we would never be in a position to know or even make a reasonable guess what is going on in another person's mind, relying as we must on the observation of the other's bodily and behavioral states alone. (Similarly, mass and velocity are interacting variables, but no law allows the calculation of the mass of a body from its velocity or vice versa.) A correct view of the relation of mind to body must make it possible for us to know what goes on in another's mind, as we sometimes do, and must not entail its impossibility.

The other realistic possibility is precisely that the causal connection between mental states and bodily ones is entirely "captured" by laws of coexistence. Thus on such a view the physical world is causally closed; in order to explain any occurrence in the physical world, only physical variables *need* be mentioned. Adopting our earlier symbolism, let f_1, f_2, and f_3 constitute the physical world which by assumption is causally closed. Let f_3 be those physical variables which are connected to the mental ones by laws of coexistence. Finally, let the mental variables be represented by f_4. We saw earlier that if for every differing value of f_3 (that made a difference to f_1 and/or f_2) there was a different value of f_4 and vice versa, then if f_1, f_2, and f_3 constitute a causally closed system, so do f_1, f_2, and f_4. In short, if every time the body was in a different state that made a difference to other physical variables, the mind was in a different state, then the physical variables, less those connected by laws of coexistence to the mental ones, and the mental ones would jointly constitute a causally closed system. But of course the assumption is not true in empirical fact. For there are an indefinite number of relevantly different body states which correspond to the same mental state of no consciousness at all. Hence such a "substitution" of mental for certain physical variables could not be carried out in a systematic fashion.[5] But such a substitution can be and usually is made in most of those situations where (a) the person is conscious and (b) we believe his conscious state "had something to do with" the physical event we want to explain. Is this consistent with this view that I am developing here, a view commonly known as *psychophysiological parallelism*? It not only is consistent with but indeed follows from this theory that mind "makes a difference," assuming that the corresponding physical variables interact with other physical variables, as of course they do. For if my present choice were different from what it is, it follows from the theory of parallelism that my brain state (or whatever bodily state is relevant) would be different and so my behavior would be different, and so on.

Though these two views are usually called *interactionism* and *parallelism* respectively, it may be noticed that, as I defined 'interaction' in the last chapter, both views countenance interacting minds in spite of the fact that parallelism is sometimes described negatively as the doctrine of noninteracting minds. For on both views, the values of the mental variables "make a difference" to earlier and later, not to mention simultaneous, values of some physical variables. Once this verbal incongruity is taken note of, no harm will come from our retaining the traditional terminology.

It should be clear by now that either parallelism or interactionism can be true whether determinism is true or not. For, to take the nondeterminist case first, the laws of the mind/body connection, whatever they are, could hold even if not all phenomena have complete lawful explanations. And perhaps even more obviously, to take the determinist case, these laws, though not themselves process laws, could be derivable from such laws. That is simply to say that the mind and the body, though not by themselves constituting a system with process and whether they interact or not in the sense just characterized, may very well be part of a larger system with process. More technically, in the interactionist case, the mind/body laws would be part of the process laws themselves, or, if you like, the mental and body variables would be among those in a system with process. In the parallelist case the mind/body laws, being only of the coexistence type, would *not* be derivable from the process laws of the physical variables alone. But one may still reasonably say that in such a case minds are "in" a system with process, in that with the process laws and the coexistence laws together one could, given the state of the relevant variables at a given moment, calculate the earlier and later values of the mental variables.

Only parallelism makes possible our everyday knowledge of what is going on in other persons' minds (whether that knowledge stands up to certain philosophical criteria or not) and is consistent with the great deal of scientific knowledge we have of the connections of bodily and mental states. Since there is also a looser parallelism between a person's thoughts and his behavior as well as between his relevant neurophysiological states and his behavior (both in contrast to that of thoughts and neurophysiological states), we can generally take a person's linguistic behavior as an expression of his thought, his pain behavior as accompanied by feelings of pain, and his blushes as roughly simultaneous to feelings of embarrassment. But the stricter (as well as the looser) parallelism of mind and body is assumed in the practice of lie detection; in anesthesiology so far as its purpose is not just the quiescence of the body for the convenience of the surgeon, but also the prevention of pain or consciousness; and in almost all attempts to change, bring about, or prevent certain states of consciousness by changing the body whether by sleep, exercise, drugs, alcohol, or anything whatever. If the connection between mind and body were that as envisaged by the interactionist, we would never have any assurance that producing some specific change in the body would produce a desired "effect" in one's mental states. In short, only parallelism is consistent with common sense, properly understood, as well as the more systematic knowledge we have of mind and body. Or, not to forget the somewhat paradoxical nature of the situation, the very idea of investigating scientifically the lawful connections of brain or bodily states to mental states presupposes parallelism. I conclude that parallelism is true and shall henceforth assume it to be so in this essay.[6]

Behavior and Action

We may now proceed to take note of an allegedly fundamental distinction between what is usually labeled as behavior on the one hand and as action on the other. So distinguished, the idea is that behavior is just the physical movements of an organism whereas an action is meaningful, has a point, is significant, and the like. Various theories have been based on this distinction, such as the view that in contrast to behavior descriptions action descriptions are always value-laden or culturally relative or otherwise peculiar. Another theory holds that actions, unlike mere behaviors, are by their "nature" not causally explainable. It is only this latter theory that I wish briefly to examine here.

What I want to maintain is that granted that an action is not just a piece of behavior, nevertheless an action can be described without any special problems in principle and that since this is so we have here no reason why actions cannot be given lawful explanations. Since the argument for this position has already been made in detail by someone with whom I agree, I shall not make it again.[7] But I shall in a few paragraphs sketch the idea of the matter as I see it.

Consider then two actions: signing a letter to a friend; putting one's name to a bank loan. The relevant behaviors, that is, the physical movements of the arm and hand, are, we may suppose, qualitatively identical. But the actions are enormously different and not just numerically. Wherein lies the difference? If the difference is not in the behaviors, it must be in something other than the behaviors. This something will, according to the description of the action, include variously the intentions or desires of the one who acts, the effects on other people including how they perceive the action, the causal effects on other things, and so on. The point is that, in a certain sense, it doesn't matter what the "other" is, and that at any rate will depend on the case, so long as it is something which can itself be described. Thus we might say that an action is a behavior that takes place under certain, specifiable circumstances, perhaps including some earlier and later ones. The matter is further complicated by the fact that the "same" action, agreeing to be somewhere at a certain time, for example, might be undertaken by quite different behaviors — by speaking, by writing, by nodding the head, and so on. Here it is not so much the behavior itself one is interested in, if at all, but the intentions of the actor and the perception or understanding of it by others.

Many things besides actions are described partly by their relations to other things and no one supposes this means that the existence or behavior of the thing stands beyond the realm of scientific description or explanation. Correctly describing an object as an artificial satellite, for example, makes "reference" not only to some other body to which it is spatially and lawfully related in a certain way but also to the nature of the satellite's origin. It may be objected that in the case of action at least part of the additional "elements" besides the simple behavior is its *meaning*. I agree, but I don't take it as an objection. What *is* the meaning of an action? Whatever it is, it is something in the world and therefore describable. If it is, for example, the *thoughts* typically associated with the behavior in question or the thoughts that would be associated with it if people reflected on what they are doing,[8] then we have two possibilities. If it is the former, then we have another momentary fact to account for along with the behavior. If the latter, then there is a disposition as well. Here I only say that whether it is the occurrent thought or the disposition thereto or some combination of the two, whether in the actor or in the perceiver (or in anyone else), there would seem to be no reason why they cannot be described and therefore lawfully explained. The same goes if the associated dispositions are only behavioral. To be sure, the description may be very complex, even involving reference to the origin of the association of the thoughts or dispositions to the behavior. (The association will not ordinarily in itself be a lawful one but rather will be conventional. So one may want, in a particular case, to explain not only why the action occurred at this particular time but also how a certain kind of behavior came to be conventionally associated with a certain "meaning.") The point is that *whatever* one takes an action to "include" — thoughts, dispositions, effects — they are analytically isolable elements in a particular case, thus providing no obstacle in principle to description and explanation.

Though the issue of the distinction will come up again somewhat obliquely in later chapters, I shall for the most part ignore the distinction between behavior and action in what follows. I shall usually speak simply of the explanation of human behavior in a broad sense which will ordinarily mean what are called actions and not just the simple physical motions. However, if I am not mistaken, most of what there is to say about several aspects of the explanations or possible explanations of human behavior doesn't depend on some of these finer, though of course in some contexts crucial, distinctions, since the logical structure of certain possible theories about human behavior is completely independent of the distinction. It may seem odd, especially in these days, for a philosophical theorist of society to play down the distinction between behavior and action. The intention is in no way, as will be seen, to denigrate the role of mind in human affairs, but only to affirm the possibility of the scientific explanation of those affairs. Put another way, the distinction between action and mere behavior is fundamental only to the extent that the distinction between thought and non-thought, or the mental and the physical is fundamental, and not, as some would have it, to the extent that the distinction between the scientifically nonexplainable and the scientifically explainable is fundamental.

Belief and Action

Several philosophers in recent years have been arguing that the case of human action faults the Humean conception of causation in that its correct analysis shows, according to the philosopher in question, that some distinct events are "logically" or "conceptually" and not only "externally" related, or that causation is not mere "constant conjunction," or that some occurrences are "conceptually" outside the causal realm. MacIntyre makes some of these arguments in his "Mistake about Causality in Social Science." In this final section of this chapter I shall take partial issue with some of MacIntyre's arguments and especially with his suggestion that his argument shows there to be something wrong with the Humean conception of causation. Then I shall also be in a position to dispute his idea of what is causal and what is "logical" in the social sciences.

MacIntyre apparently wishes to maintain (a) that "the relation of belief to action is not external and contingent, but internal and conceptual"[9] and (b) that the Humean view of causality is false at least as being the only kind of causality. From these conclusions he goes on to draw some consequences for the social sciences. Actually MacIntyre is somewhat confusing on this second point. Sometimes he seems to be arguing that since the connection between belief and action is not Humean, but is causal, then causality cannot be merely Humean. Some causality, as it were, clearly is Humean for MacIntyre, even some causality having to do with the explanation of human behavior. At other times, however, the argument appears to be that the connection between belief and action is not causal at all, and, incidentally also that not all causality is Humean. But finally, he seems most commonly to be maintaining that Hume was wrong in asserting that the only connections to be found in nature are "external and contingent" since the connection between belief and action is not of that sort. In any event, while I shall agree with MacIntyre that in a sense belief and action are "logically" or "conceptually" connected, I shall also argue that this does not show there to be anything wrong with the Humean conception of causation by which *I* mean the view that any two "distinct" properties are only externally related and that causality is mere "constant conjunction." It is not easy to find any passages in which MacIntyre expresses his views in a nutshell, so the following will have to do:

> It [the "conceptual scheme" of many classical sociologists] contains two elements at least worth noticing and challenging. The first is the view that beliefs and actions are distinct and separately identifiable social phenomena. The second is the view that causal connexion consists in constant conjunction.[10]
>
> It is worth pointing out that, if you hold the Humean view of causality, and you wish to investigate the relation of belief to action, you will probably involve yourself in treating belief and action as separate phenomena, since it is only between such that causality in the Humean sense can hold.[11]

Minds, we said earlier, consist of states of consciousness and dispositions.

Sometimes only states of consciousness are called mental. This calls attention to the fact, I presume, that dispositional "mental" acts are not really mental at all in the primary sense; not because dispositions are nonexistents as Ryle and others would have it, but because these dispositions are dispositions of the body and are not in themselves constituted even in part of conscious states.[12] Thus a person may know or believe even when he is asleep or unconscious. Memory, too, is generally a set of dispositions, although a sudden remembering — for example, to pick up some bread on the way home — is not a disposition but a conscious state. But what are such dispositions dispositions *to*? Solubility, as we all know from our philosophy of science books if from nowhere else, is the disposition to dissolve when put in water. A dispositional "mental" act is commonly analyzed simply as the disposition to act in certain ways under certain conditions, and for scientific purposes this is both necessary and adequate. Indeed, even occurrent mental states must be so treated, that is, as the tendency or the acquisition of the tendency to act in certain ways under certain conditions. This is, of course, the idea of *methodological* behaviorism. But I want to suggest that, for philosophical purposes and as an accurate description of reality, a "mental" disposition must be treated as the disposition *both* to act in certain ways *and* to have certain occurrent mental states under certain conditions. Thus a person's hope that all people may someday soon have enough to eat is the disposition not merely to act and to speak in certain ways under certain conditions, but, under some of those same and also other conditions, to have certain specific thoughts, feelings, and other conscious states.

The status of this suggestion may seem to be a bit peculiar. I do not intend to be analyzing the *meaning* of, say, 'hoping', at least as that activity (of analyzing) would ordinarily be understood, but to give a "theory" of mental dispositions designed to reflect the causal reality, that is, the fact that there is an intimate lawful relation between the bodily state which "grounds" the disposition in question and the conscious states which, as I am treating dispositions, are its partial realization. According to the analysis of dispositions I would defend, and not trying to say any more precisely what the status of such an analysis is, 'x is soluble', for example, "means" that 'x has a certain, nondispositional property and whatever has that property and is placed in water dissolves'. Using a familiar notation, in which 'S' stands for 'soluble', 'W' for 'being placed in water', 'D' for 'dissolves in water', and 'f' is a predicate variable, we have

$$Sx \text{ means } (\exists f)[fx \cdot (y)([fy \cdot Wy] \supset Dy)].$$

The virtues and shortcomings of this analysis of dispositions I propose to ignore in going directly to the problem of belief, for what follows doesn't depend on the details of the analysis.[13]

Belief is a disposition. On this it is easy to agree with the *metaphysical* behaviorist Ryle. And, as he has also forced on our minds, a given belief is not the disposition to do a single, specific thing (or, I would add, to have a single, specific thought) under a single, specific condition, but rather the disposition to do a somewhat vaguely specifiable number of things under a somewhat vaguely specifiable number of conditions. Thus the belief that the Christian God exists is the disposition, among other things, to pray on certain occasions, to attend church services when possible, to say certain things in response to certain questions, and so on. In the case of belief, as contrasted to some other dispositions, the linguistic aspect is crucial, of course. For what some call the "logic" of belief and what I would rather say is the nature of what we happen to label as belief is such that a person who believes that x is F "must," if he answers at all and if he answers honestly to the question whether he believes that x is F, answer affirmatively. This is part, no doubt, of what MacIntyre means when he says the connection between belief and action is internal and conceptual, not external and contingent. But let us look at that a little more closely. When one maintains that all properties are *only* externally connected, the properties in question are only *simple* properties. Thus if someone tried to refute this doctrine by pointing out, say, that the properties of being a bachelor and being a male are not so connected for it is a matter of definition or of "logic" and not of lawfulness that nothing can be a bachelor without being male, he would have misunderstood the doctrine. Here we see the crucial importance of the distinction between simple and complex properties. In the case at hand, we should expect that the "names" of some particular kinds of actions will occur in the definition of 'believing so-and-so' whatever so-and-so might be. Here, to be sure, there is a definitional, or what some call a "logical" or "conceptual," connection between belief and action. *But the simple properties that are involved in the definition(s) are only externally connected.* Thus if 'Ba' stands for 'a believes x', and 'E' for all the vaguely specifiable, relevant conditions, and 'A' for all the vaguely specifiable, relevant actions (and conscious states), and 'f' is a predicate variable, we get

$$Ba \text{ means } (\exists f)[fa \cdot (y)([fy \cdot Ey] \supset Ay)].$$

Here the connection between belief ('B') and action ('A') may, if one wishes, be described as "internal and conceptual" (I would rather say it is simply definitional) since '*A*' occurs in the definition of '*B*'. But the connection(s) between *f*, *E*, and *A* may be taken to be straightforwardly lawful, that is, merely as "external and contingent." Thus the connection between belief and action is internal and conceptual in the sense in which the connection between solubility and dissolving is internal and conceptual. I conclude that the sense in which belief and action are "conceptually" related does not show that the significant doctrine that any two simple properties are such that (a) they are only externally related to each other and hence (b) they may be lawfully connected in any manner whatsoever is false.

At this point it may seem that with respect to the social sciences I have granted everything to MacIntyre. To be sure, I have argued that MacIntyre's conclusion about causality in general has not been established; nothing he has said proves that any two (simple) properties may not have any lawful connection whatsoever. On the other hand, MacIntyre's ultimate aim in his paper is to show that any investigation such as those of Marx or Weber or Pareto into the connection between beliefs and actions which imagines itself to be a causal one misconceives its own nature. And in granting to MacIntyre that the connection between belief and action *is* in a sense "internal and conceptual" (definitional) I may seem to be granting this point as well.

We could, I suppose, define (the name of) a given belief in a way that it would cover any situation whatsoever, in principle. But this would be silly for any practical as well as for any scientific or analytic purposes. And in any case we could always ask about the lawful connections between and among the properties (the names of) which make up the definitions. Thus if we limit the definition of (the name of) a given belief to what a person with that belief would do under certain, relatively few circumstances, we can always ask what a person who would do so-and-so in such-and-such circumstances would do under such-and-such other circumstances. And this is, or may well be, a question of lawful connection and by no means a priori or conceptual or internal or definitional. Thus the question of the "lawful" connection between belief and action really resolves itself into one of the lawful connections of behaviors in the same persons. Thus too the questions of Marx, Weber, and Pareto were not only perfectly good questions (with which, in his way, MacIntyre agrees) but they were or could have been questions of lawful connection. In holding, as I do, that the classical sociologists were or may have been investigating the question of the lawful connections between belief and actions (though not the actions (the names of) which occur in the definitions of (the names of) the given beliefs), I am not committed to holding that they succeeded in coming up with laws of nature. For, as we observed in the last chapter, the Humean view of causation properly understood does not imply that when there is a lawful connection between *A* and *B* there must also be a simple, true law of nature which mentions only *A* and *B*. (I am not speaking, of course, of what Hume himself may have believed.)

Let us consider for a moment, then, the Weberian case of Protestantism and the rise of capitalism. We may ignore how he came to know or believe in the connections he claimed to exist (MacIntyre says he used Mill's method of difference) in asking whether or not the connections in question are or could be lawful ones. Now the case of religious belief is particularly odd (MacIntyre might have called this to our attention, if he were aware of it, rather than treating it as typical) for at least two reasons: in the first place religious beliefs typically include both "factual" and moral components, and in the second they have a kind of comprehensive nature. We tend to consider a person's religious beliefs as having to do with what he would do (or not do) in nearly all situations. This is in very strong contrast to the belief that light travels at about 300,000 kilometers per second, for example, for this belief is the disposition to do only a few things in some very specific and numerically small circumstances. *Even so,* it is possible to characterize Protestant belief in a way that tells us what a Protestant would do in certain, specific circumstances, but not what he would do in other, specific circumstances (whether Weber succeeded in practice in doing so or not). And then we may ask what if any lawful connections hold between the tendency to act in certain ways relevant to being a Protestant and those circumstances relevant to having the opportunity to pursue certain economic practices. MacIntyre's claim that Weber was unknowingly making explicit the *logical* implications of Protestantism for economic activities, which implications the Protestants *lived*, so to speak, may be correct. But it does not establish his general point; it only shows that Weber did not define belief in Protestantism narrowly enough to raise the lawful question even if he thought that was what he was doing. Is it an "internal, conceptual" matter, for example, that the so-called Christian nations should have been the most warlike in the last few centuries? This is not a question of the logical implications of Christian belief, but of the lawful or at least the external connection between different aspects of the behaviors of people in such nations.

To put it another way: That a person who would act a certain way in a certain situation would act another certain way in another certain situation is a matter of lawfulness or at least of fact and not one of logic, provided both situations and actions are characterized in narrow enough terms. If one or both of the actions is described in a way that makes it an instance of a class of actions of which the other is a member, then the connection between them may appear to be "logical" so that a person who would act the one way in a given situation "has" to act the other certain way in another situation. But even where the connection is of this sort, which I have argued shows nothing of metaphysical significance except the importance of making the simple/complex distinction among properties, there is presupposed, as MacIntyre recognizes, that the person is rational, not in the sense that his beliefs are necessarily well founded, but in the sense that his beliefs are consistent with one another, or to speak more to the point perhaps, that his various actions are not expressions of inconsistent beliefs. But of course, as MacIntyre also realizes, not all people are rational and no one is always rational. To take an extreme case, if a person professes one thing but acts in a way which, as we ordinarily speak, is inconsistent with the belief, then we say he is irrational. The fact that we may so characterize such a situation leads MacIntyre to claim (a) that the use of the words 'rational' and 'irrational' shows that the connections involved are logical and not lawful, and (b) that since a person may act irrationally, that is, inconsistently with his professed belief, there is not a constant conjunction between any belief of a certain kind and any action of a certain kind, hence showing once again that the connection is not lawful. The second point we may dismiss immediately, for, once more, the notion of causation as constant conjunction does not require that any two lawfully related variables themselves exhibit a constant conjunction in their values. With regard to the first point, though we may and reasonably do use the words 'rational' and 'irrational' to talk about such matters, this only suggests (a) that the connections between the "elements" or simple properties of the person's belief must be external after all or else that he doesn't really have the belief, depending on how we *decide* to use the word, and (b) that we might look for the conditions under which people are rational and irrational respectively.[14] This too will be a search for lawful connections. Being rational is itself a disposition of a person, so there is always the lawful question: Under what conditions will a person who professes belief in so-and-so act in such-and-such a way (a way we call rational)? This may or may not be a question for the social sciences depending, I suppose, on the answer. This is not to be confused with the question of rationality in the other sense of having well-founded beliefs, for here the social scientists and historians can tell (and have told) us a good deal about the social conditions under which people are more or less likely to accept, say, millenarian fantasies (irrational) or a belief in scientific method (rational). One suspects that the answer to the first question lies more in psychiatry and matters of body chemistry, drug intake, and the like, though again one can always ask under what social conditions people are more or less likely to do or have done to them the kinds of things that make people irrational in this sense of not acting consistently.

If I have understood MacIntyre correctly, his view would seem to entail that if one knew what, say, a person's religious beliefs are and assuming that person to be rational, one could calculate how that person would act in whatever situation might arise. If that consequence is absurd for religious beliefs, it is all the more so for any less comprehensive set a person may have, not to mention a "single," specific belief. Thus it would seem after all that the social scientist may very well inquire about the causal connection of beliefs to actions in the sense of trying to find out what a person who happens to be disposed to act in certain ways in certain situations may tend to do in other, definitionally unrelated circumstances. There is nothing a priori about social science as such.

IV Reduction — The Nature of Social Objects

Although the issue of reduction has received much attention in the literature in recent years, it is, nevertheless, one which, at least in the case of the social sciences, no one has taken apart thoroughly.[1] In this and the next chapter I propose to approximate that undertaking, limited here by the merely pedantic, there by the extent of actual empirical knowledge, and elsewhere, no doubt, by my own imagination. The first section of this chapter gives a systematic reason, in addition to that of convenience of format, for breaking the material into two chapters. In this chapter our main concern, briefly put, is with the question whether there is a distinct realm of social objects. Its section headings are as follows: *reduction of objects and reduction of explanations*; *descriptive individualism*; *descriptive emergentism*; and *Durkheim and Ortega y Gasset on social objects*.

Reduction of Objects and Reduction of Explanations

The rough idea of reduction, as it is relevant to the various sciences, is that of eliminability or at the least of conflation. But eliminability or conflation of what? Of laws or theories, of entities or supposed entities, of suppositions or beliefs? This is part of the issue to be explored. Broadly speaking, in the case of the social sciences we can distinguish two contexts of reduction: One is that of whether there are social objects in addition to particular persons and things and, if so, how they might be related to those particular persons and things. The other context is that of whether the "usual" explanations of social phenomena can somehow be reduced to or replaced by explanations of a different sort. For reasons that will become clear as we continue, I shall refer to the first context as having to do with reduction in the *weak* sense, the second context as having to do with reduction in the *strong* sense. Reduction in the weak sense is the subject of this chapter, reduction in the strong sense of the next chapter. The weak sense has to do, we may say, essentially with what there is — the context of description — while the strong sense has to do with what laws may or may not hold — the context of explanation. But as we shall see momentarily, laws are also involved in the former context though not in a way that vitiates the distinction.

The main argument of this chapter (as distinguished from its main subject) will be that there are no social objects above or beyond or alongside individual persons and things. It will keep with historical reality as well as suit our analytic purposes if at this point I begin using the term 'sociology' to include all the social sciences and such that the subject matter of its putative explanations are things like and the properties of groups, institutions, nations, average persons, and the like; and the term 'psychology' to refer to that science the putative explanations of which are concerned with individual persons and their properties and relations. So put, we may say that the main argument of this chapter will be that the property terms of sociology can be reduced to those of psychology. (From this point on *in this chapter,* I shall use simply 'reduction' for 'reduction in the weak sense'.)

As we shall see, the notion of reduction does not really require that there be a full-blown, reliable theory about what is to be reduced. Indeed, in one form, it is not logically necessary that the relevant predicate expressions be known to enter into any significant laws of nature at all. But it is useful nevertheless to introduce the idea of reduction abstractly by way of assuming that one has theories about both that which one is reducing (the reduced theory) and that *to* which one is reducing (the reducing theory). I shall initially speak, then, of reducing one theory to another or of eliminating one theory in favor of another.

Assume, then, that we have two theories, T_1 and T_2. Let T_1 be the reducing theory and T_2 the reduced theory. (To anticipate, T_2 would be sociological theory, T_1 psychological theory.) Further, let A be the system(s) that T_1 is about, and $a_1, a_2, \ldots, a_n$ be states of those systems. Let B be the system(s) that T_2 is about, and $b_1, b_2, \ldots, b_n$ be states of these systems. Furthermore, assume that the a_i and b_i are such that they can recur, so that a given succession of states in a system of A might be a_7, a_3, a_4, a_7, a_3, for example. In order for a reduction of T_2 to T_1 to take place, a "connection" must be found or established which satisfies the following three conditions:

(1) Each *b* is coordinated to one and only one *a* which occurs at the same time. (It is not required that every *a* have a *b* coordinated to it.)
(2) No *a* is coordinated to more than one *b*. (Thus every *a* is either coordinated to one *b* or not coordinated at all.)
(3) For every *a*, if it is coordinated to some *b* at a given time, it must be so coordinated every time it occurs and vice versa.[2]

The question now is what kind of "connection" could satisfy these conditions. The answer may possibly be apparent from what has already been said in earlier chapters. There are two such connections, namely, (a) definitions and (b) laws of coexistence.

If sociology is to be reduced to psychology, then the property terms of sociological theory are connected either by way of definitions or else by way of laws of coexistence to the property terms of psychological theory; that is, the properties of groups, institutions, and the like must be related in one of these two ways to the properties of individual people and things in order for reduction to be achieved. Which is appropriate to the social sciences? Laws of coexistence can hold only between properties or variables which are distinct from one another to begin with. To put it roughly, before one can raise the question whether the properties of groups are related by laws of coexistence to the properties of individual people and things, one must assume that the properties of groups, or at least those in question, are entirely other than those properties of people and things. There can be a lawful connection between a given two properties only if logically either could exist without the other. Hence the question of reduction in the social sciences presupposes the more basic question of the nature and status of social objects and properties to begin with. Are all social properties such that they (or, to speak precisely, their names) can be defined in terms of (the names of) the properties of individual things and persons?[3] Or are there some properties of social objects which cannot be so analyzed? These precisely are the questions to be pursued in considerable detail in the remainder of this chapter.

Descriptive Individualism

"There are no simple properties of social objects." I wish to defend this proposition as true and to argue that its negation is the only plausible meaning to be given to the view that, ontologically speaking, there are social objects in addition to individual people and things. As examples of social objects we may list: trade unions, the Buddhist religion, a government, the working class, the ideology of the working class, the average-sized family of American couples, the voting behavior of Unitarians, the foreign policy of France. Speaking commonsensically, we may say that of course "there are" many different kinds of social objects; speaking ontologically, it is problematic and controversial whether "there are" social objects. What is the dispute about? Or rather, what can it only be about, whatever some may have thought they were disputing?

Put very roughly we have those on the one side who say that social objects are really just ways of behaving and other properties of individual persons and other particular things. On the other side we have those who say that at least some social objects, such as the State for example, are "more than" or "other than" any properties and relations of individual persons and things. There are, so far as my imagination can construe, only three remotely possible interpretations that could be given to the second of these views — that, ontologically speaking, there are social objects. They are (a) that some social objects can exist without there being any people, (b) that some social objects have properties which no individual person or thing has, and (c) that some social objects have simple properties.[4] Let us consider each of these separately.

Although the meaning of the first of these is passably clear, its difficulty as a reasonable interpretation of one side of a genuine dispute is that no one is apt to maintain it. I can think of no clear-cut historical example of anyone who would hold, for example, that a trade union might exist even though it had no members or there were no people at all; or that France might have a foreign policy even though no particular people were involved. Among major thinkers only Durkheim, of whom I shall be saying more in the last section, could, to my knowledge, be said to have written some things that might conceivably be so interpreted. Some philosophers such as Plato and Hegel have, to be sure, held that the "real" Idea of the State or of Freedom might exist without people. But the Idea of the State, whatever it might be, is not an actual or even a possible state and the Idea of Freedom, whatever it might be, is not any actual or possible social condition in which one might find oneself. Thus we must reject this understanding of the proposition that there are social objects on the grounds that it makes it too absurd for anyone really to believe.

The difficulty with the second interpretation of the theory that social objects have a reality beyond that of individual things and people is not that no one believes it but that everyone does. Anyone can give an example of a property of some social object that no particular person exemplifies; here a single example will both establish that point and lead to the argument. A political party may be said to be united or, contrarily, disunited. No particular person is united or disunited except, if at all, in quite a different sense. So some social objects clearly have properties which no individual person or thing has. At the same time, it will surely be agreed all around that a party's being united, say, *is* just the ways in which most of its members feel and believe, act and are prone to act, speak and are prepared to speak. In brief and details aside, saying that the party is united is indeed but a shorthand way of talking about various properties of the majority of the members of the party.

I may now express this idea more technically by stating that the property of the social object can be defined in terms of the properties of individual people. And just as no one will dispute that there are properties of social objects which are not properties of any individual, so no one, surely, will dispute that some of those properties of social objects can be defined wholly through the properties and relations of individual persons and things. But can all properties of social objects be so treated? Can every property of every social object in principle be defined in terms of the properties of individual persons and things?[5] This precisely is the issue, and if the answer is affirmative we may be justified in saying that, ontologically speaking, there are no social objects; all that exists are individual persons and things.[6] Social objects will only be, as some speak, convenient fictions or logical constructions. They will not, however, be of the status of such nonexistents as unicorns and mermaids; it is not the distinction between exemplified and unexemplified properties which is at issue here but rather the distinction between simple and complex properties. For the linguistic reflection of the distinction between simple and complex properties is, as argued in the first chapter, exactly that between undefinable and definable predicate terms respectively. Perhaps at this point I may reasonably claim to have established that the only issue is indeed whether there are simple properties of social objects and a fortiori that, without a real distinction between simple and complex properties to begin with, there is no way to formulate a genuine issue.

I shall label the view that, ontologically speaking, there are social objects, that is, that there are simple properties of social objects, as *descriptive emergentism.* The contrary view that, ontologically speaking, there are no social objects, that is, that all properties of social objects can be defined in terms of the properties of individual persons and things, I shall refer to as *descriptive individualism.* In the literature these two views have sometimes been called "metaphysical holism" and "methodological individualism" respectively. But there are two good reasons for avoiding this terminology. For one, these expressions are often, if not more commonly, used to denote views about *explanation,* about whether the laws of the social sciences can somehow be reduced to or deduced from those of psychology, with which views those of *descriptive* emergentism and *descriptive* individualism are sometimes confused. For the other, the expressions more than suggest that what I have labeled descriptive emergentism is an old-fashioned metaphysical position (bad) while what I have referred to as descriptive individualism is the modern, methodological outlook (good). This terminology in which the metaphysical seems to be unfavorably contrasted with the methodological only embodies the illusion of some of the positivists that they were not themselves taking a metaphysical position but only suggesting to the scientists how they should proceed. Positively, descriptive individualism is, like its opposite, a metaphysical theory. It presupposes some of the traditional dialectic of existence and the stand it takes makes sense only within that dialectic.[7]

Descriptive individualism is, I believe, true. The argument in its favor is, in one sense, very simple; in another, we must admit that it presupposes a whole philosophical frame of reference which cannot here be defended except insofar as this whole book is a defense of it. The argument, negatively stated, is simply that we are not acquainted with any simple properties of social objects nor do we have any reason to "postulate" such properties. Positively, we may say that a predicate term can have a clear meaning only if it either refers to a property with which we are acquainted or can be defined in terms of properties with which we are acquainted. Clearly, the emergentist could challenge either the criterion itself or the way it is applied by the individualist in this particular case. That is, either the emergentist may argue that the criterion of meaningfulness is too narrow to begin with or he may deny that we are not acquainted with simple properties of social objects. In the next section I shall examine the emergentist's position a little more; here I want to develop the sense and the implications of the individualist's view.

The individualist holds that we are not acquainted with any simple properties of social objects. Naturally there will be some odd cases. Although one does not see a trade union or feel a state, one can, for example, see and hear an orchestra. And an orchestra would seem to be a collective or social object. The individualist may respond in two ways. First, so far as one can literally perceive an orchestra it is the orchestra only as a physical and not at all as a social object that is perceived. And we have not denied that physical "collectives" may not exemplify simple properties. But secondly, one might possibly grant that we can sometimes perceive what are really complex properties as simple. I doubt that we ever perceive any of the genuinely social properties of social objects as simple at all or even that we ever literally perceive them, but an individualist could consistently maintain his position even if he granted that sometimes some persons perceive some social properties as if they were simple.

Descriptive individualism, therefore, is the view more in the empiricist tradition. For it, there can be no possibility of lawful connections — whether laws of coexistence or any other kind — between the properties of social objects and the properties of individual persons and things for we do not have two distinct sets of properties to begin with. Being a bachelor has no lawful connection to being a male. Similarly, the anger of the crowd has only a definitional and no lawful connection to the anger of the persons who make up the crowd.[8] Here the details do not matter. According to the very theory of descriptive individualism, then, a connection of the sort exists which satisfies the conditions for reduction given a few pages back. Unlike the case of descriptive emergentism, it is not for the individualist still an open question whether reduction is possible; in the sense defined, reduction follows from the very theory.

And what of eliminability in this case? One might say that we have "eliminated" the social entities by making the definitions, though literally of course we cannot eliminate what was never there. Do we eliminate any laws? The answer is that we do not; we have merely reformulated them in individualistic terms.[9] We still have the same basic number of laws we had before, only instead of having one set which mentions only the properties of individual people and things and another set which mentions properties of groups, governments, religions, and so on, we have only one set, all members of which mention only the properties of individual people and things. What has been "eliminated" is only the need for the *names* of certain properties and not any laws of nature or entities. Whether it is desirable or even always possible in practice to make the definitions such that the laws or putative laws mentioning properties of groups can be so reformulated is primarily a methodological question, one which I have no intention of pursuing here and probably couldn't answer anyway dependent as the answer is partly on the ingenuity of practicing social scientists, partly on the state of the technology of investigation.[10]

Descriptive Emergentism

We have seen that the position of the descriptive individualist entails that a definitional connection or set of connections exists which satisfies the conditions for reduction abstractly stated. In the case of the descriptive emergentist, clearly no such entailment obtains. But even though the emergentist is not logically committed to reduction and may even be reluctant to embrace it, it is important to see that even on his position reduction is possible in principle. If for every simple property of social objects, there exists a law of coexistence such that that property is exemplified if and only if a certain state of affairs occurs at the level of individual persons and things, then we have, in the sense defined above, the grounds for reduction. This reduction may be possible even when we do not have theories at the level of the reduced and the reducing, since the rough idea of eliminability would remain. For if there *are* any laws at the level of the reduced, they are eliminable when such reduction takes place in the following sense: that from the laws of the reducing theory *and* the laws of coexistence, the laws of the reduced theory will follow logically. There is no possibility of making the *de*duction from the laws of the reducing theory alone. This can easily be seen by considering the fact that whatever laws may exist at the level of the reduced will mention properties the names of which won't occur at all in the laws of the reducing theory. The laws of coexistence are the bridge, so to speak, by containing the names of the properties at both the level of the reduced and the level of the reducing.

But even if there are no laws at the level of the reduced, the essential idea of reduction and "elimination" remains. Assume that the laws of the reducing area are process or near-process, that is, that from them and the statement of some initial conditions one can reliably predict the future states of affairs in the area in question. Then one could predict future states in the area of the reduced by first computing the state in the area of the reducing by means of the laws of the reducing theory, and then by using the necessary law of coexistence. This could be done if reduction has been achieved whether laws exist at the level of the reduced or not. But it is useful to see that the heart of the idea of reduction is preservable even in the case where the variables of the area of the reduced do not, by themselves, constitute any laws of nature. Now even though we are officially talking about the case of reducing sociology to psychology, or in this case of reducing social properties to properties of individual persons and things, it may be worth noting that the kind of connection I just mentioned, while it does not hold in the case of the social and the individual since there are no simple social properties to begin with, is exactly the connection which holds between mental properties and physical ones. That is, the mental variables by themselves do not make for any laws of nature; there are, however, laws of coexistence which connect any given mental state to a certain physical state but not so that for every *different* physical state, there is a *different* mental state. Since this is so, the laws of the physical realm so far as they in conjunction with some set of initial conditions in the physical realm permit us to predict future, relevant, physical states also would enable us to predict future mental states in conjunction with the laws of coexistence. I am not, of course, about to announce the real possibility of reliably predicting future states of mind in an interesting sense — some of them we surely wouldn't even understand — but only to explain further by means of what should be possible in principle my view of the connection of mind to body.

But let us return to our descriptive emergentist, not with respect to mind, but with respect to social properties. I have shown a clear sense in which such an emergentist can also be a reductionist. But historically speaking, an emergentist of this sort is likely to be anti-reductionist. Why is that? It may help if I recall that such a person is apt to express his view in words such as "the group is more than the individuals in it," "the State is higher than any person in it," "the collective is more important than the individual," and so on. (Of course these sentences may express only moral or political values; but not infrequently they express a confusion of what is believed to be the case with what is held to be desirable.) In any event, and this is the point, such a person would, if he were to articulate his view in my terminology, say that the "emerging" properties — in this case, the properties of social wholes — are not merely parallel to certain properties of individual persons and things, but are such that they interact "back" with these properties of individual persons and things in a way that the latter do not constitute in any case a causally closed system. Hence the State might be said to be "more than the sum of" or even "prior to" the individuals which "make it up." In short, those who postulated or even claimed to be acquainted with simple properties of social wholes are not likely to be satisfied with those properties as "merely" parallel to configurations at the individual level; they will want them to "make a difference" to what happens at the individual level in a stronger sense than seems to be provided by "merely" parallel properties. *We* can keep in mind, however, that the values of "merely" parallel variables do nevertheless make a difference in that as they vary, so do those of the parallel properties in the other realm; thus parallelism is consistent with a thought's having any effect whatsoever on the physical world, for example. And the same would go in the case of "merely" parallel social properties.

A final comment about eliminability is in order, although it is hardly more than a repetition of what was said before in a somewhat different context. What is eliminated by reduction as we have been talking about it, that is, by laws of coexistence, is a theory or rather the need for a theory or laws at the level of the reduced. No *entities* are eliminated or defined or explained out of existence. Specifically the social wholes or the simple properties thereof, if they existed "in the first place," are not eliminated by showing that there are laws of coexistence connecting them with properties or configurations of properties of individual persons and things. One might rather say that lawfulness presupposes existence, without, however, as some more scientistically inclined philosophers seem to think, constituting its "meaning" or being a decisive criterion for it. What properties there are, whether they are simple or complex, is prior to all explanation, to all matters of lawful connection, though we sometimes, as in the case of atomic and subatomic particles, for example, *discover* certain properties in a situation where we are looking for explanations.

As I have already hinted, two arguments have been made in favor of emergentism. One of them has it that we are or can be acquainted with the (simple) properties of social objects. It will be further held that this acquaintance is not by the usual senses, but rather is by some special faculty of the mind. To this extent, and especially insofar as an operative faculty of this kind seems to be quite rare, the theory and the argument are analogous to intuitionist theories of ethics with all their attendant epistemological difficulties. So there is little I can add to those arguments which have already shown the implausibility of intuitionist views in general. These arguments have to do primarily with the problems of confirmation of and public access to the alleged results of the use of the intuitive faculty.

The other argument is that (simple) properties of social objects must be "postulated" in order causally to explain certain phenomena. Certainly there is nothing wrong in general with an argument of this kind; it is after all the basis of atomic and quantum physical theory in which entities of a certain sort, that is, as having certain (simple) properties, are assumed to exist in order to account for certain observable phenomena.[11] One may doubt, however, that in the case of social objects such a "postulation" is necessary. Durkheim believed that it was, and we may now turn to an examination of his and Ortega y Gasset's views on the matter.[12]

Durkheim and Ortega y Gasset on Social Objects

It may further illuminate the issue of the status of social objects to consider the views of Durkheim and Ortega y Gasset on it. Both appear to hold that certain social objects or social facts cannot be reduced to the properties and relations of individual people. Hence in my terminology, they both seem to deny the position of descriptive individualism, though I do not think this is really so in the case of Ortega. Naturally they do not use my language; neither one of them ever says that there are or are not simple properties of social objects. Both are struck by the coercive nature of society — that much of what any person does appears to that person, if he reflects on it at all, to derive from externally imposed obligations. These obligations do not typically arise from freely entered into agreements on the part of the individual (in any case the obligation to live up to one's agreements cannot derive from any such agreement), but appear to be "just there," not coming from or owed to anyone in particular.

Even though Durkheim agrees that "society is composed only of individuals,"[13] he also insists that "the states of the collective consciousness are different in nature from the states of the individual consciousness; they are 'representations' of another type. The mentality of groups is not the same as that of individuals; it has its own laws."[14] Durkheim provides a definition of 'social fact' as follows: *"A social fact is every way of acting, fixed or not, capable of exercising on the individual an external constraint;* or again, *every way of acting which is general throughout a given society, while at the same time existing in its own right independent of its individual manifestations."*[15]

Although Durkheim does not clearly distinguish the issue of what exists from that of what explains what and the status of such explanations, he certainly appears to believe that there are *entities* which are neither physical objects nor individual states of minds, entities the properties of which enter into lawful relations with the properties of individual people. Yet these entities are not completely other than people. They are properties of "the collective consciousness" (*l'âme collective*). This, I think, is best interpreted as saying that there are simple properties of collectives. It would appear that the root reason Durkheim has for believing in such entities with such properties derives from the individually felt phenomenon of external, impersonal, nonphysical restraint on our behavior. (He also cites the states of mind and actions one finds oneself undergoing and undertaking in crowds, states and actions which seem "foreign" to one's nature.) So he concludes there must *be* something which does the restraining, something with causal efficacy, something, I say, with simple properties that is not a person, but not for all that a physical object either.

Ortega begins with the same kind of phenomenon. He considers the felt obligation to shake hands with everyone upon entering a room (under certain conditions and in certain cultures) as his prime example of just such an obligation — again, one which presents itself to the individual as externally imposed, impersonal, and nonphysical. The felt obligation one has on entering the room does not arise from some spontaneous, internal desire or decision to shake hands with everyone, nor does it come from the orders or requests of any person in particular — by his authority or power — nor, finally, is one being physically coerced against his will to lift his arm, palm open, and place the hand into that of another. Still one does it, and if by chance one does not, he knows and feels his transgression of a social obligation. In some ways Ortega wants to consider his conclusion the opposite of Durkheim's and in any case to be clearly distinguished from the idea of a collective consciousness. The following, lengthy passage expresses his negative intent quite clearly and offers some useful, though not always indisputable, historiography:

Since the end of the eighteenth century, it has been arbitrarily and mystically supposed that there is a social spirit or consciousness, a *collective soul,* which the German romanticists, for example, called *Volksgeist,* or "national spirit." It has never been sufficiently emphasized that this German concept of the "national spirit," the *Volksgeist,* is simply the heir of the idea that Voltaire suggestively launched in his masterly *Essai sur l'histoire générale et sur les moeurs et l'esprit des nations.* The *Volksgeist* is "the spirit of the nation."

But I repeat, this idea of the *collective soul,* of a *social consciousness,* is arbitrary mysticism. There is no such *collective soul,* if by *soul* is meant — and here it can mean nothing else — *something* that is capable of being the responsible subject of its acts, *something* that does what it does because what it does has a clear meaning for it. But then will the characteristic of *people,* of *society,* of the *collectivity* be precisely that they are soulless?

The collective soul, *Volksgeist* or "national spirit," social consciousness, has had the loftiest and most marvelous qualities attributed to it, sometimes even divine qualities. For Durkheim, society is veritably God. In the Catholic de Bonald (the actual inventor of collectivistic thought), in the Protestant Hegel, in the materialist Karl Marx, this collective soul appears as something infinitely above, infinitely more human than man. For example, it is wiser. And here our analysis, with no special effort or premeditation, with no formal precedents (at least so far as I am aware) among philosophers, drops into our hands something disquieting and even terrible — namely, that the *collectivity* is indeed something human, but is the human without man, the human without spirit, the human without soul, the human dehumanized.[16]

What, then, is this force which, according to Ortega, moves us to perform such actions? We are told that it is "an action that is performed by us but that is not ours — it has an anonymous, extra-individual origin."[17] But what is this origin? Is it some apparently distinct *entity*, like Durkheim's? We are warned by Ortega not to believe that his view is even similar to Durkheim's:

> When someone had a confused and momentary glimpse of it [the "extraordinary reality" of the phenomenon of social coercion], like the Frenchman Durkheim, he did not succeed in analyzing it and above all was incapable of thinking it, of translating it into concepts and doctrine. To anyone familiar with Durkheim's thought, I recommend that when my analysis touches the two or three momentary points at which my doctrine *appears* to coincide with Durkheim's — I recommend that he reject the suggestion, because it would completely prevent him from understanding my concepts.[18]

Since Ortega clearly takes Durkheim to hold that it is an *entity* which is not a human individual and which has causal efficacy, the passages just quoted invite us to interpret Ortega's view to be something different. On the other hand, Ortega would seem to be quite mistaken in interpreting Durkheim as holding that *l'âme collective* is "*something* that is capable of being the responsible subject of its acts, *something* that does what it does because what it does has a clear meaning for it." His mistake is not, if I understand Durkheim correctly, in saying it is a *something*, but in ascribing to it a consciousness of its own. Nothing Durkheim says, except for calling it *l'âme collective*, should lead one to that conclusion, and much of what he says about it should lead one to the contrary. In any event, because Ortega so interprets Durkheim and because of what he says about his own view with respect to Durkheim's, one may be tempted to suppose that his is exactly that which I say is Durkheim's, that is, that there are simple properties of social wholes, but social wholes are not themselves minds or conscious entities. Still it is Ortega's emphasis on 'something' in the passage just quoted which suggests that he wants to deny that what he too is willing to call a "collective" and also "society" and "people" is a something, an entity other than particular people and their properties and relations. To be sure, he does characterize this force as "extra-individual," treats it as if it were causally efficacious, and claims that his analysis has "no formal precedents . . . among philosophers." What then, positively, is Ortega's view of the nature of social objects?

I have spent this time in preparing an interpretation of Ortega's view because if the interpretation is the right one, then it does, in addition to affording me an opportunity to make some more general comments with respect to the explanation of social phenomena, provide the basis for a partial answer to Durkheim. That is, it yields a way of accounting in terms of descriptive individualism for the same kinds of phenomena that led Durkheim to his emergentism. Even though Ortega refers to the origin of certain of our actions and the feelings that surround them as "extra-individual," I don't think he means by this that that origin is extra-human or even that it does not come from some individual human(s); but only that, in the first place, it is external to the particular person who performs the action, and secondly and more importantly, its origin typically is to be found in people who are not among those in whom the action has the characteristics that lead to a problem in the first place.

Ortega spends a lot of time on the origin of the handshake as a form of salutation, this action that we all perform but do not "understand." Partly his interest is in the history for its own sake and in disputing another account of its origin. More importantly, he is interested in showing, whatever the historical details, that the handshake was originally an "intelligible" act, one which made sense to the participants, not just as *a* form of salutation — in that sense the handshake still makes sense to its employers — but in its particular form of grasping the hand of the other, moving it briefly and slightly, and dropping it. In short, the only way we can understand the handshake today is not by examining *it* more closely or by studying those who shake hands more carefully but only by looking at its historical origins.

There are clearly several issues involved here. In the first place, there is the question of what it is to understand an action. As I have indicated earlier, especially in the first chapter, I do not take my task to argue that there is only one kind of understanding which is possible or even, apart from any context, appropriate of human action or behavior. Quite ignoring the question whether such kinds of explanation are causal or not, we may agree that Ortega would seem to be correct in maintaining that there is a sense of 'understand' in which we understand the handshake only when we do know its historical origins, including most importantly the *reasons* those who originated it had for doing so. We may consider this example, insofar as it involves knowing the reasons its first employers had for shaking hands as a form of salutation, to be paradigmatic of what some have called *historical understanding*. But we must be prepared to accept the likelihood that some forms of human action, perhaps even some forms of salutation, have no explanation whatsoever in terms of original human reasons for originating or indulging in the convention. This kind of understanding which I have just labeled as historical understanding is that which, if I understand him rightly, Lucien Goldmann in his *Human Sciences and Philosophy*[19] believes is the only appropriate way of approaching human behavior and the disregarding of which he deplores as being characteristic of the social sciences in advanced capitalist societies such as the United States and increasingly his native France. We must now see that such understanding is not the only possible one of a human action.

If to understand a kind of action is to be able to predict its occurrence in the sense of knowing the circumstances in which it will occur, then it is obvious that we can understand the handshake without knowing its historical origins. On the other hand we know that the correlation between those circumstances by themselves which permit the prediction and the action is itself a conventional one in need of causal explanation. "Why do human beings in certain circumstances shake hands?" asked as a causal question could conceivably again be interpreted as a historical question in Ortega's and Goldmann's sense, but it need not. The idea is this: if we want to understand causally why in certain circumstances this organism extends his hand to another and grasps his, in one sense it is a full-blown explanation merely to cite the social and perceptual environments in which he has heretofore existed. Or to put it another way, the schema of the relevant law would be that if a human organism with standard perceptual and intellectual equipment has existed in environments with such and such characteristics[20] and he finds himself in such and such circumstances, he will perform the action we call "shaking hands." It may be noticed that this law-sketch itself mentions in its antecedent events which occur at several different times. Thus it is, as it stands, an example of what Bergmann calls historical laws and what I prefer to call polychronal laws. But since the events mentioned are all in the life of the subject whose behavior is being explained, it would not, I presume, satisfy Ortega's or Goldmann's conception of a "real" explanation.

But I shall go even further. Can this polychronal law itself be "eliminated" or reduced to a law which is not itself polychronal? The answer is affirmative provided that the relevant events which occurred in the social and perceptual environments of the subject left a physiological "imprint," presumably in the brain or nervous system. If there were enough of an isomorphism between the events (as perceived) and the "imprint," the isomorphism itself being a lawful relation of the coexistence sort, then the polychronal law could be eliminated in favor of one which has the form: if a human organism has such and such characteristics (features of the brain or nervous system) and is in such and such circumstances, it will perform the action we call "shaking hands." Whether in this case and all logically similar ones (for example, Freudian laws of adult neurosis), there is such an "imprint" is of course a question of fact. Freud himself assumed there was, and we may agree that it is the "frame of reference" of modern psychology and neurology that all such polychronal laws could in principle be eliminated, although in explaining particular cases it may be much easier to find out the past event in the subject's life than the present state of his nervous system.

What I have endeavored to show is that there is a sense of 'understand', a perfectly good sense, in which the handshake, for example, can be understood without reference to events beyond the life and perception of the particular subject whose action is being explained. More than that, the schema of a possible kind of explanation of the subject's behavior makes no reference to *reasons* — the subject's or anyone else's; at most it assumes that the organism is a sentient and conscious being. But we must now return to the "subjective" aspect of the action, for it was this in the first place which led Ortega and Durkheim to suppose that there is some kind of problem. The characteristics which strike Ortega are that we don't understand our action in the sense explained, that we nevertheless feel obliged to perform it, and that the obligation is, as it were, general and impersonal and not specific. Ortega gives the impression that he has explained these phenomena by his pointing to the historical origins of the kind of action in question and so is able to avoid the kind of emergentism which Durkheim embraces. But I think we must insist that he has left out a crucial part of the story as far as Durkheim is concerned. At most Ortega has explained how there comes to be a kind of action which is sometimes performed and which we do not "understand" and why, *given* that there is a sense of obligation on the part of the subject to perform the action in certain circumstances, that obligation appears as general and impersonal. What he hasn't explained at all is why any sense of obligation should attach to the action at all, and it was exactly the feeling of an external force acting upon one but coming from no person or physical force in particular that led Durkheim to postulate *l'âme collective*.

What remains to be explained, then, in order to avoid Durkheim's emergentist solution is how it is that the felt obligation to shake hands in certain circumstances, for example, arises and most importantly why it presents itself to the subject as an externally imposed obligation. So far as we are looking for a causal answer to the question how people come to have certain states of consciousness, we should look to psychology for the answer. And indeed psychologists do have something to tell us about the mechanisms by which what are initially for the child the "do's and don'ts" of specific persons become internalized, that is, take on the aspects of felt obligations. Although the obligation is the "internalization" of the initial person-specific authority, that "internalization" may still present itself to the subject as an impersonal, externally imposed duty. Durkheim seems to have supposed that since the obligation so presents itself, there must be some *entity* external to the subject which exerts the "force." This would be acceptable only if the feeling of imposition presented itself as a direct awareness of the entity doing the imposing, the more general principle being that if one is directly aware of a simple property of something, then *there is* something with the property. But in fact the phenomenology of such experience is such that while the something may (wrongly) present itself as external to oneself, it is in any case nothing very definite and specific. I conclude that together Ortega and I have satisfactorily answered Durkheim, and have therefore established the adequacy of descriptive individualism.

We may return finally, by way of leading into the next chapter, to a point I suggested earlier: that Durkheim confuses the question of the *existence* of groups with that of the *explanation* of group behavior. His claim that "the mentality of groups is not the same as that of individuals; it has its own laws" appears to be intended as an argument for the existence of groups as something more than the individuals which make it up. But this is really a separate question. For the descriptive individualist may well grant that the laws of group behavior are different from, and not reducible to, the laws of individuals *in a sense*. In addition to the feeling of externally imposed obligation which I have discussed at some length, Durkheim cites the feeling one sometimes has in a crowd of being "swept along," of participating in actions and feelings which are not really one's own. Again we may ask the psychologist how it is that human beings happen to have certain states of consciousness, but here it is more a question of whether the fact, if it is a fact, that such phenomena have their own laws entails anything about the existence of groups. The full answer to this question requires lengthy preparation and will come in the next chapter. It is obvious from what I have just said, however, that I believe that the individualist can consistently maintain the autonomy of the laws of group behavior, not as distinguished from the laws of the behavior of individuals in groups, but rather as distinguished from those of the behavior of individuals not in groups at all or in "small groups," as the sociologists call them. But with this we are ready to turn to the issue of explanatory reduction.

V Reduction — The Nature of Social Explanations

Descriptive individualism entails reduction in the weak sense. This we saw in the last chapter. But those who speak of reducing sociology to psychology typically have something more ambitious in mind than "mere" definitional reduction. Roughly what is conceived is that the "new" laws of psychology — those "former" laws of sociology to which, so to speak, definitional reduction has been applied — should be deducible from the "old" laws of psychology. This is the idea of explanatory reduction or reduction in the strong sense. What are the conditions which must obtain for this deduction to take place? I shall attempt to begin to answer this question in the first section of this chapter, *reduction and composition rules*, by considering the paradigm of Newtonian mechanics. Then I shall apply those considerations to the issue at hand, *the reduction of sociology to psychology*. We will then have arrived at a point at which it will be useful to summarize the findings of the last chapter and the first two sections of this chapter under the heading of *four issues; twelve possibilities*.

Reduction and Composition Rules

If, as argued in the last chapter, all that exists (in the relevant sense) are individual things and persons, then the question of explanatory reduction becomes the question whether the laws of the behavior of *individuals* in certain more complex situations can be deduced from those of the behavior of individuals in certain less complex situations. There is no such thing as group behavior except as a purely physical phenomenon, and so we can avoid the misleading way of formulating the issue of explanatory reduction as that of whether the laws of group behavior can somehow be deduced from the laws of individual behavior. Examining the paradigm of Newtonian mechanics will help us to understand these points more clearly.

Consider the two-body case. Given the masses, positions, and velocities of any two bodies for any given moment, Newton's laws of motion allow us to compute positions and velocities of the two bodies for any other time. This is again the idea of process. But suppose we add a third body to the system and wish to compute the positions of the three bodies for some future time. With the assistance of Newton's laws we can do this in one of two ways, which logically amount to the same thing: (a) With the help of a law sometimes called a *composition rule*,[1] we can analyze the three-body case into three two-body cases, then "put it back together again" so to speak, and make the computations. In other words, given the law of the two-body case, the composition rule, and the values of the relevant variables of the three bodies, we can make the desired computations. (b) From the composition rule and the law of the two-body case we can *deduce* the law of the three-body case. Then given this law and the values of the relevant variables of three bodies we can make the desired computations. Although the first of these procedures better describes what actually and ordinarily goes on in physics as well as in the analogous situations in psychology, I prefer the second way of describing the situation in which one deduces a law. Several comments will further bring out the implications of this idea.

First. The composition rule is itself a law of nature, and although it takes the form in Newton's system of a quantified law, it is nevertheless a law and not a mathematical truth. Given the law of the two-body and the law of the three-body cases, it is of course a *logical* fact that a certain proposition in conjunction with the former will yield, deductively, the latter. But the proposition itself is not a logical truth. It might be said at this point that the notion or employment of a composition rule is trivial. In Newtonian mechanics with *one* composition rule and the law of the two-body case, it is possible to deduce not only the law of the three-body case, but those of the four-body case, the five-body case, and so on, varying only the number of variables of the same function. That the laws of all these cases should be such that *one* composition rule allows their deduction makes it anything but trivial, and it is an empirical and contingent fact and not a logical one that they be so. Here then we have a paradigm case of explanatory reduction, in which the laws of the behavior of bodies in larger groups are deducible from the law of the behavior of bodies in the smallest group in conjunction with the composition rule.

Second. Definitional reduction is assumed in this whole procedure, of course.[2] Or rather, since the behavior of "groups," the solar system, for example, typically is already talked about in "individualistic" terms — that is, in terms of the properties of the individual bodies and the relations among them — the issue doesn't usually arise in macro-mechanics. In micro-mechanics or statistical mechanics, it arises almost backward, as it were, for it is a matter of correlating, though not in a definitional way, the observed or measurable properties of gases (the macro-objects) with a certain distribution of the properties of molecules or atoms (the micro-objects).

Third. The composition rule might "break down" at a certain level of complexity, the 1000-body case, for example, and the computations no longer be accurate. Apart from inaccurate observation which, except in very special contexts, is of no theoretical significance, this "failure" could be from any one of a number of reasons. (a) It might be that at the 1000-body level there is no determinism, so to speak, that is, that the behavior of 1000-body systems simply is not lawful either strictly or relatively. There might still be true statistical laws of the system, but none by which one could reliably predict the behavior of individual bodies. (b) It might be that a "new"[3] variable "begins" to interact at that level, that is, that the system is causally closed with respect to mass, position, and velocity up through the 999-body level, but at the 1000-body level only the addition of some other variable — color, for example — makes for a causally closed system. Technically, in the way we defined these notions earlier, color would be an interacting variable from the "beginning" since some value of it makes, by assumption, a difference to some values of mass, position, and velocity, but with the added complication that the *number* of bodies with the properties also makes a difference. Cardinality is not, of course, a relevant property of any body, but only of the group itself. The full articulation of this idea need not concern us; let us simply speak loosely and say that a "new" property "begins" to interact at a certain level of complexity. (c) But it might be also that the sheer complexity is what matters and that a "new" law is needed for that reason. Indeed one might imagine the possibility that, while the law of the behavior of the 1000-body case is not deducible from the law of smaller cases and any composition rule, from the "new" law of the 1000-body case and a "new" composition rule we could deduce the laws of the 1001-body case, the 1002-body case, and so on. Or it might be simply that one needs a "new" law for each case beginning with the 1000-body case and that no composition rule exists for the deduction of the laws of more complex from those of less complex cases.

The second and third of these possibilities are, it is easily seen, compatible with determinism. I emphasize this because all three cases, including the limiting case where lawful explanation breaks down, are what are called those of *explanatory emergence*. Hence, contrary to what some thinkers have claimed or implied, explanatory emergence does not imply indeterminism. Explanatory emergence then obtains when, for one reason or another, the laws (or, in the limiting case, the lack of lawfulness) of the more complex case are no longer, by virtue of any composition rule, deducible from that or those of the less complex case(s).

Fourth. Explanatory emergence takes place, if at all, only relative to some given theory or law(s). For whereas, say, the laws of the 1000-body case and those of higher cardinalities might not be deducible from the two-body case and any composition rule, they might be deducible from the 500-body case or any higher one through the 999-body case and some composition rule. There would, therefore, be explanatory emergence for the 1000-body and all higher cases with respect to the two-body case but explanatory reduction with respect to the 500-body case. Thus to speak of explanatory emergence or reduction absolutely makes no sense.[4]

Fifth. It is to be emphasized that the law of the three-body case is *not* deducible from the law of the two-body case alone, nor is the law for any more complex case deducible from the law of any less complex case alone. It is logically possible that there be no composition law at all, that is, that there be a "different" law for each level of complexity such that no formula allows the successive deduction of each law for the more complex situation. If this were so, the science of mechanics would be quite different from and infinitely more complicated than the way we know it, but it would still be deterministic. Considering these possibilities though makes it clear that whether explanatory reduction is possible or explanatory emergentism true is a purely factual or empirical matter to be decided by the science in question. No philosophical, moral, or ideological considerations are relevant to deciding in a particular case whether reduction can be achieved once the issue is clearly put. In this, the issue of explanatory reductionism versus explanatory emergentism is quite unlike that of descriptive individualism versus descriptive emergentism, for the latter, as we saw, is essentially a question of metaphysics and meaning, though conceivably certain empirical findings could have a bearing on the matter.

We are now in a position to see quite clearly that explanatory reductionism does not follow from definitional reductionism, even if we add determinism as an additional premise. For the former is a matter of empirical fact and the latter a matter of metaphysics and meaning. Thus explanatory emergence in any form whatsoever is compatible with definitional reduction. This is worth stressing because some have insisted that in the case of sociology and psychology explanatory reduction *must* be achievable. Those who make this insistence do so, I believe, as a result of one of three errors: (a) they confuse explanatory with definitional reduction and so believe that their empiricist metaphysics commits them to explanatory reduction; (b) they mistakenly believe that the thesis of explanatory reduction follows logically from the thesis of definitional reduction or, more often, from the latter and the thesis of determinism;[5] or (c) they mistakenly believe that their moral or social values of upholding individual dignity commit them to explanatory reduction.

Before I turn to the application of these ideas to the case of sociology and psychology, this might be an appropriate place to distinguish various reasonable meanings of 'holism' in terms of the ideas we have developed.[6] What we may label as *holism*$_1$, then, will be simply the doctrine that there is explanatory emergence. It may be and has been applied to the case of the group in relation to the individual (or rather the behavior of individuals in groups relative to some other kind of behavior) as well as to the case of the behavior of the organism relative to the behavior of either its physiological components or its physical-chemical constituents. (In this second case the question of emergence is whether there are laws of coexistence such that the laws of the behavior of the organism are deducible from the laws of the behavior of the components or constituents rather than of composition laws, the latter of which presupposes that all the properties are on the same "level.") Explanatory emergence at the level of the organism is also one meaning of 'vitalism' about which there used to be much controversy. But a second meaning of 'holism', call it *holism*$_2$, would have it that all the variables of the system in question — society or organism — interact with one another. As theories in psychology, holism$_1$ and holism$_2$ are two clear meanings that can be ascribed to *gestalt* doctrine, that is, that organisms are wholes in one or both of these senses. (Another part of *gestalt* psychology deals with the *perception* of organisms as wholes, which may or may not have to do with their actually being wholes in the senses defined.)

Holism$_3$ we may characterize as the doctrine that wholes have properties which their "parts" do not have. If we make the distinction of properties into simple (undefinable) and complex (definable) and consider the two cases again of organisms with respect to their "parts" and groups of any kind with respect to their "parts" which will ordinarily be individual persons, the only controversial case will be that of whether there are simple properties of groups, which we have already discussed at some length. In all the other cases, $holism_3$ is obviously but trivially true. *$Holism_4$* presupposes the truth of $holism_3$ and is a special case of $holism_1$. According to it, there are properties of wholes which interact "back" with their parts such that no system which includes the variables which characterize the "parts" can be causally closed unless it also includes the property or properties of the whole. It may be observed that $holism_4$, which I doubt to be true at any level of things but which is, nevertheless, a factual matter, is perfectly compatible with determinism and process knowledge of the world.

To refresh our memories and to sum up before we turn to the issue of the explanatory reduction of sociology to psychology: Within the empiricist context and the tradition of descriptive individualism, explanatory reduction takes place, first, by assuring that all the relevant property terms mentioned refer to the properties of and relations among individual people and things and, second, by finding a composition rule such that it in conjunction with the law(s) of the less complex case(s) yield deductively the laws of the more complex cases.

The Reduction of Sociology to Psychology

When we apply these ideas to the human sciences, we immediately encounter various complications and problems. Some of these problems are technological and methodological, some are terminological and definitional, some are logical and philosophical. Naturally I shall not try to solve them all. I can at best only describe problems of the first and second kinds. Those of the third I shall try to solve. It is useful to begin by discussing the idea of the explanatory reduction of sociology to psychology in its strongest possible form. I say this because I am convinced that it is the only reasonable explication of what many mean who speak of the reduction of sociology to psychology, even though they do not, possibly, realize all the problems in and implications of what they are maintaining.

The behavior of a group is, except in the purely physical sense, just the behavior of the persons in the group. Let us label the behavior of an individual in a group *social behavior*. And let us contrast this with behavior "outside" any group and label that sort *solitary behavior*. Explanatory reduction then is no longer best described as deducing the laws of group behavior from those of individual behavior, but rather one of deducing the laws of social behavior from the laws of solitary behavior. As in mechanics there is no possibility of doing this directly, of course, that is, without composition rules. One can put the idea simply to begin with then: Is there a composition rule such that it, in conjunction with the laws of solitary behavior, yields deductively the laws of social behavior? This is the question of the explanatory reduction of sociology to psychology.

But we must now ask ourselves what precisely is involved in these notions of social behavior and solitary behavior. It is not, of course, a matter of discovering what social behavior and solitary behavior really are. It is, rather, one of deciding how to draw the distinction. To suit any precise scientific purposes, the distinction must, I suggest, be drawn in a way that satisfies the following three criteria. First, it must more or less correspond to the somewhat vague distinction of the same kind that already exists in ordinary discourse. Second, it must make it possible to decide in the typical case whether a given piece of behavior is social or solitary. Third, it must make it possible for the question of explanatory reduction to be raised significantly once the laws of each kind of behavior were known. It may be that my almost casual way of drawing the distinction in the previous paragraph already satisfies these criteria, but in any case it will be useful to hear from some others. Consider first how the sociologist Max Weber makes the distinction by way of a characterization of social action:

> Sociology (in the sense in which this highly ambiguous word is used here) is a science which attempts the interpretive understanding of social action in order thereby to arrive at a causal explanation of its course and effects. In 'action' is included all human behaviour when and in so far as the acting individual attaches a subjective meaning to it. Action in this sense may be either overt or purely inward or subjective; it may consist of positive intervention in a situation, or of deliberately refraining from such intervention or passively acquiescing in the situation. Action is social in so far as, by virtue of the subjective meaning attached to it by the acting individual (or individuals), it takes account of the behaviour of others and is thereby oriented in its course.[7]

The most important feature of Weber's characterization is that according to it a social action need not involve another person in a causal or spatial sense but only by way of the actor's considering the possible behavior of others. This "connection" to others is only intentional. A social action then can take place in physical isolation from other people. One may wonder whether, as a matter of empirical fact, we ever act, even in Weber's broad sense, without considering negatively, positively, or even neutrally the behavior of others. If we do not, then for this reason alone the manner of drawing the distinction does not satisfy our criteria; that should be obvious. On the other hand, it might appear that some such definition of 'social action' is almost "necessary," for no piece of behavior described solely in terms of the physical activity (or lack of it) is either social or not social, or for that matter even an action, as some speak. Again, this is not an intuitive insight into the "real" nature of social behavior, but the imperfect reflection of a piece of empirical fact — that to know the causes but more especially the effects of a given piece of behavior in a given society, one must know what the act "is" in terms of its "subjective meaning" to the participants. Or rather, one must know (to indicate my own point of view once more) the behavioral-dispositional or physiological correlates of that "subjective meaning."

The significance of this fact — that an *action* is not adequately characterized solely in terms of the physical movements — of which so much is made in some quarters must not be overestimated, as I argued briefly in the third chapter. In any case it must not be taken as a reason for saying that an action is not the sort of thing which is susceptible to scientific explanation. If the "something more" of an action over a "mere" piece of behavior is indeed *something*, then there can be no reason in principle why it should not with the behavior itself be amenable to scientific explanation. And *for the purposes of scientific explanation* those behavioral-dispositional or physiological correlates both can and must be taken as the "something more." For those purposes, "having such-and-such attitude" and "having such-and-such belief" and even "having such-and-such thought" and "having such-and-such feeling" will be treated as dispositions to behave in certain particular ways under certain particular environmental and physiological conditions. Hence the fact that an action is "more than" a piece of behavior is no objection to a strictly behaviorist account of human behavior including social behavior.

Weber's way of drawing the distinction between solitary and social behavior may or may not be adequate, depending on how it is taken. In any case, it will be better for our purposes to draw it more as a contemporary psychologist would do so, for, as we shall see, the issue of explanatory reduction really comes down to the question of whether there is something special about social stimuli. Skinner, for example, is content simply to say that "social behavior may be defined as the behavior of two or more people with respect to one another or in concert with respect to a common environment."[8] Gerwitz is correspondingly loose: "The *social environment* consists of those functional stimuli which are provided by people; and *social behaviors* are those under the actual or potential control of social stimuli, in either their acquisition or maintenance, or both. It is arbitrary whether learning that occurs in a social context, but that is, or subsequently comes, under the control of nonsocial stimuli, is labeled social.''[9] It is, of course, possible to tighten up one's characterization so that fewer behaviors come under the heading of the social. For example: ''For these experiments the definition of a social situation included the following: (a) two or more persons must have at their disposal responses that result in reinforcement for other persons; (b) the principal sources of reinforcement for any person depend on responses made by other persons; and (c) the responses controlling reinforcement are subject to learning.''[10]

There would seem to be no way usefully to characterize social behavior in terms of an observable feature of *it*. But rather than adopt Weber's definition which requires us to know what is going on in the actor's consciousness, we can better, along with the psychologists, characterize it in terms of its causes. The crucial feature is, of course, that other persons are somehow involved in the stimuli of social behavior; and since our purposes are logical and philosophical rather than scientific, this necessarily rough characterization will be adequate for us.

Assuming then that we have already made our distinction between solitary and social behavior, consider first a major empirical complication in the attempt to find a composition rule such that the laws of solitary behavior in conjunction with it will entail the laws of social behavior. People typically behave differently at funerals than at political rallies. Moreover, behavior at a funeral of a given person ordinarily would not differ according to whether there were 356 or 357 people in attendance, nor at the political rally according to whether there were 63,300 or 65,900. Of course some differences in numbers make a difference to our behavior, but it is more the ''social situation'' than the numbers that would seem to matter.[11] The ''situation'' in turn will involve any number of variables — the expectations and attitudes of the participants, the biological relations of the participants to each other, the similarity in views, race, religion, sex, and nationality of the participants, and so on. These facts by no means entail that explanatory emergentism is true and explanatory reductionism false; indeed we are still looking at the issue in somewhat ''global'' terms, those of the sociologist rather than the psychologist. But it must be admitted that these facts make the discovery of whatever composition rule or rules there may be exceedingly difficult. Or better, they make extremely difficult a precise enough formulation of any laws of social behavior to begin with so that one could, assuming one already had the laws of solitary behavior, raise significantly the question of reduction by way of composition rule(s).

We will begin to come to the very heart of the issue when we observe that a condition for reduction by way of composition rules is that the laws of the reduced theory can contain the names of no variables which are not already in the laws of the reducing theory. In the case at hand, that means that no property terms can occur in the laws of social behavior that do not also occur in the laws of solitary behavior. For the composition rules add nothing descriptive, that is, no "new" property term occurs in them; so if the conclusion of a formally valid argument — the laws of social behavior — is to contain, nontrivially, the name of any given variable, then its name must occur somewhere in the premises, and that can only be in the laws of solitary behavior. That is only to say formally what is intuitively evident anyway — that if explanatory reduction is to be possible, all the relevant variables in the explanation of human behavior must occur in the laws of solitary behavior themselves.

This logical fact about reduction might seem to render utterly hopeless the attempt to reduce sociology to psychology and so to make the thesis of explanatory reductionism highly implausible. It implies in the first place that a way of talking about human behavior must be found such that every instance of it can be characterized as the combination of values of the same variables. This problem, however, one might reasonably say is simply one of the ingenuity of the investigators themselves and indeed one which is in the process of being overcome.

The real problem lies in the question of what the relevant variables are in the explanation of the many kinds of human behavior. In the case of mechanics, the laws which, given the values of the relevant variables, permit the calculation of later (or earlier) values of those variables mention only properties of the bodies themselves and a relation (distance) between and among those bodies. In the case of human behavior, as a matter of empirical fact, the environmental variables, but including those which characterize the appearance and behavior of other humans, are of such importance that it would be entirely futile to expect to achieve a science of human behavior if that were taken to mean a set of laws which, given any set of initial conditions, would permit reliable predictions of human behavior, solitary or social, and which mention *only* properties of humans and relations among them. What this means for the issue at hand is that, if explanatory reduction of sociology to psychology is to be possible, no relevant environmental variables can be mentioned in the laws of social behavior which are not already mentioned in the laws of solitary behavior. If there are environmental variables which make a difference only to social behavior, one could, trivially, always stick them into the laws of solitary behavior, standing by, as it were, to make their needed appearance at the level of social behavior. It is simply a case of the sort we discussed in the second chapter where not all different values of a given variable make a difference to the values of some other variable. But, and this is the point, if there are environmental variables whose values make a difference only in the case of social behavior, then it would become doubtful in the extreme, if not simply impossible, that there be any composition rule(s) which would allow the deductions necessary for explanatory reduction.

But are there any such variables? It may seem patent that there are; is it not obvious that we respond to other human beings in a different way from that in which we respond to the nonhuman environment? Surely, it may be said, the social situation does involve "new" environmental variables — those that constitute the appearance and behavior of other people — so that the laws of social behavior will have to mention variables which do not or need not occur in the laws of solitary behavior. And if this is so, then there can be no composition rule which when conjoined to the laws of solitary behavior would yield deductively the laws of social behavior. It must be granted that these observations have an initial plausibility of a very high degree, but we must now see how a contemporary psychologist might dispute their plausibility with observations of his own.

The essential point to be made against the argument of the explanatory emergentist is that he has taken the relevant environmental variables too "globally" to begin with. Speaking of another person's race or religion, for example, as affecting a given person's behavior is quite adequate not only for everyday purposes but even for those of the sociologists. But, our psychologist may continue, if we are going to get down to the serious business of analyzing precisely both the elements and the causes of behavior, we must operate on a different level. On this different level of analysis we may reason as follows. First, every human behavior is some combination of learned and unconditioned responses to a given situation. The character of learned responses will naturally depend in part on the nature of the unlearned. Second, the responses — both learned and unconditioned, and in "combination" — will, of course, vary with the stimulus. So it is not surprising that we respond differently to people than to other things. We also respond differently to trees than to trucks. Third, nevertheless our responses to other people come about in exactly the same way and can be explained in terms of exactly the same processes as our responses to nonhuman things, that is, as some combination of learned and unconditioned responses. Hence, in any case there is nothing special about the character of the laws of social behavior; they have the same logical forms as the laws of solitary behavior. Fourth, the appearance or behavior of another person as presented to a given person, although it may in a short time come to present itself phenomenologically as having a certain unity or simplicity,[12] is ''originally'' a combination of several distinct stimuli. This is true of most other objects as well such as trees. Therefore, we may assume that ''simple'' stimuli which are the ''elements'' of a social situation themselves have nothing peculiarly social or even human about them. Fifth, in mechanics one analyzes the complex situation into a number of simpler ones and then ''puts it back together again'' according to a rule — the composition rule — in order to calculate the behavior of a given body. Similarly in the case at hand, there almost certainly exists some composition rule(s) by which we could, having analyzed the situation in which a complex stimulus occurs into a number of situations of simple stimuli, ''put it back together again'' in order to calculate the response of the organism in question.[13] Sixth and finally, human social behavior is but one kind of behavior in which the stimulus is complex. Hence the laws of social behavior can after all be deduced from the laws of solitary behavior, or certain crucial ones among them, and some composition rule(s).

Having brought the issue of the explanatory reduction of sociology to psychology to this point, I have but three comments. First, it must be admitted that the case of the psychologist for explanatory reductionism is after all quite reasonable and that he may very well be correct. At the same time it must be insisted that no one has yet proved, even in the scientific sense, that explanatory emergentism is false. Second, the issue is a rather straightforward, empirical one. It is not, like that of scientific determinism, one which, while empirical in a broad sense, admits of no likely, future resolution, but rather one about which further experimentation, observation, and the ingenuity of the psychologists could well make belief in explanatory emergentism unreasonable. Third, having analyzed the issue as we have, we are in a position to see clearly that little except the cold, scientific fact itself seems logically to ride on the answer — not whether our social responses are different from our nonsocial ones, not whether we are basically driven by instincts or not, not whether our loves and hates and commitments determine our behavior in large measure, and certainly not, as we have already argued, whether society is something more than the properties and relations of individual persons.

It will have been noticed that I carried the idea of explanatory reduction by way of composition rule(s) from mechanics to the human case in a manner that made it even stronger in the latter situation. For in mechanics we cannot deduce by any composition rule the laws of the behavior of bodies in groups from that of bodies in isolation. That is, we cannot by any composition rule get the Newtonian laws of motion from the law of inertial motion which we may take as the law of the behavior of an isolated body. Thus if we were to reason by strict analogy, we might have concluded in this way that just as in mechanics the laws of the behavior of bodies in groups cannot be reduced to the law of the behavior of bodies in isolation, so the laws of human social behavior could not be reduced to the laws of human solitary behavior. We have just seen, however, that this is not by any means certain. In any event this distinction between the one-body case — whether in mechanics or in the human sciences — and all others hints at another distinction and a somewhat different notion of reduction which may possibly have been in some minds when they spoke of the reduction of sociology to psychology. The distinction is that between (monadic) properties on the one hand and relations on the other. The idea is, first, that whereas psychology deals with persons "in themselves," though perhaps including relations to the *physical* environment as in the psychology of perception, sociology deals with persons in their relations to and interactions with other people. Some such idea of the province of sociology is by now to be found expressed in almost every American textbook in the social sciences. This part of the "argument" we may take as stipulatively true. The second part is the heart of the matter for it holds that these relations can somehow be reduced to or eliminated in favor of the monadic properties of people.[14]

Put so starkly, the proposal sounds utterly implausible. And so I think it is. To be sure, every relational predicate can, as a matter of formal logic, be correlated to a monadic predicate and even, in a sense, "defined" in terms of it. But in so doing one does not reduce the number of basic predicate terms, whereas the vague idea behind what I am talking about is that of reducing or defining the predicates that express the relations between and among people to the relatively few and admittedly nonrelational predicates that hold for humans "independent" of society. (The very distinction between the two classes of predicates can, I think, be reasonably drawn but it is difficult to do so in a few words. All we need is the rough idea.) More technically, it sounds like the doctrine of internal relations. This doctrine has several different versions but in the end all of them seem to come to the idea that the fact that something stands in a certain relation to something else can always be deduced from some statement or statements about its nonrelational properties. This is not the place to refute the doctrine of internal relations, that is, that *all* relations are internal; that I think has been amply done by many writers already.[15] If even *some* relations are external (at the basic ontological level, I believe *all* are), it is not unreasonable to suppose that some of the social relationships of people to each other are external. The relation, for example, of *being the next door neighbor of* would seem to be just such a relation or, if that sounds too much like a purely spatial relation, then that of *being the parliamentary representative of* would seem also to be a purely external relation. If what I have said does satisfactorily explicate what was *meant* by reducing sociology to psychology in this sense, then I think we can conclude that such a reduction is impossible.

There are, finally, the possibilities of various sorts of partial and less powerful explanatory reductions. The simplest one of these would be (a) to be able to deduce some but not all of the laws of social behavior by some composition rule(s) from the laws of solitary behavior. Other possibilities are as follows: (b) to be able to deduce by way of some composition rule(s) the laws of the behavior of persons in larger groups from the laws of their behavior in small groups, possibly even the two-person situation; (c) to suppose that there are various natural levels of complexity in terms of the cardinalities of the groups within each of which but not between which some composition rule(s) apply; and (d) to suppose that there are distinct realms of behavior in terms of social situation within each of which some composition rule(s) apply. Each of these when taken as all that can be achieved gives up in some measure the idea of a complete explanatory reduction of sociology to psychology. Indeed, all but the first refer only to reductions within sociology itself. So far, however, as these last three possibilities are *not* taken as the limit of what is possible, the first and third of them, (b) and (d), are both formally compatible with a further reduction of sociology to psychology as we discussed it at length earlier in this section.

Four Issues; Twelve Possibilities

This will be an appropriate place to summarize our discussion to this point by listing the various possible views concerning the nature of the realm of the social and its relation to the psychological. I shall also have occasion in this section to raise the substantive question of the relation of reduction to process. I begin by setting up the four issues.

Consider again the sociological variables alone. They may or may not all be definable in terms of the properties and relations of individual persons and things. This is the *first issue*, that between the descriptive individualist and the descriptive emergentist. We saw earlier that in the case of descriptive individualism once the definitions are actually provided, it follows as a matter of logic that one has achieved reduction. But in the case of descriptive emergentism, we still have an open question whether reduction can be achieved or not by laws of coexistence. The question whether or not reduction by definitions and/or laws of coexistence can be achieved then is the *second issue*.

We have just been discussing the question whether or not the laws of social behavior can by some composition rule be deduced from the laws of solitary behavior, that is, whether explanatory reduction is possible. Such a question is apt to interest the descriptive individualist more than the descriptive emergentist, but, as I noted earlier, the emergentist will also have to agree to the distinction by which the question of explanatory reduction is raised, for it is prior to and not dependent on any philosophical position. This, then, explanatory reduction or not, is the *third issue*. But now it is worth noticing that compatible with all the possibilities so far generated is the assumption that there exists *process* among the sociological variables alone, the properties and relations which belong only to groups. This would mean that given the values of the sociological variables at some given moment, there exists a set of laws such that it is possible to calculate any later or earlier values of those same variables. Let this be, whether or not process obtains among the sociological variables alone, the *fourth issue*.

With respect to the last-mentioned issue, consider first the context of descriptive individualism. Although we wish to keep in mind that all that really exists are individual persons and things and their properties and relations, we may still wonder whether, without knowing which individuals have which properties and without being able to predict the (possibly unique) properties of individuals except insofar as we can predict the occurrence of those sociological properties in the definition of which occur those properties of individuals, one can, given knowledge of the values of the sociological variables alone, by any laws calculate earlier or later values of those same variables with any great reliability. If we take the question strictly, the answer would seem to be patently in the negative as a matter of empirical fact. For to ignore for the moment those properties of individual persons which may make a difference to the values of the sociological variables but which are not included in their definitions, factors such as floods and earthquakes, for example, seem obviously to be variables or values of variables which interact with the sociological variables and which are not themselves sociological variables and do not occur in their definitions. Still one wants to know within what limits and to what degree we might expect to approach process knowledge of the sociological variables alone. This does indeed touch on the question of the "role of the individual in history" to which I shall devote a later chapter in the perhaps absurd belief that I might have something new to say on that well-worn topic. Even those who did seem to maintain something like a process view of the sociological variables — certain Marxists, for example — almost certainly did not mean that even if the sun exploded tomorrow, capitalism everywhere would still be succeeded by communism. Reasonable doctrines of historical inevitability (and I believe there are some) do not commit one to the view that history and society are insulated against the larger processes of nature.

In the case of descriptive emergentism, the question of process on the level of the sociological variables is also very complicated, but not just for "empirical" reasons. As we noted earlier, no one including the descriptive emergentist is going to deny that some sociological variables can be defined through the properties and relations of individual things and persons. Thus for the emergentist there are several abstract possibilities regarding process: (a) that the simple (undefinable) properties alone yield process, while the definable ones alone do not; (b) that the definable ones alone yield process, while the simple ones alone do not; (c) that both the simple ones alone and the definable ones alone yield process; (d) that neither the simple ones alone nor the definable ones alone yield process, but jointly they do yield process; and (e) that neither separately nor jointly do the simple and the definable sociological variables yield process. Perhaps the "strongest" of these possibilities would be where each group separately yields process. I doubt that anyone ever held a view to be interpreted in such a way, but this is perhaps because those who hold that there are simple, social properties to begin with are not apt to be very much interested in the definable properties anyway.

Let us suppose, however, in order to consider the question for the descriptive individualist and emergentist simultaneously, that there exists process among the definable sociological variables alone. Is this supposition consistent with explanatory reduction as I discussed it in preceding pages? Can we suppose both that among the sociological variables alone there exists process and that the laws of these variables are, once the definitions have been supplied, deducible from the laws of what I called solitary behavior and some composition rule? To ask whether it is abstractly possible, we will be well advised to consider again the case of mechanics. We already know that as a matter of empirical fact, explanatory reduction does exist in mechanics, if we take the two-body case as our most elementary one. If we now had a way of talking about complex systems in ''group'' terms so that, say, a three-body system has the property *F* when there is such-and-such distribution of mass and such-and-such distances and velocities involved, then we would have process at the level of the group variables alone. And we could in fact do this if we cared to construct the appropriate definitions of such ''group'' variables. Thus the answer to our question seems to be in the affirmative, provided that the laws of the most elementary case are themselves process laws as they are in the case of mechanics. *It is not possible to deduce process laws from a given set of laws and any composition rule unless the given set are themselves process laws.* Thus, to return to the case of human behavior, even if the laws of group behavior are process laws, they might still be deducible from the laws of solitary behavior by way of definitions and composition rule provided that the laws of solitary behavior are themselves process laws. I believe, as I have indicated before, that we are now very far from empirical fact, but we are here exploring mere logical possibility.[16]

With four issues of two values each we have sixteen combinatorial possibilities of the natures of and connections between sociology and psychology, or better, between sociological variables and psychological variables. But since descriptive individualism entails definitional reduction, there are only twelve logically consistent positions. In describing those positions let us use the following terminology: *individualist/emergentist* for the issue whether or not there are simple properties of social wholes; *reductionist/nonreductionist* for that of whether or not reduction is possible (for the individualist by definitions, for the emergentist by laws of coexistence); *process/nonprocess* for that of whether or not there is process among the sociological variables alone;[17] and *monism/pluralism*[18] for that of whether or not the laws of social behavior can be deduced from the laws of solitary behavior and some composition rule. The twelve possibilities are as follows:

1. *individualist, reductionist, process, monist.* There are no simple properties of groups; all social properties can be defined in terms of the properties of individual persons and things; there exists process among the sociological variables alone; and the laws of social behavior can be deduced from the laws of solitary behavior and some composition rule(s).

2. *individualist, reductionist, process, pluralist.* There are no simple properties of groups; all social properties can be defined in terms of the properties of individual persons and things; there exists process among the sociological variables alone; and the laws of social behavior cannot be deduced from the laws of solitary behavior and some composition rule(s).

3. *individualist, reductionist, nonprocess, monist.* There are no simple properties of groups; all social properties can be defined in terms of the properties of individual persons and things; there does not exist process among the sociological variables alone; and the laws of social behavior can be deduced from the laws of solitary behavior and some composition rule(s).

4. *individualist, reductionist, nonprocess, pluralist.* There are no simple properties of groups; all social properties can be defined in terms of properties of individual persons and things; there does not exist process among the sociological variables alone; and the laws of social behavior cannot be deduced from the laws of solitary behavior and some composition rule(s).

5. *emergentist, reductionist, process, monist.* There are simple properties of groups; all simple properties of groups are connected by laws of coexistence to properties of individual persons and things; there exists process among the sociological variables alone; and the laws of social behavior can be deduced from the laws of solitary behavior and some composition rule(s).

6. *emergentist, reductionist, process, pluralist.* There are simple properties of groups; all simple properties of groups are connected by laws of coexistence to properties of individual persons and things; there exists process among the sociological variables alone; and the laws of social behavior cannot be deduced from the laws of solitary behavior and some composition rule(s).

7. *emergentist, reductionist, nonprocess, monist.* There are simple properties of groups; all simple properties of groups are connected by laws of coexistence to properties of individual persons and things; there does not exist process among the sociological variables alone; and the laws of social behavior can be deduced from the laws of solitary behavior and some composition rule(s).

8. *emergentist, reductionist, nonprocess, pluralist.* There are simple properties of groups; all simple properties of groups are connected by laws of coexistence to properties of individual persons and things; there does not exist process among the sociological variables alone; and the laws of social behavior cannot be deduced from the laws of solitary behavior and some composition rule(s).

9. *emergentist, nonreductionist, process, monist.* There are simple proper-

ties of groups; not all simple properties of groups are connected by laws of coexistence to properties of individual persons and things; there does not exist process among the sociological variables alone; and the laws of social behavior can be deduced from the laws of solitary behavior and some composition rule(s).

10. *emergentist, nonreductionist, process, pluralist.* There are simple properties of groups; not all simple properties of groups are connected by laws of coexistence to properties of individual persons and things; there exists process among the sociological variables alone; and the laws of social behavior cannot be deduced from the laws of solitary behavior and some composition rule(s).

11. *emergentist, nonreductionist, nonprocess, monist.* There are simple properties of groups; not all simple properties of groups are connected by laws of coexistence to properties of individual persons and things; there does not exist process among the sociological variables alone; and the laws of social behavior can be deduced from the laws of solitary behavior and some composition rule(s).

12. *emergentist, nonreductionist, nonprocess, pluralist.* There are simple properties of groups; not all simple properties of groups are connected by laws of coexistence to properties of individual persons and things; there does not exist process among the sociological variables alone; and the laws of social behavior cannot be deduced from the laws of solitary behavior and any composition rule.

It has been argued in this and the last chapter that of these possibilities either the third or the fourth, the *individualist, reductionist, nonprocess* views, is correct. And I have also indicated my belief that the issue between the *monist* and the *pluralist* is still quite open and unsettled.

So much for reduction. We have seen that the two basic issues are (a) what there is (what simple properties there are) and (b) what laws "there are" and what logical relations they have to each other. It is a metaphysical question whether there are simple properties of social wholes for it involves the more general philosophical questions of how we get knowledge of the world, how we can confirm it, and the like. The questions of what laws there are and their mutual logical relations, though much less fundamental philosophically, seem nevertheless to have generated more philosophical and ideological fervor. Partly this derives from a desire to enhance the dignity of the individual or the authority of the state by "scientific" arguments, partly from the felt necessity to challenge or to affirm the institutional form and role of the social sciences in society and academia, partly from other sources. Be all that as it may, the only way to rational understanding of the issues is clear logical analysis of the notions of reduction. It is that which I have attempted to provide in these two chapters.

VI History and Social Laws

This chapter may, in some respects, be considered the most important of this book. For one thing, it spells out in detail my commitment to the deterministic frame of reference and the idea of lawful explanations of human affairs. For another, it indicates, in light of what shall have gone before, what kinds of lawful knowledge of society are possible and likely to be discovered. I have found it useful to pursue these matters, at least initially, in the context of an issue which has received a good deal of attention in recent years — that of the nature of historical explanation. The three sections of this chapter are, accordingly, as follows: in the context of what must seem to many by now to be the wearisome issue of *historical explanation,* I shall raise what I believe to be the deeper issue behind it; I shall, in spite of a strong disposition to the contrary, discuss briefly an aspect of the free-will "problem" under the heading of *"free will" and historical explanation*; and under the heading of *the imperfection of society*, I shall examine in its own right what I take to be the implications of the deeper issue involved in the relatively superficial one of historical explanation.

Historical Explanation

In a nutshell, the "problem" of historical explanation, as discussed in the last several years, is this: historians very frequently give explanations of historical events which are or seem to be or purport to be causal explanations. The word 'cause' or its variations may not actually be used in many of these explanations, but there is nevertheless much use of "causal language" in historians' writings. According to received doctrine in Anglo-American philosophy of science, an adequate causal explanation "really" has the form or at least ought to have the form of a deductive argument in which there occur as premises (a) the statement of at least one law of nature, and (b) the description of the event or circumstances said to be the cause, and as conclusion the description of the event being explained. For the argument I am going to develop, the refinements some would wish to make in this formulation of what I shall call the *deductivist model* of explanation do not matter.

Now the "problem" arises from the fact that rarely if ever in the historians' actual explanations does there occur the statement of a law of nature. This unhappy circumstance would seem to yield the following four jointly exhaustive possibilities: (a) the explanations of historians are systematically defective; no one of them, so far as it fails to mention a law of nature, is in fact an adequate, causal explanation; or (b) the deductivist model of causal explanation is defective; some adequate and proper causal explanations simply do not in any sense have the form which advocates of the deductivist model insist on; or (c) the deductivist model has been misunderstood somehow; it was not intended to rule out or perhaps even to apply to explanations of the sort in question; or finally (d) historians' explanations, or at least some of them, really do fit the model despite appearances to the contrary; the explanations make an implicit, though, to be sure, not an explicit, reference to some law or laws of nature.

Each of these four possibilities has been adopted by someone or other. Usually, however, it is granted on all sides that at least some historians' causal explanations are adequate and in some sense complete, so that the major sides of the dispute have maintained *either* that the deductivist model is defective *or* that the explanations in question really do fit the model or at least don't tell against it. Thus the question has frequently been put as: are laws of nature *implicit* in historians' arguments granted that they are not *explicit* in them? This somewhat infelicitous way of describing the issue unfortunately suggests that the issue may have something to do with what historians have in mind when they think of or write such explanations. In fact, what historians have in mind when they write their causal explanations, whatever interest it may have for the psychologist or the biographer of historians, is of no philosophical significance whatsoever. But it is necessary, before I try to state what precisely the philosophical issues at stake are, that I dispose of some other trivial or philosophically minor matters that tend to be confused with the real philosophical issues.

Having claimed that the issue in no case has to do with what goes on in historians' minds, I might go even further and say that it has nothing special to do with historians at all. The kinds of explanations historians give are in fact for the most part precisely the same kinds that each of us offers constantly in his everyday life. Nor does the fact that the events in question are ''historical'' in any way distinguish in a philosophically significant way the kinds of events historians explain from the events we all try to explain and do explain every day. For what makes an event ''historical'' is nothing intrinsic to the event itself but only its human importance combined with the fact that it is past or present relative to those who describe it or think of it as ''historical.'' (But I do not pretend to have given a complete or even, as far as it goes, an entirely accurate account of how the word 'historical' is used.) In short, whatever philosophically interesting issue there is here with respect to explanation and the way the world is can be raised about my saying that the cause of my daughter's present pleasure is her having found a new friend at school, or for that matter, that it's raining now because cold air is moving down from Scandinavia into the warm air already here. Whenever a causal explanation is proffered without an explicitly stated law of nature, one may ask what we are to make of it vis-à-vis the deductivist model of explanation whether that explanation be offered by historians or not and whether the explanation be of human behavior or other characteristics or not.

In the second place, we must take note of, only then to dismiss, the obvious but irrelevant fact that there are many kinds of explanations other than causal ones. There is no point, however, in my rehearsing the list.[1] That historians (again, like everyone else) undertake to give many of these other kinds of explanations in their professional tasks is indubitably true. But they sometimes give explanations which are or at least are supposed to be *causal* explanations. Furthermore, it is not necessary to argue for the natural superiority of causal explanations to any or all other kinds. Such an argument can very possibly be made. But we must not assume, as many of the arguments on both sides sometimes seem to assume, that there is (are) ''real'' meaning(s) of 'explain' any more than there is a ''real'' meaning of any other word.

Finally, some would approach the questions I am raising in this section by means of an investigation into what they call our ''concept'' or ''concepts'' of explanation. At times this manner of speaking is just a harmless but needlessly roundabout way of talking about the world — the mere remnant of a certain dogma about the nature and possibilities of philosophy. Otherwise it may embrace that dogma itself: that we cannot as philosophers talk about the way the world is directly but only of our ''concepts'' of its many aspects.[2] In some the dogma has a Kantian flavor; our fundamental ''concepts'' are just part of the way we "must" think about the world if we are to think about it at all. In others "our" concepts are admittedly culture-bound, a "form of life," but as such beyond philosophical criticism. Here I can only say that I reject these "conceptual" approaches to philosophy and assume that the real philosophical issues have to do with the way the world is and not just about how we think about it in the sense just indicated.[3] Let us return to the issue itself.

Those who advocated the deductivist model often *did seem* to be saying or inadvertently implying some or all of the following, all of which are false: that whenever anyone thinks about causation he automatically also thinks about lawfulness; that no explanation of any kind is any good unless it contains explicitly a law of nature; that no *causal* explanation is any good unless it contains explicitly a law of nature; or that no causal explanation which does not contain a law of nature explicitly is any good unless there is a true law of nature which mentions only events of the kind mentioned in the explanation. What the advocates of the deductivist model *should have been* saying are the following, all of which are true: that there cannot in the world be a causal connection without there being a lawful one; that probably every event is in principle capable of an explanation of the sort the deductivist model describes; and that a nontrivial explanation of an event in accordance with the deductivist model is, in *some* specifiable ways, the strongest kind of explanation of that event we can have. I suggest that part of the reason many of the advocates of the deductivist model could not really say about it what needed to be said derived from their illusion that the model was merely a methodological device, a tool for doing or even a description of science. In fact, the model embodies a certain metaphysics of causation and, I think, a commitment to a deterministic frame of reference, both of which were too metaphysical in tone to be explicitly embraced by many of the more positivist philosophers of science. I believe the metaphysics of causation in question, broadly the Humean, is correct and the frame of reference the most rational; but in any event, we have here another case in which the practitioners of "ordinary language" philosophy or "conceptual" analysis were able to create *their* illusion, in themselves and others, that they had significant criticisms to make of the deductivist model, an illusion which could persist only in face of the failure of the "methodologists" of science explicitly and candidly to recognize and defend the metaphysical implications of their doctrines.

I am now ready to state what I believe are the three significant, primary questions to be asked with respect to the "problem" of historical explanation.

They are as follows: (1) Can there be a causal connection in the world without that connection's being an instance of a lawful connection? (2) Is the world such that everything that happens in it is capable in principle of an explanation of the sort championed by the advocates of the deductivist model? (3) If the answer to the first question is negative and to the second affirmative, why is it that historians, among others, rarely if ever give or are able even to produce an explanation of the sort championed by the advocates of the deductivist model?

As every reader who has come this far will know, my answer to the first question *is* negative and to the second *is* affirmative; so I am obliged to answer the third. My defense of a negative answer to the first question occurred in the second chapter; here I would like only to recall the obvious but, in light of many arguments on both sides of the issue of historical explanation, very important point that there can be a causal and therefore a lawful connection between two events without there being a true law of nature which mentions only events of the kind in question. Hence, if some historian maintains that the cause of the French Revolution was an ''incompatibility'' between feudal social and production relations on the one hand and the development of actual productive forces on the other, it is *not* required, according to the analysis of causation I have embraced, that there be any true law of nature mentioning only events of the kind mentioned in the explanation, but only that there be a nontrivial true law of nature in which both are mentioned along with other variables as well.

The second question is that of the deterministic frame of reference. It will be relevant to spell out the relation between it and the metaphysics of causation I believe to be true.

Every major analysis of causation except some variation on the Humean one is, I believe, either unacceptably anthropomorphic or inherently unintelligible. Still I want to imagine a view in which, say, a causal connection is not an instance of a particular lawful connection or of anything else except of causal connections in general, so that it occurs in the particular case in which, as we speak, this caused that. This will enable us to see more clearly the logical connections between determinism and the Humean view of causation. If determinism is loosely treated as the idea that every event has a cause, it is clear that this might be true even if causation is non-Humean. Of course no one has ever denied that there are laws of nature even if he considered causation to be something other or something more than lawfulness. Could a non-Humean then answer affirmatively to the second question? The answer, in strict logic, is that the non-Humean could indeed hold that every occurrence has an explanation of the sort espoused by the advocates of the deductivist model. I can think of no historical example, however, probably because those who are consciously non-Humean are so frequently those who are anxious to prove that we are, in a special philosophical sense, "free."

The deductivist then could consistently be either a Humean or a non-Humean with respect to causation. Now we must ask: Can a Humean be a nondeductivist? Or, to put the question a little more clearly, can a Humean deny that every occurrence is such that it is in principle capable of an explanation along the lines of the deductivist model? The answer would seem to be patently affirmative, for surely it is possible for causation to be nothing but lawfulness and yet for some states of affairs not to be capable of lawful explanation. Yet before this can be answered definitely we must ask a little more clearly what is to be meant by "capable of a lawful explanation." I characterized determinism as the thesis that every event is in a system which has process (where the occurrence of *any* property is an event); from this it would follow that every event is such that it could have been predicted from some earlier states of affairs and some laws of nature. This would seem to be the idea of the deductivist model. But here is the catch: it is quite possible for an event to be lawfully related to other events without its being in any system which has process (though I doubt that it is so). Even the most radical libertarian is unlikely to deny that the favored mental or behavioral states have *some* lawful relations to the state of the body, for example that if the brain were not alive, one would not be making the choice one is making or engaging in the behavior one is engaging in. Thus while it is not a priori that every event has some lawful relation(s) to some other event(s), it is difficult to imagine an event's occurring in our world which was utterly unrelated causally to anything that came before, such that no matter how different the world had been at any earlier (or later) time the event in question could still have occurred. Certainly the moral choices of the philosophical libertarians do not satisfy those conditions; in fact they don't even come close. Thus everyone can agree that every event has at least a "partial" explanation.

But does this mean that every event is, after all and on everyone's views, capable of the sort of explanation urged by the supporters of the deductivist model? Here is part of the difficulty not only in the discussions of historical explanation but in other circumstances as well. In some contexts, usually the philosophical, we mean by a lawful explanation one which necessarily makes use of process laws so that in few cases of any sort do we have something approaching a lawful explanation of anything. In other contexts, including the scientific, to give a lawful explanation of an event is ordinarily only to cite *some* of its lawful relations to other, usually earlier, events such that we do not have, in strict logic, a deductive argument. Or we might say that what is put in the place of the law in the explanation is not strictly a universally true generalization since it is not entirely without actual or (causally) possible exceptions. This difference Bergmann and others have characterized as the difference between "perfect" and "imperfect" knowledge.[4] The failure to make this distinction and to realize its implications can easily become the source of a special kind of scepticism regarding scientific knowledge. For it is easy to show for almost any generalization that we usually regard or which might be proposed as a law of nature, especially if it is a law of succession, that it has actual or possible exceptions and so, as some speak, is not really a genuine law of nature at all. What is shown is that such generalizations are not process laws and if "perfect" knowledge is what is required before we are entitled to speak of lawful knowledge of the world, then indeed we have very little of it. But let us now see how these ideas we have developed apply to the case of historical explanation.

The only remaining question, then, with respect to historical explanation is the third; namely, if determinism is true and if even in the strongest possible sense an explanation on the deductivist model is possible for every event, why is it that rarely if ever is an explanation produced which conforms to the model? Why, further, is it that historians do not but also cannot produce such explanations? My answer is perhaps obvious by now. From the claim that every event is in some system which has process (from which it follows that every event has a lawful explanation) it does not follow that every "system" of events has process. More specifically, from the proposition, which expresses my view, that every historical event is a part of some system which has process, it does not follow that the "system" of historical events has process. How can this be? Simply by supposing that the process system to which historical events belong embraces other phenomena besides historical events, perhaps events of quite a different order altogether. But at the same time, historical events do not by themselves constitute a system which has process. Or to speak a little more technically: the social variables (in which we may include the psychological ones of the sort that characterize individual human choice and behavior) do not constitute a causally closed system but are only part of a larger set of variables which does have process. I am even prepared to suggest that if by a law of history or a law of society we mean one which mentions only characteristics of people and events of the sort we ordinarily call social or behavioral characteristics, and which admits of no actual or "hypothetical" exceptions, then strictly speaking *there are no laws of history or society*! Of this very likely possibility, I shall make much some pages hence. For now, let us emphasize once more that this is perfectly compatible with the deterministic frame of reference, with the view that every event has a lawful explanation of the sort the deductivist requests.

In any event my answer to the crucial question is clear. The reason we cannot usually come up with the law(s) which the deductivist claims is "involved" in every historical causal explanation is that to get a truly airtight law we would have to go beyond mentioning those characteristics of things and people we usually think of as social (or "historical"), even, I suspect, beyond the behavioral to the physiological in the case of humans and to the minutely physical in the case of events such as earthquakes and tornadoes, all of which affect the historical realm. The laws are there, but they are exceedingly "complex," or if you like, there are many of them, and may involve many "levels" for the utterly "complete" explanation of a single historical event. A historical event is, after all, by most measures itself an extremely complex phenomenon.

"Free Will" and Historical Explanation

If I understand Alan Donagan correctly, he has quite a different account of the phenomenon of our and the historians' failure to come up with genuine laws of history and society from the one I just gave.[5] In the longish quotation from an article of his below, we see that he makes his explanation of the phenomenon almost into a methodological principle of historiography.

> . . . most historians would be sceptical of a proffered explanation in which it was assumed that all agents of the same psychological type, or in the same sociological position, when confronted with a situation of the same kind, will act in a certain kind of way. . . . [T]hey would not easily be persuaded that a certain factor in an agent's psychological type or sociological position, taken together with certain factors in his situation, must give rise to certain factors in his response to that situation. They take account of the possibility that, in the same situation, a man may act differently from other men of the same emotional dispositions, habits, character, psychological type, or sociological situation or status; and that he himself may act differently at different times. . . .
>
> By affirming this possibility historians allow that the traditional moral doctrine may be true that a man ultimately has an unconditional power to choose how he will act. There is, of course, much in any man that he cannot

> alter. In large measure, his emotional dispositions are no more a matter of choice than the kind of body he has. Nor can habits once formed be changed except by vigilant effort. The moral tradition holds that a man is responsible, not for everything in his character or inclinations, but for what he does: hence it denies that his character and inclinations finally determine what in given circumstances he will do. According to it, a man simply chooses the ultimate principles on which he will act, and he may choose them either in accordance with or against his own inclinations, either reasonably or unreasonably. Most choices are explicable, because they are conditioned by prior choices; but the only explanation of a man's ultimate choice of principle is: that is how he chose. While historians do not as such affirm this traditional doctrine of free will, they proceed as though it could be true. They accept it methodologically, although they may reject it philosophically.[6]

I have chosen this passage because I think it makes explicit much of the source of the attacks on the deductivist model of explanation: the concern with "free will." I must not leave the impression, however, that Donagan himself altogether rejects the idea of explanation, even scientific explanation of a sort, of historical events. But it is evident that so far as historical events involve certain kinds of human choices, Donagan does not believe that a "complete," a deterministic, explanation of them is possible and furthermore that historians proceed this way in practice too. Indeed he even seems to suggest that a historian is inconsistent if he explicitly rejects the philosophical doctrine of free will. This is inconsistent, Donagan suggests, with his methodological assumption of its truth as a practicing historian.

But is any of this really true? I agree that the philosophical doctrine of free will — that there are choices which are not "completely" caused — is *compatible* with most if not all of what historians write. Rarely, if ever, do historians propose deterministic explanations of the type which I have claimed are nevertheless in principle available. But presumably Donagan wishes to claim something stronger that that; otherwise one might say that most historians assume methodologically that the human race originally descended from elves, for nothing to be found in a typical historical study is logically incompatible with that assumption. What Donagan must mean is that what historians say presupposes the truth or at least suggests the truth of the philosophical doctrine of free will. Donagan's argument, so far as it goes beyond affirming a mere *compatibility* of the philosophical doctrine with the historiographical process, seems to be that since the historian admits (in practice) that two persons of the same psychological type and in the same social situation along with "certain factors in his situation" (?) may act differently, he is presupposing that the "traditional moral doctrine may be true that a man ultimately has an unconditional power to choose how he will act.'' But he is no more presupposing this than he is the contrary. For that assumption to the contrary — that all human choices, like all other events in the universe, have ''total'' explanations — does not imply that two persons ''of the same emotional dispositions, habits, character, psychological type or sociological situation or status'' must act the same in the same situation. The deterministic thesis implies nothing whatsoever about what in particular is lawfully connected with what. I would like to suggest that just as historical events, while fully explainable, are not so solely in terms of ''historical'' factors, so individual human events, including human choices, while fully explainable, are not so solely in terms of factors we would ordinarily call psychological and sociological. Of course if we include under psychological dispositions an account of how one would act in every possible circumstance, then it becomes trivially true that an account of any behavior will be psychological, but it will still be true that what ''triggers'' some of those dispositions will be nothing psychological, that is, nothing of which the person is conscious. How a person acts may be affected by his digestion of which he may or may not be aware. Other physiological factors of this sort surely are relevant to any deterministic explanation of a piece of human behavior.

In short, then, because historians often leave off their explanations when they arrive at individual choices, or because their explanations of those choices themselves are only partial, or finally because they may ascribe different choices to two persons they have described as being or who are in fact of the same psychological type — none of this implies that the philosophical doctrine of free will is true, though, to repeat, it may all be compatible with that doctrine. I conclude that it is not true in any interesting sense that historians methodologically assume that doctrine. I would go even further and say that what historians discover and write and the way in which they do it have virtually no *philosophical* significance whatsoever. Whatever philosophical problems there are with respect to determinism and explanation, free will, knowledge of the past, and so on can be raised quite independently of the historians. It goes without saying that this is in no way to depreciate their enterprise, but only to insist that paying close attention to what historians actually do will no more give us general philosophical insight expect per accidens than will the close attention to what ordinary people say, so much admired by some philosophers.

I have studiously stuck with the expression '*philosophical* doctrine of free will' because I believe that the doctrine has little or nothing to do with the ordinary distinction we all make between acting freely and acting under some kind of compulsion or "acting," if that is the word, involuntarily altogether. There are many kinds of actions that we generally lump under the nonfree from the knee jerk caused by the doctor's hammer to behavior under the influence of certain drugs to kleptomaniac behavior. Different cultures and, for that matter, different persons in the same culture draw the line, somewhat blurry to begin with, between the free and the nonfree in different places. But one thing seems to me to be certain: When, for example, one takes an oath in which he is asked whether he does so of his own free will, he is not being asked to judge whether or not his choice is without full causation, that is, he is not being asked to judge whether or not the philosophical doctrine of free will is true. The philosophical doctrine of free will may possibly be true, though I doubt it very much. In any event, neither the way we ordinarily speak in general nor historians' explanations in particular imply that it is true.

The Imperfection of Society

The provocative title I have chosen for this section is not intended to indicate any of the many moral blemishes every society has, nor is it an anti-utopian manifesto; it is rather a way of referring to the fact that the social variables alone do not form process. Hence process knowledge of society, as that would usually be understood, is impossible not just because of moral and technological obstacles, but because of what causal connections actually obtain in reality. I follow many others in referring to process knowledge as perfect knowledge and to *certain* kinds of lawful knowledge which are not process knowledge as imperfect knowledge. Though I have here adopted the epistemological mode of discourse, it is well to realize from the beginning that imperfect knowledge can be the result of two quite different circumstances: human inability or unwillingness to discover certain lawful connections that exist in the world, or the lack of certain lawful connections in the world itself. It is of course with the second kind of situation that I shall be concerned. Although much is made of the first circumstance in some quarters, I fail to see that it has much philosophical significance, unless one treats moral reflection itself as philosophy. In any case one may talk of the logical relations that do or might obtain between laws which reflect imperfect knowledge and process laws, even if, in a given area, there are no process laws.

Process fails to obtain among those variables which we call social, behavioral, or "historical" either separately or jointly. As some speak, a law of nature is a law and a true one only if it is entirely without exceptions and if it has no vagueness or ambiguities in its formulation and in the predictions which it, in conjunction with some statement of initial conditions, yields. If, finally, we mean by a law of society or of human behavior or of history one which mentions only variables of the sort we usually call social or behavioral or "historical," we may safely conclude that there are no laws of behavior, society, or history. This, to repeat, is not because determinism is false or because the kinds of events in question are not in (a) system(s) which has (have) process, but because they are being considered only as members of some subsystem which does not have process. It is in this sense and for this reason that we can never expect to have a comprehensive, precise, and reliable social theory of the sort we have had in physics-chemistry. This point is worth further emphasis. If by a scientific theory we mean a body of laws deductively connected such that there are more and less comprehensive statements in it, that is, an axiomatic system, such a theory may be said to be comprehensive of its area — in this case human behavior, primarily — if (a) all the property terms of the area either are "in" the propositions of the theory, defined or undefined, or are definable in terms of those property terms "in" the propositions of the theory, and (b) all the laws of the area, whether known or not, are deductive consequences of the propositions that make up the given theory.[7] There will never be a true and reliable social theory of this sort, not for the reasons usually advanced, but, again, because among the determinants of human behavior and therefore of the "behavior" of societies are factors (variables) which lie far "outside" the realm of those ordinarily and perhaps ever investigated or considered proper to investigate by sociologists, historians, psychologists, and other students of human behavior.[8]

The behavior sciences, like physics, investigate by observation and experiment, and there is no reason in principle why that knowledge should not be objective. In short the social sciences are like the natural sciences in all relevant and nontrivial senses except that, unlike physics-chemistry at any rate, we can never hope to have a comprehensive and reliable social theory. The fact that this is so, I think, explains the failure of social scientists to come up with anything like such a theory and not because, as other philosophers would have it, that we are "free" in the philosophical sense or because the (causal?) explanations of human behavior are trivial or "rational" or whatever or because the "concepts" we use in describing human behavior are necessarily value- or culture-laden. It is therefore necessary to emphasize, too, how lawful knowledge of society and human behavior is possible even though there is nothing approaching process at the social level. This then is the question what kinds of imperfect social knowledge of a lawful sort we may expect to have, taking as the only ''limitation'' the way the world actually is.

Let us first consider laws of succession and the ways in which such laws may fall short of process laws. There are three such ways and more often than not the first two of them will be combined. They are as follows: (a) a lack of precision with respect to the time between succession of events; (b) a lack of precise specification of the conditions under which the law ''applies'' or, alternatively said, a failure to specify all the relevant variables in the law(s) to the one(s) we are interested in; and (c) a failure to specify precisely the properties that are supposed to be involved in the lawful sequence. The second of these ''shortcomings,'' in a way, is the root of all the problems and it is, in a way, what I have already described as *the* reason we cannot ever have a comprehensive and reliable social theory. Since the conditions under which the social laws ''apply'' themselves often lie beyond the social realm itself, we cannot expect social theorists ordinarily to take cognizance of those conditions when they report what lawful knowledge they have discovered. This form of imperfection inevitably carries with it the first — a lack of precision with respect to time. This hardly needs further explanation. The ''law'' that feudal society gives way to capitalist society, for example, is surely imperfect in both respects (if it is to be regarded as true at all), for we know that there are conditions under which it doesn't hold, even social conditions, and it obviously is not precise with respect to time, except for the order.

The third kind of imperfection may be of two kinds, but only one is of the sort owing to the way the world is. The one that isn't has to do with the vagueness in meaning of certain notions with the result that we don't know or haven't decided precisely what phenomena are to be considered as instances of our property term. Such imprecision is not always a fault; it may in fact be suggestive of avenues of investigation that a premature ''tightening'' up of the notions involved would, psychologically or even institutionally speaking, cut off. Who is the philosopher to declare exactly what conditions — institutional and social, but also psychological and ''conceptual'' — give rise to the most fruitful lines of thought? This rhetorical question is not a plea for imprecise thought or for any methodology whatsoever, but only for recognition of the fact that the conditions under which scientific investigation and the discovery of lawful knowledge flourishes is itself largely a causal question and not one to be settled a priori by the philosopher or anyone else. I think we already know many of those conditions, at least of the social and institutional sort.

But in any event it is not this sort of imprecision that is relevant to my story here. It is rather, *for example*, the sort of law that tells us that if such and such occurs then either this *or* that will happen. In the context the "this or that" (the disjunction may of course have more than two disjuncts) may be different values of the same variable or even different variables altogether. Such a law, it is important to emphasize, is not, as I put its schema, a statistical law, for no definite assignment of probabilities is given to each disjunct. Thus we might be said to have the lawful knowledge that feudalism in any given society which has it will be succeeded either by capitalism or by socialism, which is probably imperfect in all three ways — with respect to time, with respect to conditions, and with respect to property.

This sort of law, which deals with successions in time like a process law, but which is "imperfect" in one or more of the ways I have mentioned, is sometimes called a *developmental* law. (Sometimes that notion is used to *include* process laws; furthermore, there is sometimes built into the notion the idea of progress.) The kinds of examples one sometimes comes across of developmental laws make it quite clear that they are not statistical laws. For example, the law of the "development" of an acorn into a sapling and then into an oak tree tells us nothing about how many or what percentage of acorns ever make it. So too for the "law(s)" of psychological maturation. At least in the *history* of the notion — we can *decide* to what extent we wish to retain it in ours — there is the idea of a "natural" or "normal" sequence even though, as in the case of acorns, this sequence may be realized only in a minority of cases. We may go even further and connect the idea of a developmental law with that of the philosophical notions of nature and what typically goes with them — a substance metaphysics as well as a moral scheme according to which it is good for things to realize their natures.[9]

The point of this discussion, it may be recalled, was to discuss, in light of the fact that there is not process among the social variables alone, what kind of lawful knowledge is possible if we restrict ourselves essentially to considering the social variables. Developmental laws of society are an obvious candidate. But one may wonder whether such laws are possible, whether such "laws" are really laws, and if so, what is their "status." The answers depend in part, I think, on which kinds of "imperfections" are involved. If the only "imperfection" is that the times are not exactly specified, but the law is otherwise intended to be without exceptions, one may, for reasons to be developed at length in the next chapter, doubt seriously whether there are any such laws. Even if the "imperfection" has to do with time and property or even the latter alone, the same considerations cast doubt on the possibility of there being nontrivial developmental laws. (They will be trivial in one sense if the disjunction of properties gets too large; so, for example, the "developmental law" that feudalism will be succeeded by some different kind of society, while no doubt true, is not specific enough to be very interesting — at least not to us.)

Still, and this is the important point, as long as the range of variables which is taken into account includes only those which are ordinarily considered social or "historical" or behavioral, the only kind of lawful knowledge one can expect to have of the successive "states" of society is of the sort expressed by developmental laws. At the same time these laws, if there are any of a nontrivial sort, will be deducible from the laws of the larger set of variables which does have process and of which the social variables are a subset. The fact that this is the only sort of lawful knowledge that one can reasonably expect to have of the successive states of society under the condition in question is of course an empirical and not a logical one. This fact, however frequently and even systematically ignored by philosophers, social scientists, and ideologists is, I think, patently the case. Many a social thinker, including Marx, has in his cooler moments been aware and even specifically mentioned some of the "nonsocial" variables such as climate and natural resources that make a difference to the social systems they affect, only to ignore these facts later in their more theoretical formulations of the "function" or the "nature" or the "goal" or even simply the possibilities of the social sciences. The sources of this oversight are themselves, in many cases, ideological, I suspect, though one might also hazard the guess that the logical implications of the known empirical facts about societies and their "evolution" were not clearly understood simply because they hadn't been thought through. But I now risk talking the point into the ground.

Another kind of law, one which we have already come across and which, in light of the lack of process among the social variables, may still be available to our discoveries and which mentions only social variables, is laws of coexistence. For the issue at hand it doesn't matter whether these laws are "imperfect" in either or both of two of our three ways (since they obviously won't be with respect to time), in which case many of the things we have already said about developmental laws could also be said, in the same respects, about laws of coexistence; or whether they are "unconditional" laws of coexistence. Certainly the lack of process among the social variables alone does not preclude the possibility of there being such "unconditional" laws of coexistence which mention only social variables. The "unconditional" law of coexistence that when the brain has no blood in it there is no consciousness does not in the least imply that "brain variables" and "consciousness variables" constitute a set which has process as indeed they do not. So, too, to consider a social theory for a moment: even if Marx in both his theoretical assumptions and his concrete predictions about the *successive* "states" of society was completely wrong, even wrongheaded, he could still be right both in his theoretical assumptions and in his concrete instances about cross-sectional connections of the sort having to do, for example, with ideologies and the relations of production. (This example suffers from the fact that Marx himself never intended it to be or wrote it as an "unconditional" kind of connection and also from the fact that it isn't clear from his writing what he thought the connections were exactly anyway.) It very well could be that a specific form of religion always — actually and "hypothetically" — accompanies a certain mode of economic organization without its being true that there are any "laws of historical development" or even any developmental laws. This, I think, is obvious once it is stated clearly.

Finally, I must discuss what could have been discussed at some earlier point — a kind of law which is not "imperfect" in any of the senses mentioned above, which does connect earlier with later states of a system, but which is not a process law. The idea is that according to the law two or more different states of the system are the "initial conditions" which, given the law, explain some given event. For example, a law which allowed one to explain a given neurotic symptom might tell you to look *both* for some childhood experience *and* for something in the recent life of the subject as the "cause." More generally the Freudian "laws" are of this sort in which appeal is made to the events at two distinct times in the life of the subject as explanatory of the events at yet a third. (Of course the "second" and the "third" times will, in these cases, often be roughly the same. The point is not whether the event to be explained occurs at some other time from the events which explain it, but only that the latter themselves occur at the least at two different times.) Another example would be the classical "laws" of association in which my present mental content may be explained by the facts of my having had another, certain mental content immediately preceding the one to be explained *and* that these two mental contents occurred roughly together sometime in the past for whatever reason.

Laws of this sort have been called historical laws,[10] but this can be a very misleading name. I propose instead to call them *polychronal* laws. The reason for mentioning such laws here is that while I daresay we have no unconditional laws in the social sciences, nor anything very close to them, of a sort that connects events through time, the approximations we do have and can reasonably expect to get in the future will more likely be approximations of polychronal laws rather than of process laws. The reason for this will be somewhat clearer if I proceed to discuss some of the logical features of polychronal laws.

In the first place what has been called our "frame of reference," that is, the frame of reference of modern science, implies that polychronal laws are "temporary" in virtue of the fact that there is always a "trace" of the earlier event(s) in the later. So that, to take the Freudian case again, "ideally" we would, for purposes of scientific explanation, appeal not to the earlier childhood experience but rather to its presently existing "imprint" on the subject. (For purposes of therapy it might be quite otherwise.) Although I have used several metaphors to explain the idea in a few words, I think it is clear. But it must now be emphasized that while the frame of reference suggests that the scientist can always look for the "trace," there is no *logical* necessity that there be one to be found. There may be systems which, by use of polychronal laws, permit precise and reliable predictions of each of its states from two or more of its earlier (or later) states, but which do not have process as it was earlier defined, unlikely as this may seem in empirical fact. If there are process laws for a system, on the other hand, then any polychronal laws it may also have will be deducible from them. In this sense polychronal laws are always "expendable" in a system that has process. (One may wonder, by the way, whether the laws of coexistence of a system which has process are always "expendable." The answer is that they are not, although there are certain conditions under which some of them may be deducible.)

The fact that a system may not have process and yet be such that every state of it is an exact function of two or more of its earlier states suggests that it might be useful to modify our definition of 'determinism' to cover such an eventuality. For it surely would be included in any rough-and-ready formulation of the deterministic thesis. So we may now define 'determinism' as the thesis that every event (the having of a specific property by something) is, by some law or laws of nature, a computable function of some earlier state *or states* of affairs; or, if you like, every event is in a system which has process or for which "unconditional" polychronal laws hold.

We are now in a position to see, especially in view of the notion of a "trace," why, in practice, we may expect to have approximations only of polychronal rather than of process laws in the behavioral and social sciences. The point is simply that the "traces" when they exist will frequently be "inside" human beings either as physiological states of the body or as certain, perhaps sporadic, mental states or, finally, as dispositions to either. Thus, to remind ourselves once more of the Freudian case, the limits imposed on us by technology and morality make it easier to determine that a person had a certain traumatic episode in his childhood than that his brain or nervous system is now in a certain, relevant state. In the case of the social sciences, too, it may be easier to determine that a certain society previously had a certain social structure and certain rituals which no longer exist than to observe directly their "remnants" or "traces" in the perhaps sporadic but still causally efficacious thoughts and feelings of the present members of the society. So, for example, historians and social scientists often may explain certain facts about the United States and certain Western European societies in terms of the facts that they *are* both representative democracies *and* that whereas the latter *were* once feudal societies, the United States never *was*. Again, the idea is clear even if the details are not precise.

I have attempted in this chapter, however imperfectly, to draw out some of the implications of the fact that the social variables alone do not even approach being a system with process. This fact can and has led to two quite opposite kinds of responses, equally mistaken, I believe. On the one hand we have those who insist that *a* science must have "unconditional" laws and a highly structured theory based on them or at least the reasonable expectation of them if its investigations are to be rational and scientific. Since, if I am correct, such knowledge is not possible in the way in which the social sciences have traditionally defined their range of investigations, the result is often either disillusionment with all social investigation or a dogmatism to the effect that either we (or someone) already know the laws of social development or at least that they are there to be discovered. On the other hand we have a considerable assortment of those who claim that scientific understanding of human behavior is not possible even in principle or not "appropriate," whatever that could mean. Their characteristic motive, sometimes explicit, is obvious. Both responses — that of denying, despite all evidence to the contrary, the importance of extra-social factors in human affairs, and that of defending the philosophical doctrine of free will — derive themselves, in the final analysis, from temperamental factors, or so I believe.[11] So, no doubt, does my view. But I do believe myself to have shown that both of these responses may be mistaken; in any event, they do not have the a priori status often claimed for them. It is possible to be, in a good sense, ''scientifically'' minded without believing that we shall ever have a ''full-blown'' science of society, on the one hand, and to appreciate the commonsense core of the idea of free will, on the other, without believing that human beings have miraculously made a partial escape from the causal realm.

VII Laws of Historical Development

The problem of the possible existence and status of what I shall call laws of historical development continues to intrigue philosophical analysts as well as political thinkers and actors. One recent attempt to provide an analysis of such laws is Mandelbaum's "Societal Laws."[1] I mention that article because this chapter in large measure has it as its starting point and in order to acknowledge my debt to it once and for all. More exactly what I shall do in this chapter is to introduce my topic properly by presenting a *general characterization of laws of historical development* along with a very brief historical background of the notion; to develop and discuss the *three major possibilities* with respect to the existence and status of laws of historical development; to relate what will have gone before to the notion of *historicism*; and to discuss critically certain aspects of Karl Popper's view of laws of historical development, historicism, and the "function" of the social sciences — all under the heading of *Popper on historicism.*

General Characterization of Laws of Historical Development

By a law of historical development I mean, first, one which has human societies as its subject matter, and second, one which is *either* of the form 'If any society is now in state *A*, then it will sometime in the future be in state *B* and then state *C* . . . and so on' *or* of the form 'If any society is now in state *B* then it was in state *A* sometime in the past and will be in state *C* sometime in the future . . . and so on'. The law could mention any from two to several states of society. Roughly speaking, we may say that a law of historical development is one which, given the appropriate "initial conditions," would permit the prediction (or postdiction) of succeeding (or preceding) states or "stages" of society. Such laws have also been called historical laws of development, laws of social development, social laws of development, laws of the motion of society, laws of social progression, and so on. Mandelbaum calls them "global laws of directional change."

Although I have chosen the phrase 'laws of historical *development*' I do not intend it to carry anything normative in its *meaning*. Or, to put it another way, a (historical) development can be good, bad, or indifferent. To be sure, some have used the word 'development' or the phrase 'law of historical development' so that a development of a historical sort is always good. Or they have maintained, not as part of the meaning of the word or phrase, but as a matter of "fact" that all historical developments are good. But I need not and shall not make either of these assumptions. The notion of a law of historical development is best clarified, at least initially, if one self-consciously removes any value content that may suggest itself or may have attached itself to the notion in the course of its own history. Similar comments apply to the ideas of a "state" or "stage" of society.

It is clear that the notions of a "society" and of a "stage" or "state" of society are contextual. For certain purposes we treat ethnic or racial groups as societies, for others nation states or geographical areas, for yet others the whole of the human race. As for "states" or "stages," we could speak of each succeeding moment as a different state, or we might (as has more often been done) distinguish successive "states" or "stages" in terms of methods of production or political institutions or religious beliefs. But little of this matters much for what I want to do. For what I shall say applies equally well for the most part regardless of the "units" taken as societies and their states or stages.

The opinion that there are laws of historical development has its parallel in biology, where it is sometimes claimed that there are laws of biological evolution. Sometimes, too, the idea is applied to the "development" of the individual organism. My analysis will naturally have some application to these ideas as well as to that of social "evolution," but I shall put my analysis in terms of the latter only.

The claim that there are laws of historical development is one made not only by nineteenth-century German historians, social thinkers, and philosophers and others of that time, but also by many in our own time.[2] More specifically, many Marxists, especially those inclined to the Stalinist version of Marxism, claim that there are laws of historical development (at least some of which they "know") and which allow the reliable prediction, among others, that the next "stage" of human society is to be world-wide communism. Given their origin and content, naturally much ideological confusion abounds on these issues in all philosophical and political camps. All I wish to say about the Marxist case(s) for the moment is that one can distinguish the claim that there are laws of historical development from the specific content that some Marxists would maintain them to have. Hence those who reject laws of historical development or, more absurdly, a science of society itself because they don't believe Marxism or because they don't like communism only deceive themselves.

But in any case, Marxism is not the only contemporary school of thought to maintain that there are laws of historical development (unless one defines 'Marxist' as anyone who believes in such laws, as some have done). Much of American anthropology, particularly the school around Leslie White,[3] holds there to be laws of the successive "stages" of society. Naturally the content of such alleged laws is usually different from that alleged by the Marxists; one might say with some point that the methodology owes much to Marx and Engels, however. Be that as it may, my analysis applies as much to the doctrines of the anthropologists in question as to the Marxists.

One more historical observation with philosophical comment will lead us into the analysis of the notion of a law of historical development that I wish to propose. Hegel and many of the philosophers of history whom he influenced such as Dilthey and Croce held that human history should be understood as successive and in some cases "progressive" manifestations of the One or the Spirit or of certain Ideas or whatever — something in any case which is not natural. In consequence, they also believed that each society or world "society" itself went through a succession of "stages" toward some goal, perhaps never to be realized. But then on such a view the connection between successive states or stages may or may not be lawful; certainly the connection between the One and the natural world is not lawful, although it may have, historically speaking, been expressed in the language of causality. Hence while Hegel et al. might reasonably be and have been called historicists, they did not, strictly speaking, hold there to be laws of historical development. But the full meaning of that anticipates my analysis.

What I would take to be an "ordinary" science of society would try to discover among the variables which "constitute" society as it is ordinarily conceived which interact with which and the laws of their interactions, and among those same variables which interact with "nonsocial" variables and the laws of their inactions. In this respect at least, there is no difference between mechanics and social science, except in subject matter. The *scientific* ideal of such an "ordinary" science of society would be a process theory such that given the values of the variables which "constitute" society and of whatever other variables are relevant at any given moment one could predict or postdict the values of those social variables for any other moment. Indeed, as we know, there is not process among the social variables alone and our lawful knowledge of society still ignores many of the relevant, nonsocial variables. Still, let me call whatever laws or approximations to laws that we can obtain about the social variables — the laws, that is, of this "ordinary" science of society — *the laws of the interaction of the elements of society*.[4] This use of the term 'element' presupposes nothing about the connection of the elements of a society to society itself, whether, in terms of our discussion of an earlier chapter, this connection is lawful or definitional or even something else. These laws of the interaction of the elements (Mandelbaum calls them *abstractive* laws) may involve either a connection of variables *over* time (Mandelbaum's *directive* laws), which we have called laws of succession, or a connection of variables *at* a time (Mandelbaum's *functional* laws), which we have called laws of coexistence.

Three Major Possibilities

We are now ready to turn to the logical analysis of the notion of a law of historical development. Broadly speaking there are two possibilities: either there are laws of historical development or there are not. But the first possibility has two distinct alternatives; namely, that the laws of historical development are (logically) deducible from the laws of the interaction of the elements or they are not. So I shall discuss three major possibilities: no laws of historical development; deducible laws of historical development; and nondeducible laws of historical development.[5]

No laws of historical development. In this case the world is simply such that however a "state" or "stage" of society is characterized, there are no laws such that a state of a certain kind is *or would be* invariably followed by a state of a certain other kind. But under certain conditions, there may be the illusion of a law of historical development and the italicized phrase calls attention to that. That is, it may follow from the laws of the interaction of the elements and the way the world actually is — its initial conditions — that, for example, every *existing* capitalist society (characterized in a certain way) will be succeeded by a communist society (characterized in a certain way); but the same laws might also show that *were* a capitalist society to exist under conditions which in fact have never and perhaps will never obtain, it *would not* be succeeded by communism. In this case the statement that all capitalist societies are succeeded by communist societies is, so far as it might be true, simply an accidental generality and not a law at all and hence not a law of historical development.[6] Of course, as far as political and social decision-making goes, it may make little difference: if it is *true* that all existing capitalist societies will be succeeded by communist societies, it doesn't matter much in those contexts whether that truth is a law of nature or an accidental generality. But the theoretical point stands that one does not have to maintain that there are laws of historical development in order to maintain consistently *any* given prediction about the future of societies. Marxism in particular, unless by definition, does not require that there be laws of historical development for its predictions, whether accurate or not, to make sense.

At this point it might be suggested that one could simply amend the definition of 'capitalism' so that it excludes those features which, according to the laws of the interaction of the elements, would "prevent" a capitalist society, as originally characterized, from being succeeded by a communist one, were such a society to exist. And then it would seem that we would have a genuine law of historical development. There are two kinds of questions here: factual ones and linguistic ones. The factual questions involve: (a) how many different features of society would have to be included and how many specifically excluded in the definition of 'capitalism' with the intention that the existing societies which we ordinarily call capitalist will fit the definition and the bothersome hypothetical case will be excluded by the definition; (b) whether at least some of the bothersome hypothetical cases may result not from peculiar features of certain hypothetical capitalist societies but rather from factors external to society altogether; and (c) whether any such definition can be found such that it is a *law* that all capitalist societies will be succeeded by communist ones and such that the meaning of the word 'capitalism' retains some recognizable connection with its meaning in ordinary usage or even in technical, scientific usage. The linguistic question concerns at what degree of complexity in the definition we would *decide* to cease calling the corresponding law(s) "a" law of historical development. In the limiting case, the definition would require a complete state description in order to preserve the law and then the "law" of historical development would be one with some of the laws of the interaction of the elements. Furthermore, the definition would not be satisfied by more than one society unless it involved a disjunction of complete state descriptions given that no two societies are exactly alike. But now I am anticipating some points of the next section.

Deducible laws of historical development. In this case any laws of historical development would be deducible from the laws of the interaction of the elements. Let us assume for the moment that there is process or something approaching it among the social variables alone. Now this deducibility could be taken simply as a trivial result, for if one has process laws of a system, that is, if the system has process, then it will be true that whenever a state of a certain kind occurs in that system, it will always be followed by another state of a certain kind. In other words, if our states or stages are what are referred to by complete state descriptions of the system, then the laws of historical development, if that system happens to be a society, will be the process laws themselves. But this *is* trivial, and moreover the social variables alone don't have process. What are the other possibilities?

What are called states or stages of society usually are defined in terms of only one or a few features of the social order and hence are not what would be referred to by anything near a complete state description. To stick with our example, we might say that 'capitalism' is defined as 'a social order in which the means of production and distribution are predominantly owned by nonpublic persons' and 'communism' as 'a social order in which the means of production and distribution are predominantly owned by public bodies and in which there are levels of production sufficient to a policy of "From each according to his ability; to each according to his need" and which is in fact public policy'. It is clear, however one might wish to amend these definitions for analytical purposes or to make them fit with actual usage, that only a very few features of society are picked out. Now it is by no means a priori that there are no laws of historical development where the subject matter of those laws are characteristics of societies such as "being capitalist" and "being communist." But in order for there to be such laws, it is worth pointing out, the properties in terms of which the "stages" are defined would have to be, if I may so express myself, relatively noninteracting variables. By 'relatively noninteracting' I mean that the other features of society would make a difference only in time and perhaps in "intensity" (that is, for example, in how long the capitalist society lasts and in exactly what percentage over 50 percent of the means of production and distribution are owned by nonpublic persons) and not in "existence" (that is, once capitalism exists, then no matter what the values of the other social variables, including human beliefs and attitudes, it will be succeeded by communism). This observation may make it doubtful whether, as a matter of empirical fact, there are any nontrivial laws of historical development so understood. But with some slight modifications we can consider another possibility.

We have been assuming, it will be recalled, that there is something approaching process among the social variables alone. This assumption, as a matter of empirical fact, is false. There could still be laws of historical development deducible from the laws of the process of which the social variables are a (proper) subset. But the other possibility is that there are laws of the sort which mention a number of "nonsocial" conditions which must obtain before the laws of historical development "apply," so to speak. For example, there could be laws to the effect that *if* there are no "acts of God" beyond a certain destructive power, and *if* there are no socially crippling diseases, *then* if there is an existing capitalist society, it will be succeeded by a communist society. But that means, as most of us speak, that strictly the law of historical development is not a law at all. Or, if one wishes to speak in the way some others do, it is a "law" with limited application; but the conditions of its application should be considered to be part of the "law" even so.

The question whether there are any deducible laws of historical development is a purely factual one, but we have just seen that it can be seriously doubted whether there are any nontrivial, "unconditional" laws of historical development. On the other hand, "conditional" laws of historical development may very likely exist; indeed, it would seem that many such laws are known. For example, the "conditional" law that every society will become industrialized might seem to be such a law. First of all, if it is true at all, it would be deducible from the laws of the interaction of the elements (including the nonsocial variables); and, secondly, stated as mentioning only social variables, it is "conditional" in that it assumes that the sun won't explode tomorrow, that there will be no widely destructive human disease, and so on. But this is all merely "empirical." When it comes to nondeducible laws of historical development we have an unlikelihood which is much stronger; it is, so I shall argue, ontological.

Nondeducible laws of historical development. Here the idea is that there are laws of historical development which cannot be logically derived from the laws of the interaction of the elements. We just noted that the social variables do not in fact form a causally closed set of variables, and so we might not really expect laws of historical development, if there were any, to be derivable from the laws of the social variables alone in any case. But I want to consider the possibility that there are laws of historical development which can be deduced from *no* set of laws of the interaction of elements, not even from that broader set of which the social variables form a subset and which, we may assume, does have process. Now if these laws, or rather the properties they are about, are to have anything to do with society as it is ordinarily conceived, then there can be only one reason why there would be nondeducible laws of historical development. It is that there are properties of social wholes which interact back, so to speak, with the elements, thus making the set of the variables of the elements causally incomplete in themselves and so making a "complete" science of society, in the "ordinary" sense, impossible.[7] It is impossible because one could never find a set of laws which mentions only properties of the elements of society and perhaps diseases, weather, and so on, which, given any set of initial conditions, would fully explain or predict any other state of the elements.

This all fits with the historicist idea that an "ordinary" science of society is impossible. Georg Lukács, for example, maintains in his *History and Class Consciousness* that although there are laws of historical development (or at least conditional ones: there is an element of voluntarism in his thought, at least at this time),[8] a science of society is impossible. Or in any case such a "science" will inevitably be distorting — the last and greatest of bourgeois illusions, according to Lichtheim's account of Lukács[9] — because it fails to take account of the whole; it fails to see the increasing "irrationality" of the "whole" of capitalism because it studies only the "parts" of capitalism, "parts" which may be increasingly "rational."

What is presupposed by the doctrine of nondeducible laws of historical development then is that there are properties which characterize a state or stage of society which are not definable in terms of the properties of the elements of society. This, of course, is the doctrine I labeled as descriptive emergentism in the fourth chapter. For if there were (true) laws of historical development all of whose property expressions were definable in terms of those of the properties of the elements, then those laws would ipso facto be deducible from the process laws of the interaction of the elements possibly by being some among them. And then we are back to the second possibility. So the doctrine in question is committed to a form of holism (holism$_4$ as defined in the fourth chapter), the doctrine of nondefinable or simple properties of social wholes which interact back with the properties of the "parts."[10] That is why I called it an ontological doctrine, since it must hold there to be properties which are not given to the senses and which cannot be otherwise "hooked up" to the properties which are given to the senses. This locates the doctrine squarely in the anti-empiricist camp, whatever the intentions of some of its advocates. For apart from some sort of a priori argument (which I can't imagine) to the effect that there *must* be such properties, this doctrine can be plausibly maintained only if it is sustained by some theory of intuitionism, that is, some view to the effect that while not by the senses to be sure, nevertheless we are able to grasp or intuit or know those properties which are the subject matter of laws of historical development. But to know any such *laws*, we should have to intuit not only the particular properties, but also their specific values, just as in mechanics it isn't enough to know that the relevant variables are mass, position, and velocity: we must also know specifically how they interact in order to know the laws, and, in order to know that, we must be able to determine the specific values of those three variables.

Now it could be consistently, if somewhat irrationally, maintained that there are nondeducible laws of historical development even though we don't and couldn't possibly know any of them in particular. And we might conceivably, if only barely, have empirical grounds to believe that there are the relevant kinds of properties; namely, if we found that the properties of the elements were not a causally closed set and suspected "nonelemental" interacting variables.[11] But even if we had some slight reason to believe that there are such nondefinable properties of social wholes, it still would not follow that there are laws of historical development, for generally it does not follow from that fact that one has a set of variables that they are in themselves lawfully connected, much less that they are connected in the form of autonomous laws of succession.

A few paragraphs back I mentioned "society as it is ordinarily conceived." This was my way of alluding to a further logical possibility. There could be properties of social wholes which do not interact with the properties of the elements and which are causally irrelevant to anything but themselves. In this case there could be laws of historical development if one took those properties as characterizing states or stages of society; only since they would neither be defined in terms of nor interact with the properties of the elements of society, they *would* be irrelevant to society "as it is ordinarily conceived." They would have nothing to do with wars or economic systems, legislation or forms of government, the institutions of family, religion, education, and so on; nothing, in short, to do with anything that we ordinarily take as "constituting" society. And of course the same problems of how we could ever know these properties, not to mention their lawful connections, remain.

To return a bit from the remotest regions of logical possibility, there is yet one final possibility, with respect to the status of laws of historical development, which is, in a sense, somewhere between the deducible and the nondeducible. Suppose that we did have independent and direct access to properties of social wholes, and suppose again that it is these or at least some of these properties which are taken to characterize states of society. Then we would have the possibility of laws of coexistence stating a connection of temporal simultaneity between values of these variables and values of the variables of the elements. If *every* state of the social wholes could be lawfully coordinated to a state of the elemental variables, then any laws which mention the variables of those wholes alone would be deducible from the laws of the interaction of elements and the laws of coexistence together. And hence any laws of historical development there might be would be deducible, not from the laws of the interaction of elements alone, but only from them *and* the laws of coexistence. This is again the idea of reduction by laws of coexistence that we came across in the fourth chapter.

There are good and, I think, sufficient philosophical reasons for rejecting any doctrine whose only plausibility would derive from a further doctrine of intuitionism. The reasons have to do with the apparently very rare occurrence of the requisite faculty, or at least of an operative one, and the consequent problems of confirmation of and public access to the alleged results of the use of intuitive powers. I conclude that it is extremely unlikely that there are nondeducible laws of historical development or ones that are deducible only by way of laws of coexistence.

One final comment is appropriate before I turn to historicism. Historically speaking, the view that there are "stages" of society and laws that account for their succession has often been tied to a teleological conception of the historical "process." Now it is clear that if teleological conceptions of history make any sense at all, they make sense in the context of a belief in laws of historical development. That is, the law would "describe" the succession, while the final goal would be the "motor force," so to speak. But it is equally clear that one can consistently hold there to be historical laws of development in *any* of the forms I have described and deny that the process has any goal whatsoever. Hence it would be a mistake to believe that the doctrine that there are laws of historical development can be refuted the easy way by showing the absurdity or irrationality of teleological conceptions of history.

Historicism

A substantial number of different and sometimes, it would appear, mutually incompatible doctrines have gone under the name of historicism. I do not wish to add to the confusion that surrounds the use of that term. But I think that in light of the foregoing discussion, it is possible for me to give a useful characterization of at least one aspect of historicism, as well as to make some other comments about it. The most famous contemporary work *about* historicism is, of course, Popper's book which I shall treat separately in a little while. For the moment I only take note of his definition of it as "an approach to the social sciences which assumes that *historical prediction* is their principal aim, and which assumes that this aim is attainable by discovering the 'rhythms' or the 'patterns', the 'laws' or the 'trends' that underlie the evolution of history."[12] Bergmann is more specific in defining 'historicism' as "the opinion that the statement of a *unique temporal sequence of events*, or of a *temporal sequence of unique events* has a status similar, equal, or even superior to that of an empirical law."[13] It is easy to show, as Bergmann immediately proceeds to do, that the alleged uniqueness of historical events is of no significance whatsoever, since in the sense in which they really are unique, everything else is too. For the rest, Bergmann's argument that "neither a unique sequence of events nor a sequence of unique events can be causally understood"[14] I shall criticize in what follows without mentioning it again insofar as my refutation of it is not implicit in what I have already said.

Historicism, I believe, can also be usefully characterized as the doctrine that *there are laws of historical development which cannot be deduced from any set of laws which mention only the elements or "constituents" of "society."* Perhaps one should add for the sake of completeness and absolute precision that such laws also cannot be deduced from the laws of any larger set of variables which might include such things as the weather and disease and of which the social variables are a proper subset. So defined it leaves quite open to what use such laws, or other knowledge of or belief in them, might be put, and whether such laws are supposed to have been instanced only one time or several times (or perhaps even no times) in actual history. These features, I believe, are an advantage in discussing historicism as it has appeared in the history of thought itself, but I shall not argue that. What I do wish to examine is the notion that such laws are not or would not be "causal" laws, that they would have a status quite unlike "ordinary" causal laws.

We have already taken note of the fact that when we are talking about nondeducible laws of historical development, we are also talking about properties which neither are given to the senses nor are defined in terms of properties given to the senses. Thus, although we might have a slight reason to believe in such properties on the basis of what is empirically given, the alleged nondeducible laws of historical development can reasonably be called "nonempirical." (The same of course cannot be said for deducible laws of historical development.) But as to their alleged noncausal nature, I shall have to say more.

Let me state at the outset that I can see no reason for *not* calling laws of historical development — deducible or nondeducible, known or unknown, with no, one, or several instance(s) in the world — causal laws. Or I might equally well say that I can see no reason for drawing a distinction between causal and noncausal laws except as a way of drawing a distinction between, say, laws of nature (including society) on the one hand and moral "laws" or "laws" that result from legislation and the like on the other hand. Or the causal/noncausal distinction among laws of nature might possibly be used, though I think not in an illuminating way, to distinguish laws of succession from laws of coexistence respectively. But at least one writer, Leon Goldstein, has another alleged distinction in mind and that perhaps may serve as a representative of some other writers.

What I have distinguished as laws of historical development on the one hand and laws of the interaction of the elements on the other, Goldstein calls "developmental" laws and "causal" laws respectively.[15] Goldstein goes on to say that developmental laws are, or would be if there were any, "categorical in application" whereas causal laws are only "hypothetical-deductive" in nature. For Goldstein, it is clear that this alleged distinction has something to do with free will and the ability of human beings to shape their own destiny. But whether it does or not, I fail to see any more (or less) "necessity" in any alleged law of historical development than in, say, Newton's law of universal gravitation or in the law that water boils at 100°C at sea level. This surely is the heart of the matter. To be sure, the law of universal gravitation does not assert categorically that there actually exist any material bodies, but then neither, so far as I can see, does the alleged law of historical development that every capitalist society will be succeeded by a communist society imply the actual existence of capitalist societies, or of the human species, or even of the universe itself. Surely this is not the truly trivial issue whether universal statements have existential import or not. Its roots are, I believe, more "historical" than "logical." Historically, historicism is indeed largely a product of the Hegelian philosophy which at least seemed to hold that there was a "logical" necessity in the mere existence of any given thing and certainly in the existence of "historical" things. But we may observe (a) that one can and many have and consistently do hold there to be laws of historical development without subscribing to Hegel's rationalist metaphysics, (b) that so far as

Hegel's metaphysics would give any "necessity" to any laws of historical development, so would it give that same "necessity" to what Goldstein calls causal laws, and (c) that Hegel was wrong in believing that there is any logical necessity in the existence of anything or in any laws that hold for what does exist. I cannot be certain that I have correctly diagnosed the source of what I believe to be Goldstein's confusion and alleged distinction between laws categorical in application and hypothetical-deductive laws, but I can think of no other basis for it.

Popper on Historicism

Popper's discussion of laws of historical development (in *The Poverty of Historicism*) suffers from at least two defects: (a) a failure to make clear at some crucial points the distinction between whether *there are* (or could be) laws of historical development on the one hand and whether we could *know* such laws (that is, could *test* for their truth or falsity) on the other; and (b) an obsession with "disclosing" what he calls the "task" of science, particularly that of the social sciences. Discussing these defects will at the same time allow me to make some further points about the logical status of laws of historical development.

Popper asks himself whether there *can* be what he calls a "law of evolution." His answer makes it clear that he believes himself to have shown not only that there are none but that there cannot be any laws of historical development.

> I believe that the answer to this question must be 'No', and that the search for the law of the 'unvarying order' in evolution cannot possibly fall within the scope of scientific method, whether in biology or in sociology. My reasons are very simple. The evolution of life on earth, or of human society, is a unique historical process. Such a process, we may assume, proceeds in accordance with all kinds of causal laws, for example, the laws of mechanics, of chemistry, of heredity and segregation, of natural selection, etc. Its description, however, is not a law, but only a singular historical statement. Universal laws make assertions concerning some unvarying order, as Huxley puts it, i.e. concerning all processes of a certain kind; and although there is no reason why the observation of one single instance should not incite us to formulate a universal law, nor why, if we are lucky, we should not even hit upon the truth, it is clear that any law, formulated in this or in any other way, must be *tested* by new instances before it can be taken seriously by science. But we cannot hope to test a universal hypothesis nor to find a natural law acceptable to science if we are forever confined to the observation of one unique process.[16]

The author begins by claiming to answer the question whether there *can* be what I have called laws of historical development, but his reasons tell, if at all, only against the claim that we can *know* such laws. In any case, it is clear that nothing Popper says here shows that there *cannot* be "laws of evolution" whether we could ever know them or not. But secondly, it may be doubted whether Popper has shown by *this* argument that it is (factually) impossible to know any laws of historical development there may be. Certainly the mere fact that the human social process is unique, if it is, does not establish that it is not or cannot be known to be the instance of a law of development, for there are known laws which have no instances. The best example, perhaps, is the law of inertial motion. By the law of universal gravitation, it is extremely unlikely that there are any bodies with no net external forces acting on them, yet the law of inertial motion is both well established and important. But thirdly, it should be added, especially in terms of Popper's professed aim of showing that historical prediction is not the "task" of the social sciences, that most of the putative laws of historical development were not to have one instance but several. This is certainly true of the Marxist theory according to which, roughly, each nation state was to undergo a certain "evolution." So it is not always a question of a unique process as far as such laws and the predictions that might follow from them go.

I think we may grant, though, that while Popper surely overstates his point, there are (or would be) immense practical difficulties in *directly* testing for any proposed law of historical development. Still, there might be laws of historical development which are deducible from the laws of the interaction of the elements and which might therefore be testable to Popper's satisfaction. I am not sure that Popper would deny the truth of that, but he might deny its significance, for he too implies, though he never says so in so many words as far as I know, that historicism can be usefully characterized as the view that there are autonomous or nondeducible laws of historical development, and it is historicism that he is interested in refuting.

In his 1957 preface to *The Poverty of Historicism*, Popper grants that he did not, in the body of the book, refute historicism. (He doesn't make it clear whether he thought he had or not.) But now he claims a strictly "logical" refutation of historicism based on essentially two premises: (a) human knowledge is an interacting variable in the social process; and (b) we cannot know now what we are going to know only in the future (in other words, the future values of the variable can in no case be calculated). Hence, we cannot know our own social future.[17] The argument is, as far as it goes, unexceptionable. It is not clear to me what Popper means by calling it "logical." Surely the first premise is factual (factually true, I should say) and surely the conclusion is factual, or else it wouldn't need the first premise. Perhaps it is the status of the second premise which, we are assured, can be proved by "purely logical" means that leads him to call the argument "logical." The second premise presumably is true a priori, that is, a logical truth. The proof of it "consists in showing that *no scientific predictor* — whether a human scientist or a calculating machine — *can possibly predict, by scientific methods, its own future results*."[18] Furthermore, the argument "applies to scientific predictors of any complexity, including 'societies' of interacting predictors. But this means that no society can predict, scientifically, its own future states of knowledge."[19] It is a logical fact, of course, that no one knows at a given time what he is going to know only at some later time, for the denial of that is the contradiction that of some specific piece of knowledge someone both knows it and doesn't know it at that time. But surely none of the following is a logical truth: (a) that of any specific piece of knowledge our knower doesn't know it now; (b) that he is going to know anything more in the future than he knows now; and (c) that what he will come to know, if anything, is a relevant variable in the process he wishes to predict. For these reasons, calling the argument a "logical" refutation of historicism is highly misleading. But perhaps I have made more of this than it is worth, and I do wish to make some other observations.

First, Popper's argument shows at best that we cannot *know* all the laws of historical development there may be. It does *not* show that there are no laws of historical development, but only that we could not know them until after their instance(s). Popper himself suggests this when he says that "attempts to do so [calculate one's own future states of knowledge] can attain their result only after the event, when it is too late for a prediction; they can attain their result only after the prediction has turned into a retrodiction."[20] That is why I used the word 'all' in the first sentence of the paragraph, for we might, so far as this argument is concerned, very well come to know that "developments" will be instances of laws of historical development without, however, knowing those laws (and so perhaps not being able to make predictions) until the future has become past. Furthermore it should be pointed out that Popper's argument itself relies on a prediction about the future, namely, that of the future relevance of knowledge to the social process. It is not *obvious* that the kinds of things which Popper's historicists wished to predict are as dependent on the state of knowledge as Popper might suppose. But *that* uncertainty in a way again supports Popper's argument, for that argument does not prevent people from guessing what the future is going to be, but only from being justified in claiming scientific certainty about their guesses, if it is based on the putative knowledge of laws of historical development.

Secondly, Popper thinks that his argument exposes a fundamental difference between social science on the one hand and physical science on the other: "This means that we must reject the possibility of a *theoretical history*; that is to say, of a historical social science that would correspond to *theoretical physics*. There can be no scientific theory of historical development serving as a basis for historical prediction."[21] This suggests that physics does or at least can, while social science cannot, provide unconditional predictions about the future. But it is not at all clear that physics can do this any more than social science can. To be sure, there are "laws" like the Second Law of Thermodynamics which constitute or yield absolute predictions about the future, but they are of about the same level of generality and reliability as the prediction that at some time in the future there will be no human race, or that present forms of social organization will be succeeded by different forms of social organization or by none at all. But at the more concrete level, where social science must fall short for the reason Popper gives (as yet unknown knowledge an interacting variable), so must physical science; for though we know how, for example, the solar system will function by the laws of mechanics "as long as nothing extraneous happens," what we don't know is whether, say, human knowledge and behavior will upset the predictions of where the moon will be on a certain date in the next century by blowing it up, for example.[22] So if Popper's distinction is on the side of making predictions, the "distinction" is, as far as I can see, none at all. Knowledge is an interacting variable with physical systems as well as with social systems.

But *perhaps* what he means is that while we can *know* all the laws of physics, at least in principle, we could never know all the laws of sociology, for, as a matter of fact, there will always be new instances of "new" laws, and we cannot in any case know each law until we have at least one instance of it. Hence we can never have a "closed" theory of social life, as we might have a "closed" theory of physics. And in this there *may* be some truth.

Popper, I said, is obsessed with "disclosing" what he calls the "task" of the social sciences. I use the word 'disclosing' because Popper's discussion seems to me to be patently ideological in that he presents as a factual (or a logical) issue what is really a value question. And the word 'task' is exactly the word that can blur the distinction between what (social) scientists in fact do or try to do or can do on the one hand and what (someone thinks) they ought to do on the other. Popper also speaks of the "function" of the social sciences, another blur word.[23] But what is this "task," this "function"? Popper says: "Why do the results achieved by a conspiracy as a rule differ widely from the results aimed at? Because this is what usually happens in social life, conspiracy or no conspiracy. And this remark gives us an opportunity to formulate the *main task of the theoretical social sciences. It is to trace the unintended social repercussions of intentional human actions.*"[24] This view of the "task" of the social sciences is contrasted by Popper primarily with the view that the "task" of the social sciences is historical prophecy, an undertaking which, in order to be successful, requires that there be discoverable laws of historical development or something close to them. (Incidentally, the way Popper formulates the "task" as he sees it, it is perfectly compatible with the thesis that social sciences *can* try to discover and "apply" laws of historical development. *Perhaps* Popper means they should investigate those actions and those repercussions which have *already* occurred at any given moment. Yet his examples[25] are of a sort which would permit prediction as well as explanation.) But my question here is not about what the "task" of the social sciences is, but about what Popper means or might mean by inquiring into the "task" or "function" of the social sciences. Certainly social scientists can and do make the kinds of investigations that Popper calls their task, and if Popper is simply pointing out that this is an area of investigation which can be expected to yield results (already presupposing a considerable bit of sociology), we may well agree. But it would seem that he is doing more than sorting out logical or reasonable possibilities.

What he is doing, I suggest, is *prescribing* what social scientists ought to do under pressure of his (perhaps well-founded) intellectual likes and dislikes. Yet it comes out as a factual claim about social science. This self-deception, disguising a value claim to oneself as a factual claim, is what I meant by calling Popper's view of the social sciences ideological. And in any case, one may wonder (if one can wonder about values) whether it is the "task" of the philosophers to tell social scientists how to go about their business.

I do not know whether there are laws of historical development. I have tried to show what the logical possibilities are, but I do not know which one of them is actual. But then I fail to see that *logically* much of practical importance rests on it. The psychological effect of belief or disbelief in laws of historical development has been and no doubt will continue to be considerable. Popper claims that once it is clear that there are no laws of historical development, or at any rate no discoverable laws of historical development, one sees that the advocacy of revolution is wrong in that it will fail to realize the perhaps shared values of revolutionaries and nonrevolutionaries alike.[26] I fail to follow Popper in his reasoning at this point: advocacy of revolution seems to me to be as futile for the industrially advanced countries as it is imperative for most of the industrially backward countries, laws of historical development or no laws of historical development.

It may be that the belief in laws of historical development has contributed to political and social actions which all reasonable people would agree were evil; but we must not fall into the error, widespread among thinkers of Popper's generation, of identifying all radical social action with either fascism or Stalinism. The attempt to ground one's values in philosophical analyses is ideological distortion. There may be reasons for opposing revolution, either absolutely or under certain conditions, but surely these reasons, if they are to be good reasons, do not depend on whether or not there are laws of historical development. For we know what we know about the future whether that knowledge is based on laws of historical development or on other complicated and perhaps more pedestrian foundations. And what we do know is not *entirely* negligible.

VIII Monistic Theories of Society

There are several ways in which one might approach a discussion of monistic theories of society, but I propose to do it as follows. After some brief *introductory comments*, I shall undertake a logical analysis of *monistic theories abstractly considered*. That will involve listing the possible meanings and implications of the statement that from a given set of variables, one of them is the sole determining or most important one, whatever the empirical content of the variables may be. Next I shall apply this analysis to social theory under the heading of *monistic social theories*, for there are, as one might suspect, many complications. In considering *Hook's objections to monistic theories* and *Plamenatz on monistic theories*, I shall argue that whether or not any monistic theory of society is in fact true, there is no philosophical reason why such a theory could not be true. I shall end the chapter with a *summary and conclusion*.

Introductory Comments

Given their importance in the history of ideas, monistic theories of society have received little serious attention in the philosophical literature. By a monistic theory I mean one which holds that in a given area one variable (or factor, as it is usually called) determines everything that happens; or, less strictly, that the one variable is the most important or the crucial one in determining what happens in the given domain. There are social theories which hold, for example, that ideas are the only or the crucially determining factor in history and theories which hold that certain ones among our ideas — religious or philosophical or scientific — constitute that factor. Other theories have maintained that a certain biological characteristic such as race or size is the major factor in the social process. And yet other, more modern, theories have insisted that certain technological factors such as the forces of production or the media of communication are the single or dominant determinant of human affairs. Each of these is what I call a monistic theory of society.

For the most part, it is, among monistic theories of society, only scientific, causal theories in which I am interested. I do not mean by a scientific theory necessarily one which has a large body of universally true, well-confirmed, logically connected laws. I argued in an earlier chapter that, as traditionally conceived at any rate, no such social theory ever has existed or ever will exist.[1] What I do mean is that in the theory in question the connections which are asserted are lawful ones. The doctrine which holds that God determines everything, and so everything in societies, is a monistic theory par excellence, I suppose. But it is not one of the sort I am interested in, for it does not conceive the connection between the crucial "variable" (God) and the other factors (everything else) as a lawful one even if such theories frequently use the language of causation.

It may be useful if, before we proceed, we ask ourselves why there is such a dearth of serious literature on the subject. There are, I believe, two fairly obvious reasons, ones which we may label the empirical and the ideological. The empirical argument maintains that it is perfectly obvious that all sorts of factors from ideas and technology to extra-social factors such as climate and biology affect the social process and any monistic theory, for that reason, is absurd. One might suspect that such a democratic attitude toward the determinants of the social process is partly bound up with the other, ideological reason for rejecting or ignoring monistic theories of society. It can be stated briefly. Marxism in some form or other is a monistic theory of society; Marxism in some form or other is the ideology of those whom many Western intellectuals along with much of the rest of society consider to be our enemies. Be all that as it may, it will be useful for us to keep in mind Marxist social theory as the most important contemporary example of a monistic theory of society.[2]

Monistic Theories Abstractly Considered

In what follows we are assuming that we have a set of variables which jointly characterize a system of some sort: astronomical, social, biological, or something else. Except where it is indicated otherwise — and this otherwise will eventually become a major consideration — we may assume that the system is causally closed, that is, that there are not any extra-systematic variables whose values would need to be known in order to account for the values of those variables which make up the system. Finally, in discussing the several abstract possibilities of the logical structure of a monistic theory, I shall, for the sake of convenience, refer to the variable which is the crucial or determining one as the *D*-variable and the remaining variables as the *R*-variables.

1. The first possibility we may consider is simply that in order for the *R*-variables to have any values at all, the *D*-variable must have some value. Depending on what kind of variable *D* is and in what kind of system, one will want, in order to give this idea any significant content, to define *D* so that it is possible for it not to have any value. Otherwise, if *D* is defined so that it "must" have some value, that is, so that its limiting cases are included among its values (for example, that no government at all is a kind of government), one runs the risk of having a completely untestable theory. Even with the restriction there is, as we shall see, the possibility of having a theory which, while testable, is still not very significant. But there are much stronger versions of monistic theories than this.

2. Perhaps the strongest possible version of a monistic theory would be one in which the values of the *D*-variable specifically determine the values of each of the *R*-variables as well as the future and past values of the *D*-variable itself. This would mean, in the most extreme case, that there are laws such that given the value of the *D*-variable at a certain time, one could compute the values of the *R*-variables at that time as well as the values of both the *D*-variable and the *R*-variables at any other time. One could not only compute, given the laws, any state of the system from any other state of the system in such a case; one could compute any state of the system from the value of a single variable in one state including of course the state of which it is a member. But it is important to see that while a system with laws of this sort could exist, it would be incorrect to say that the *D*-variable is the sole determining factor in the system, and this is for logical reasons. If there is a law which given the value of the *D*-variable permits a computation of the specific value of some *R*-variable, then there must also be a law which given the value of the *R*-variables allows the computation of the value of the *D*-variable, either specifically or, as is more likely, within a certain range. And if by determination we mean there exists a law or set of laws by which the values of one variable are a computable function, either specifically or within a certain range of values, of the values of some other variable, then the *D*-variable must itself be determined or, as one might say, partially determined by the *R*-variables in a system of the sort we are here considering. Suppose that the system is such that given the values of the *R*-variables at a

moment, one could compute the specific values of the D-variable at that moment. It follows from this strictly that the values of the R-variables alone for any given time must be a computable function of the values of the R-variables alone at any other time. And so one could ignore the values of the D-variable altogether for such computations. These computations of course would be from the values only of *classes* of variables, so the D-variable would retain its special status in such a system.

3. A third possibility lies in the idea that the D-variable determines specifically the values of all the R-variables, but not its own past or future values. Again this could mean either that the values of the R-variables are by some law a computable function of the value of the D-variable at the same moment or, at the other extreme, that the values of the R-variables at all times are a computable function by some law of the value of the D-variable at any given time. This possibility in both its variations has a very interesting consequence. Recall our characterization of a deterministic system as one for which there are laws such that given the values of its variables at any given moment, one can compute the values of its variables at any other moment. On both variations one can compute the specific values of the R-variables at a moment from the value of the D-variable at that same moment. Call such a moment T_1. Add the deterministic assumption. It follows that there are laws such that from the values of the D-variable and the R-variables at T_1, one can compute the values of the D-variable at some other time, T_2. For if one can compute the values of all the variables at T_2, then one can compute that of the D-variable. But from these assumptions it follows in strict logic that there must be a law such that the value of the D-variable at T_2 is a computable function of the value of the D-variable at T_1. Yet our original formulation of this possibility assumed that the D-variable does not determine later and earlier states of itself. It follows that such a system cannot be deterministic. (A system can fail to be deterministic, we may recall, either because the universe as a whole is not deterministic or because there are variables not considered to be in the system which interact with those in the system.) But if it is not deterministic, then the value of the D-variable at a given time cannot specifically determine the values of the R-variables at any other earlier or later time. It follows that the second variation on this ''possibility'' is not really a possibility at all. That is, it is contradictory to assume both that there are laws such that the values of the R-variables for all times are specifically a computable function of the value of the D-variable at any single time *and* that the earlier and later values of the D-variable are not a computable function of the value of the D-variable

at a given time. Thus if we want to retain the idea that we started with and still have a system where there is a favored variable, meaning in this case that there is some one and only one variable from which at a time it is possible to compute the values of all the other variables at that time, we must assume that such a system is not deterministic.

Four other possibilities I can now mention somewhat more briefly.

4. According to a fourth meaning, then, that a monistic theory might have, there are laws such that the values of the *D*-variable determine specifically the values of more variables than any other single variable in the system. For example, if there were a system of ten variables in which one of them specifically determines the values of five of the variables (including itself), a second does the same for three (including itself), and a third and a fourth jointly for themselves, there is clearly reason for saying that, all other things being equal, the first of these is the most important or dominant variable in the system. But this would be a very odd "system" indeed. If the determinations in question are through time, that is, if the relevant laws are laws of succession, then either we have four distinct noninteracting subsystems or else we haven't listed all the specific determinations in the system. More likely the laws of such a system would only be laws of coexistence. In this case, we would have a system which, if deterministic at all, would require in its laws of succession only four variables, which may or may not be mutually interacting. For if, in a temporal cross section, the value of *B* can always by some law be computed from the value of *A*, then we don't need the value of *B* in the computations which, given the laws of succession, would allow us to compute the future states of the system in which *B* occurs, but only the value of *A*. This we saw earlier in our discussion of reduction; it is the idea of "elimination" by showing a certain property to be connected to another property by a law of coexistence.

5. The fifth possibility is that the values of the *D*-variable determine the values of the *R*-variables only within a certain range and there is no other determination *in* the system except what is logically implied by this. What is logically implied is, as in the second possibility considered, that there must also be some laws permitting one to go from the values of the *R*-variables to some range of values for the *D*-variable, though that range may be much broader than the range one can get for the values of the *R*-variables from the values of the *D*-variable. If it isn't any wider then the *D*-variable may not have any special status. Now since within this system as I have described it there are no laws that allow computations of specific values for any variable given

the values of any other variable or set of variables within the system, it follows that the system is not a deterministic one for one of the two reasons I mentioned before. If the reason is that it is but a part of a larger system which is deterministic, then in the larger system what we called the *D*-variable in the smaller one may no longer be the most important variable.

6. A variation on the idea of the previous possibility, in which what distinguished the *D*-variable was the magnitude of the ranges of values computable from various laws of the system and other given values, would be that the *D*-variable is the only one in the system from which, given its values, it would be possible to compute a specific value *or* range of values for every other variable in the system. In such a system one could compute the value either specifically or within a certain range of some variable — namely, the *D*-variable itself — from every single variable. But no such variable would have the status of the *D*-variable unless from any of its values a specific determination of the value of the *D*-variable could be made.

7. Yet another variation on the same idea would hold that the values of the *D*-variable permit a computation to a specific value or range of values for more of the other variables than any other single variable in the system.

In the last three cases, I have not distinguished laws of coexistence from laws of succession. This is only one of many complications that we might consider still at the abstract level. We have already seen that a variable may be the most important in a system by virtue of its laws of coexistence, without its being possible to make computations from its values to earlier or later states of the system and this because the system is not deterministic. Thus it might be part of a larger system in which some other variable is the most important with respect to the laws of succession. But is it possible with respect to the same set of variables, that is, within the same system, for one variable to be the most important (as we have been considering that notion) with respect to the laws of succession and another variable to be the most important with respect to the laws of coexistence? The answer, I think, is negative. For if, in a temporal cross section, say T_1, I can know more about the values of the variables of the system from the value of a certain variable than from the value of any other, then so far as I can compute the values of the variables at some other time, T_2, from the value of one variable at T_1, it must be that same certain variable. Thus, while we may leave open the question whether in a given system the *D*-variable stands out because of its importance in the laws of coexistence or rather in the laws of succession or in both, we can be confident that *within the same set of variables there cannot be one variable that stands out with respect to the laws of succession and another with respect to the laws of coexistence*. Thus we may consider, in the last three possibilities above, that the *D*-variable is distinguished relative to either kind of laws or relative to both.

Are there other possibilities for the logical structure of a monistic theory in which we think of the importance of the *D*-variable only in terms of lawful connection? No doubt someone can think up more variations and complications on the possibilities I have laid out. Some of the complications I shall shortly discuss myself, including an eighth sense in which a variable in a given system may be a *D*-variable. But I can't help but think that I have identified the major and most interesting possible structures of a monistic theory. Surely, I have shown that, contrary to what some have asserted, it is not meaningless or logically contradictory to assert that in a given set of variables one is, causally speaking, the most important.

And now for a series of comments on what we have before us.

First, we should keep in mind that there are other senses than the strictly causal in which a variable may be the most important, though one of them at least is related to the causal. For example a variable in a given system may be the most important in that it is the only or the most easily examinable one in the system. Such a variable may or may not be identical with the *D*- variable of the system in any of the senses above if it has one at all. Which variable is most important in this sense might of course differ over time as a result of changes in human knowledge, skills, and technology. The same goes for another contextual notion of "the most important variable." When a system is not functioning "normally" or as someone desires it to function, one might speak of the dominant variable as that which, if manipulated, will return the system to "normal." This seems to be, as we shall see later, the only sense in which Sidney Hook thinks one can reasonably speak of a monistic theory of society. But such a situation is really an instance of a more general notion which we may now list as an eighth sense in which a variable may be a *D*-variable.

8. Roughly speaking we may say that a system is in equilibrium when it is not undergoing change. But this lack of change may be in different senses. If none of its variables change its values at all through a given period of time, this would, I suppose, be lack of change in the strictest possible sense. But a system may be said to be in equilibrium if it repeats some kind of pattern over and over or if there are certain kinds of constants in the system. In this sense, the solar system may be said at least to approximate a system with equilib-

rium. I am not interested here in refining this notion for it is not that of equilibrium per se that is important. In such a system, there may be one variable the keeping of whose values within a certain range is crucial to the equilibrium of the system. Or again one may wish to know which of the *manipulable* variables is most important for keeping the system in equilibrium. Or, to add a moral dimension, one may wish to know which of the *permissibly* manipulable variables is the most important for keeping the system in equilibrium.

A system which is functioning normally may or may not be one which is in equilibrium. A biological system functions "normally" by changing in certain definite ways. Since "functioning normally," at least in the case of organisms, is not necessarily what such systems always or even usually do, the use of such a notion may not be purely descriptive. But it doesn't matter. For once we abstract the descriptive content of a system's functioning "normally" we may always ask if there is some one variable whose values (or, again, some most easily manipulable variable whose values) are crucially important for the system to undergo just those changes considered normal. More broadly we can always ask, with respect to any given change, "normal" or not, which variable is most important to that change (or, again, which is the most easily manipulable variable or the most easily manipulable of the permissibly manipulable variables). And if a system is not in equilibrium, one may ask which variable is most important for restoring equilibrium.

We may now generalize this idea even further. In all these cases we have been talking about a system which is in a given state at one time and about which someone is wondering how it can be in or be brought to another (perhaps the same) state at another time. It is not just a matter of prediction. That is why the variable which is most important to the change (or lack of it) may or may not be identical with the *D*-variable, if it has one, in any of the senses discussed earlier. Of course if a system is deterministic, its laws will tell you not only what actually will happen given the state it is in at a certain moment, but also what would happen if the values of some of its variables were different from what they happen to be. Still there may be a difference between that variable whose values are of any single variable the most important for predicting what will happen in the system and that variable which for a given state of the system is such that if its value is such-and-such, it will bring about just a certain change (or lack of it) and no other. This notion of the most important variable is obviously contextual, depending as it is on exactly what change (or lack of it) one is interested in and the given state of a system as well. In addition, although in such a system and in the context a certain variable may be identified as a *D*-variable, one might not want to say that the theory of the system is monistic. That is why it has been proper to treat it quite separately and at a different level, as it were, from the other meanings.

Second, I have assumed here in my outline of the possible meanings to be given to the claim that one variable is the exclusive or the most important variable in determining what happens in the system that determination, or, if you like, causal determination, is nothing but lawful connection; if the values of some variable are specifically or within a certain range a computable function of the value(s) of some other variable(s) then the former are to that extent determined by the latter and this independent of any temporal relations. In the second chapter I have already defended this theory of causation to the extent I intend to do so, but it may be worth our observation that with a different notion of determination one's characterization of monistic theories might naturally be quite different. In particular, a substance metaphysics with its characteristic notion of causation as some kind of "activity" whereby a substance "produces" accidents according to its "nature" but not necessarily in a lawful manner might yield some different conceptions of monistic theories. I mention this because I think this is what we have in the Marxist case, *historically* speaking. Structurally, a monistic theory is very much against the grain of a substance metaphysics and its characteristic notion of causation. For on such a metaphysics everything has its own nature according to which it "acts." This "activity" is concerned primarily with producing its own accidents. It is typically assumed to be "unnatural" on such a metaphysics for one substance to produce accidents in another. Thus we find that, historically, in accord with the inevitable thrust of the pattern, philosophers either denied that there actually was any influence of substances on each other and tried to account for the appearance of such effects in another way (preestablished harmony, occasionalism) or they tended toward monistic theories of what there is, that is, they denied that there is a multiplicity of substances and treated the world either as one substance with its many properties or as the "accidents" of the substance they called God, which, however, is not to be considered part of the world. One is reminded of the many difficulties of thinkers in this tradition in maintaining both the immediate dependence of the world on God and the independence of God from the world. How could one be a Christian with a substance metaphysics and not fall into pantheism? At any rate one sees what I meant when I said that a monistic *causal* theory is structurally foreign to a substance metaphysics assuming that there is a multiplicity of substances to begin with. For each substance is, by its very nature, if I may so speak, an independent source of "activity," and while the natures of two given substances may occasionally conflict, on the whole all is right with the world so that this is an unusual, even "unnatural," occasion.

Third, within the lawful conception of causation I have embraced and in terms of which I discussed the senses in which a theory may be monistic, we see that *it is impossible for one variable to be the sole and exclusive determinant in any system which includes more than itself as a variable*. This impossibility is logical, for it follows deductively from the assumption that the D-variable has any possible determination on the R-variables of a sort to make it a D-variable that there must be some other determination in the system. Thus if I understand causation rightly, any theory whether social or otherwise which claims that one variable is the sole determining factor in the system is contradictory. I know of no historical example of such a theory, however. Those theories which most closely approximate it as far as the sole determining variable part of it is concerned — namely, theories of direct divine direction of the world — have a completely different, not to say completely unintelligible, conception of causation. And those theories which can be understood in terms of the correct view of causation, that is, which are stated in terms of lawful connection or its equivalent, are never of a sort to claim that there is an exclusive determining factor in whatever kind of system is under consideration.

Fourth, we see the crucial importance of the distinction between the notion of a specific value of a variable and that of a certain range of values of a variable in formulating these possibilities. Naturally the ranges of values at issue must be finite and of reasonably limited scope in order to be interesting. Naturally, too, this is not the sort of thing that can be "formalized." This is also a good place to emphasize, should someone believe to the contrary, that laws which permit computations only to a range of values and not to a specific value of some variable are not or need not be statistical laws as that notion is usually understood, though they may be evidence for certain statistical generalizations. Genuine statistical laws permit the assignment of probabilities to each of the possible values, while the laws of which I speak may or may not merit that.

Fifth, and finally, it is obvious that the D-variable could be a group of variables rather than a single variable. Too, it might be a highly defined variable, that is, have many simpler properties among its constituents, either "conjunctively" or "disjunctively" or even some other way. In these cases there would always be the additional questions, though they might not arise in the same context or the same "science," of the causal connections among the several variables or among the constituents of the "single" variable. Their answers could produce some complications for the possibilities I discussed. But except for *those* complications, on the whole the possibilities could be restated for theories which maintain that a certain *group* of variables constitute the only or crucially determining ones in some system. Whether the D-variable be one or several variables, simple or complex, we have seen that several of the possibilities I have discussed are quite compatible with all sorts of effects of the R-variables on the D-variable and, more importantly, mutual effects of the R-variables on one another. Because this is so, I doubt that the "obvious" empirical facts show that no monistic theory of society can be true. Nor, I think, can anyone doubt the scientific importance and the possible social utility in knowing whether any (true) social theories are monistic, about which kinds of theories we are now prepared to speak more directly.

Monistic Social Theories

I have considered monistic theories in the abstract initially, for I believe this better exposes their logical structure. But we must now proceed to ask whether any social theory could have the structure of any of the possible abstractions, if not why not, and what other complications may develop.

Some of the complications are those that enter into any attempt to formulate a causal theory of society or some aspect of it. These would include the problem of defining the social variables in a way that their "meanings" do not "overlap" with the result that the question of their causal connection doesn't really arise, the problem of deciding what exactly is to be a "social" variable, and the like. Some other difficulties or alleged difficulties I shall take up in the next two sections when I examine Hook's and Plamenatz's objections to monistic theories of society. Here I must again pursue a consideration which I discussed at some length in the sixth chapter. That is the fact that in no case do the social variables constitute a closed system.

The circumstance that variables outside the social system, from those of the natural environment to those of human biology, interact with those variables which do constitute the set we usually would consider social may make one wonder whether any monistic social theory could be true. Certainly there is no logical or philosophical objection to a social variable's being the D-variable in a set of variables which includes not only other social variables but any number of nonsocial variables as well, in any of our senses discussed previously. But I think we know it to be empirical fact that no monistic theory of society is true in this sense, strictly speaking, at least. To take an extreme example, if the sun were to explode tomorrow, the values of the social variables at the moment would not affect the sequence on earth one whit. Less dramatically, earthquakes, floods, disease, and the like are interacting variables (or values of such variables) with respect to the social variables. Furthermore, they interact in a way that would suggest that, at least with respect to laws of succession, their values are more important than the values of any social variables, causally speaking. Or perhaps it would be safer to say that they are just as important: if there is to be any society at all tomorrow, both the social and certain nonsocial variables must have certain values today. But it may be objected, and with some justice, I think, that this is hardly what any monistic theorists meant to deny. Everyone knows that nature may overwhelm us and has repeatedly throughout history "interfered" in the plans and predictions of human beings. The point of monistic theories of society is not to guess what nature may have in store for us (though it must be admitted that in fact we do try to embrace more and more extra-social factors in our planning and our predictions), but only to say, *assuming* that the values of the nonsocial variables stay within certain ranges, which of the social variables is (are) most relevant, causally speaking, to the values of the other social variables. I think we can agree that this is a reasonable way of thinking about the issue and we must now ask if this idea really makes sense after all.

If among a certain set of mutually interacting variables there is a subset whose values remain constant and another subset whose values change, then we may always ask, with respect to the laws of succession, among these variables whose values do change, is there one or more whose values are of crucial importance to the values of the other variables which are also in that set? Thus even though the availability of oxygen is necessary for any social change whatsoever (except the limiting case where we all die) and even though any great change in its supply could have drastic social consequences, in fact its supply is relatively constant. Thus in a sense we may ignore it. Or we may say that to explain change we must not appeal to what itself doesn't change. I would rather say that what doesn't change can't be the interesting part of the explanation. But the word 'explanation' is here slippery itself. The "full" explanation of why a given society is in the state it is at a given moment must mention as a matter of empirical fact both social and nonsocial factors. Here I may stipulate that by 'full' I mean including the value of every variable which is such that *some* (not necessarily *every*) other value of that variable would have made a difference in the values of the variables being explained. But no one is ever interested in such explanations in practice and besides we couldn't obtain them anyway.

Consider for a moment the dispute, or one form of it, whether biological or social factors are primarily responsible for this or that aspect of this or that society. The question is frequently posed with a view to testing one's politics or one's opinions on various social questions. But if we see clearly (a) that the world is what it is, whatever this or that ideologist would have it be, and, more importantly in this context (b) that we may "explain" in different aspects and, as it were, from different directions, then the "dispute" is, or ought to be, only one of scientific detail. Obviously, if we are interested in the *differences* among various societies or between earlier and later states of the same society, we are going to look for factors which themselves are not constant. Thus a person is not very illuminating if he says that "the" cause of polygamy in this society and also of monogamy in that society is the presence of oxygen in the atmosphere, though of course it is necessary for either to occur. On the other hand, if we are interested in what is common to all human societies, or in what is common to earlier and later stages of the same society, we *may* appeal to factors which themselves are constant or relatively so. (Since, as we ordinarily speak, the same effect may have different causes, aspects which are common to all societies *may* have different explanations.) Thus there is nothing logically absurd in appealing to aspects of human nature in explaining these common features. If our "innate" ability to reason and our occasional tendency to do so are part of the explanation of why we vaccinate ourselves against various diseases but, say, bears do not, then there is no reason why an "innate" tendency to aggression of a certain kind cannot be part of the explanation of why we but not certain other species have a very high incidence of intraspecific conflict. It's a question of whether we want to explain why human beings fought each other on this particular occasion and not on that or rather why human beings fight each other at all. There must first be the given organism with certain abilities and tendencies, desires and impulses before the social and natural environment can "mold" it into this or that kind of person.

But we must now return to the question of monistic theories. On the whole, constructors of social theories are interested in accounting for the differences and the changes in human societies. Since this is so, they quite properly look for variables whose values themselves change for their explanations. This, we now realize, has a certain contextual aspect to it. Still, within this context, there is no reason in logic why one should not attempt to find out whether, among the variables whose values do change, there is one which compared only to those variables qualifies as a *D*-variable in any of the senses we discussed. Thus we may, with respect to the laws of succession, have, as it were, a "conditional" rather than an "absolute" monistic theory of society, the key words referring not to degrees of certainty or of confirmation, but to the circumstance that, considering only the cases where the relevant nonsocial variables remain relatively constant in their values, there may be among the social variables whose values do change and compared only to them one or a group of variables which qualifies as a *D*-variable. Even though, of course, the former kind are not in fact absolutely unchanging in their values and furthermore some of those changes or possible changes are taken account of in prediction and planning (flood control, use of pesticides, etc.), the idea is clear. Even though, throughout human history, the sun might have exploded and ended the story, in fact it didn't, and we can now ask what changes that did occur, social and nonsocial, were in the sense(s) required responsible for the changes that constitute that history. There may or may not be a variable or relatively small group of variables that constitutes a *D*-variable as answer to the question. Indeed, the answer may be that all the changes at any given time were responsible for the changes at a subsequent time and no few of them can be picked out as crucial as a matter of empirical fact.

So far I have been considering monistic theories of society primarily relative to laws of succession, and we have seen the complications and qualifications — what I called the "contextual" aspect — of any such theory that might be true. But if we consider such theories only relative to laws of coexistence, we have a somewhat different story. Here it would seem that the empirical likelihood of there being "unconditional" laws which qualify some variable as a *D*-variable is much greater. For exploding suns take care of everything at once, and we are not left with the possibility of dangling antecedents or unfulfilled consequents, so to speak. In general it is easier to find and to formulate "unconditional" or almost "unconditional" laws of coexistence than of succession, and the same holds in the case of society. This circumstance arises from the fact that in a set of interacting variables the laws of succession, by definition as it were, must take account of the values of all those variables, whereas in the same set two variables may be connected by "absolute" laws of coexistence, completely ignoring the other variables even though they interact with them. This is because interaction is primarily a notion of making a difference *through* time.

Little more needs to be said on this score then. There would seem to be, at least in terms of anything that has been said so far, no reason why there might not be a true monistic theory of society with respect only to laws of coexistence. One hardly has a full-blown theory of society in such a case, but one doesn't have an empty bag either. Many such laws or approximations to such laws are important to social planning. Thus the law of coexistence that connects density of population with rates of mental illness is or ought to be vitally important to certain aspects of social planning. No such law or combination of laws of coexistence tells us, strictly speaking, whether there is going to be any society tomorrow or what it's going to be like. They only tell us that if there is a society with certain characteristics, then it will also have certain other characteristics. This is *not* a distinction between "hypothetical" and "categorical" laws of nature — no laws categorically assert the existence of anything — but only another way of calling attention to the distinction between laws of succession and laws of coexistence.

Hook's Objections to Monistic Theories

I shall continue my examination of monistic theories of society with a discussion of two quite different kinds of objections to them, though both seem to be of a sort one might call "logical" as opposed to simply empirical. I begin the shorter discussion, that of Sidney Hook, with a longish quotation:

> We may put the point we are making in this way. Every theory in this existential sub-type of dialectics begins with an initial monism which it is compelled to qualify by reference to the reciprocal and interactive effects of many different factors. The monism is then abandoned and it is asserted that Spirit or mode of production, technology, or the great man is the dominant (or most fundamental or most important) cause of historical or social development. But there is no way to "measure" the dominant factor in general unless this means that many more cultural phenomena can be shown to depend upon X than upon any other factor. This is a proposition about comparative frequencies and could only be established as a result of a vast statistical study of cultural dependencies which no one has ever adequately undertaken.
>
> The confusion comes from speaking of the dominant factor in relation to society or history as a whole, when it only makes sense to speak of something as dominant or most important in relation to some problem to be solved or difficulty to be overcome. There is no such thing as the most important factor in the health or functioning of the human organism. But once trouble arises, analysis may indicate that for its elimination, certain functions of the organism may be more important than others, i.e., restoration at some points is more urgent than others. So in social inquiry. What those who speak of dialectic must mean if they are to avoid tautologies or contradictions is that in reference to some problem or felt difficulty, which may vary with the different

values of different groups, the use of certain instrumentalities is more valid than others.[3]

The dialectics we may safely ignore. Hook's use of 'monistic', the reader will have noticed, applies only to those theories in which one variable is the solely determining one, but I shall continue to speak more loosely, using 'monistic' also to include those in which one variable is only the most important or dominant variable. While in one place Hook seems willing to recognize a good sense that can be given to monistic theories of society, the main burden of the passage seems to be to show that all such theories are not simply false but meaningless. His argument appears to be that those who imagine that monistic theories of society do make sense — whether any is true or not — do so because they confuse general scientific explanation with practical problem solving.

We may first agree with Hook that theories which assert the exclusive causal efficacy of a single variable are, if they ever do appear, very short-lived in the history of ideas. For they, unlike some of their cousins that I have discussed, are not only obviously incompatible with the observable empirical data, but also, as I have shown, logically contradictory. When we turn to those theories which only assert the preponderant influence of one variable relative to the others, Hook *seems* to grant the logical coherence of such a theory, but at the same time to get unusually worried about confirmation. He claims there is no way to "measure" the dominant variable unless this means "that many more cultural phenomena can be shown to depend upon X than upon any other factor." I take it this is his way of saying that such theories *make no sense* unless this means that many more cultural phenomena can be shown to depend upon X than upon any other factor, for I doubt very much that Hook is one of those who believes, as some wrongly do, that a theory can be scientific or empirical only if its variables are quantified. Hook continues by saying that such theories must be about comparative frequencies and is again worried about confirmation. I claim to have shown several logical forms which such a theory might have, at least some of which might reasonably be called theories about comparative frequencies. As to confirmation, I think we can again agree that no one has shown so far that certainly any such theory is true. At the same time, some of those who proposed such theories, such as Marx, did try to back them up with empirical data though, to be sure, they still remain somewhat in the speculative realm. But Hook seems to be doubtful that anyone might actually have meant what he, Hook, thinks could only reasonably be meant in light of the alleged problems of confirmation.

Next Hook speaks of "the confusion," something which, by my reading, he has not yet identified. I think rather it is Hook who is confused. It will be observed that he makes an analogy between the idea of "the dominant factor in relation to society or history as a whole" and "the most important factor in the health or function of the human organism." My objection is not the here irrelevant one that a society is not an organism, but the quite different one that we were interested to begin with in scientific prediction and calculation of what actually causes what in society and not simply with what may keep it "functioning." To be sure, if one is, from outside the system, trying to return it to a certain state or bring about a certain state, then which variable one would have to manipulate may vary with the circumstances. Of this kind of situation and what I called its "contextual" nature I spoke earlier. But this is *not* the same thing as simply predicting on the basis of the system itself and the values of the variables in it its future or past states, or calculating on the basis of some of the values of some one or more of its variables at a moment, the values of its other variables. Thus Hook's analogy, itself a confused result of his own "pragmatism" no doubt, fails to establish what he apparently wishes to establish. Hook tries to diagnose an error which he hasn't shown independently to be an error, but his diagnosis is itself logically at fault. Prediction of certain characteristics of a system on the basis of other of its characteristics and which is being *considered* to be a closed system is *not* to be confused with its manipulation from without.

Now it could conceivably be, though I think myself to have shown otherwise, that Hook's conclusion that monistic theories of society are logical nonsense is true and that those who thought otherwise were victims of the alleged confusion Hook points to. Hook would still not have established his conclusion, but only have shown, inadvertently, that they do not make the same necessary distinction that he fails to make.

Plamenatz on Monistic Theories

John Plamenatz, during the course of what must be one of the finest analyses of Marxism to be found, at least in the English language, argues that "any theory which postulates a fundamental causal factor to explain social change is mistaken."[4] It is a little difficult to say whether we should call his argument empirical or logical, and perhaps it doesn't matter very much, for while he seems to be arguing on empirical grounds about what actually causes what, he also suggests that if these causal features were absent, we wouldn't have anything we could recognizably call a society to begin with. But it is better to get on with his argument. He agrees in the first place that "if we take a small enough part of social life, we can easily show that it is derivative, in the sense that it is much more affected by the rest of social life, or even by some other part of it, than it affects it."[5] What he wants to show is that "if we take larger sides of social life, like religion or science or government, it is no longer plausible to treat any of them as fundamental or derivative in relation to the others."[6]

Plamenatz's argument for this conclusion we get from the following passages:

All properly social relations are moral and customary; they cannot be adequately defined unless we bring normative concepts into the definitions, unless we refer to rules of conduct which the persons who stand in those relations recognize and are required to conform to.[7]

Since claims and duties and mental attitudes are involved in all social relations, in every side of social life, no matter how primitive, since they are part of what we mean when we call a human activity social, we cannot take any side of social life and say that it determines, even *in the last resort*, whatever that may mean, men's moral and customary relations and their attitudes towards one another.[8]

We cannot pass from such statements as 'unless men had biological needs peculiar to their kind, there would be no families' or 'unless men co-operated to produce and exchange goods and services, there would be no communities larger than families' to conclusions like 'how men satisfy their biological needs determines moral relations inside the family' or 'how men co-operate to produce and exchange goods and services determines social relations inside the community'. We cannot do it because how men satisfy their needs and how they co-operate cannot be adequately defined without bringing these relations into the definition.[9]

Having arrived at this point, Plamenatz goes on to develop another kind of distinction between the fundamental and the derivative in social life which, he says, Marx and Engels might have held but never explicitly expressed, and which in some form or other must be true, I suppose. It is simply the distinction between those features which are common to all societies and existed in them before the distinction into classes (the fundamental) and those that are peculiar to certain societies and exist possibly only after the division into classes (the derivative). But this way of making the distinction "does not imply that the basis determines what is derivative from it; that the forms of social behavior which must exist before classes can arise determine the forms and features which emerge with them or after they have arisen''[10] nor that ''we can in any society, class or classless, sort out men's social activities into two groups in such a way that, as the one changes, so does the other.''[11] In short, this is not a *causal* theory of the relation of the fundamental to the derivative and therefore I shall discuss it no further. Let us turn to an examination of his attempted refutation of all causal theories of society which are of a monistic variety.

One may wonder in the first place whether, even if his argument were otherwise satisfactory, Plamenatz has made it general enough to establish that ''every attempt to distinguish, among the larger aspects of social life, between a fundamental causal factor and what is derivative from it''[12] must be mistaken. For on the face of it, it would seem that the argument at best shows only that ''men's moral and customary relations and their attitudes toward one another'' cannot be so distinguished, so neatly separated, from other aspects of social life to make the causal question of their relation to those ''other'' aspects an intelligible one. What about theories which hold that the means of communication are the determining factor of social life, for example? Does his argument even direct itself to them? It may be objected that any theory which points to something which is not at least in part a form of human behavior is not really a monistic *social* theory. And we can imagine Plamenatz agreeing, I suppose, that some extra-social factor might be the major determining factor of social life. Indeed, one version of economic determinism which defined the forces of production, not in terms of human behavior, but only in terms of the nonhuman resources and instruments of production would seem to be exempt from Plamenatz's argument altogether, however absurd it might be on simple empirical grounds to hold that the forces of production, so characterized, were the dominant variable in the explanation of social change. Let us agree, however, that a properly *social* theory of society, if it is a monistic one, is one which includes human characteristics. But I don't want to beg the question by agreeing with Plamenatz that every form of social behavior involves ''claims and duties'' in the sense he attaches to those words.

But now what is the structure and presupposition of his argument? In the first place, for Plamenatz the variables of a social theory are always forms of human behavior, or at least each includes human behavior as a ''part.'' Thus science, government, religion, and so on are, whatever else they may be, ways of acting or activities of a certain sort. So too for the ''relations of production.'' Thus a monistic theory of society, at least in the way Plamenatz is considering it, tells us that there is a variable which *is*, or has as a "*part*," a certain form of human behavior and that other forms of human behavior are, perhaps in one of the senses I elucidated earlier, a *D*-variable with respect to them. So far, so good. But now there are three quite distinct ways one might take his argument from here.

One way of taking the argument has as its basic presupposition that any monistic theory worth its salt or which has actually been held, maintains that, to speak loosely, morality is among what I would call the *R*-variables, among what, again loosely speaking, is determined and does not itself determine. But, the argument continues, this is absurd, for morality is not a variable alongside other variables to be clearly distinguished from them; it is rather part of the definition of every variable which might be considered as a candidate for a *D*-variable to begin with. So no theory which makes morality one of the *R*-variables can possibly be true and this is what all monistic social theories try to do.

The second way of taking the argument would be as follows: Since among the set of variables which are being considered, all of them have morality, roughly speaking, as part of their definitions, it is not possible for them to be causally connected, for they are related not externally but definitionally. If two variables are "definitionally" connected, then the question of their causal relationship cannot arise. This we may recognize as a variation of the argument used by MacIntyre which I discussed in the third chapter. The third way starts the same as the second, observing that each of the variables in question has morality in its definition, but concludes not that this makes the question of their causal connections irrelevant or impossible, but only that no one of the variables can possibly be a *D*-variable in any reasonable sense (possibly those I talked about?) so that again no monistic theory of society, properly so-called, is possible.

I have no desire to argue in detail which of these variations Plamenatz intended, for my purposes are philosophical and not exegetical. The first interpretation would seem to contradict Plamenatz's claim that he is going to show that *any* attempt to distinguish among the fundamental and the derivative in a causal theory of social change is mistaken. For we can construct and some have already believed theories in which morality does not play quite the role that the kinds of theories this argument would tell against demand of it. The second variation has presuppositions about causality and definition which it seems that Plamenatz would have made more explicit were this his intended argument. The third version perhaps best fits with the text, though in a way it is the least dramatic interpretation. In any case, I shall address myself to the issue in a manner that does not require my distinguishing the three variations anyway, although some comments will not apply to all three versions.

The first point to be made is that forms of behavior must be characterized in a narrow enough way so that it is not true by definition that if a person acts in a certain way in one kind of situation he "must" act in a certain way in another kind of situation. In short, one must define the behavioral variables so that it is always possible to ask whether a person who would do so-and-so in this situation would also do such-and-such in that situation. And this can be a causal question, that is, one of the lawful coincidence or at the least one of the external connections of behavioral dispositions. But secondly, even if "morality" and a form of behavior are definitionally connected, it does not follow that they cannot *also* be lawfully connected, depending on what kind of definitional connection it is. And now we had better look a little more closely at this claim itself — that morality is involved in the definition of all forms of social behavior.

In what sense is morality involved in the definition of all social behavior, if that is true at all? It's true enough that there is not a realm of behavior alongside our activities as producers, scientists, worshipers, or whatever of being moral (or immoral). What *are* a person's values? A set of attitudes, feelings, dispositions to act in certain ways in certain situations, the behavior itself. Yes, all of that, no doubt. And one must also make room for the commonsense fact that people sometimes act against their values. It is also true that morality has a kind of pervasive nature. Schematically, we may say that every piece of voluntary behavior, including social behavior, is, according to one's values, either obligatory, permissible, or prohibited. To this extent everything one does has a moral dimension. This does not mean, of course, that the social scientist's description of the behavior itself involves a moral judgment, though his *description* may mention the values and the judgments of his subjects. When Plamenatz says that social relations "cannot be adequately defined unless we bring normative concepts into the definitions, unless we refer to rules of conduct which the persons who stand in those relations recognize and are required to conform to," one is tempted to ascribe to him a confusion between the kind of thing that is going on when, for example, Jones says, "Killing is wrong," which is a moral judgment, and what is going on when the scientist says, "Jones holds that killing is wrong," which is not a moral judgment. Then one might take Plamenatz's whole argument to be a variation on the Hegelian theme that one cannot separate "values" from "facts" even for analytic purposes, and so all our "knowledge" is value-permeated, and so on.

I do not think this is Plamenatz's view, yet it is not easy to see what *exactly* he might mean by saying that normative concepts are always involved in the definition of social relations. Let us take his own example. He says that how people satisfy their material needs cannot be defined adequately without bringing in normative concepts. Surely the physical motions a person goes through can be so defined. If we see two people "cooperating" in order to assuage their hunger — one of them gathering food, the other cooking it, and then both sitting down to eat it — we can surely *describe* the situation without bringing in normative concepts, as I just did. But is it an adequate description? Adequate for what? In this case, we are assuming a description is adequate if it is useful for scientific understanding. And it is useful for scientific understanding if the properties mentioned in the description enter into significant lawful relations with other properties.

It may well be that no behavior is "properly" *called* social unless morality enters in, but this can only mean, as far as I can see, that such behavior "must" always stand in some relation to certain dispositions or intentions to act in a certain way, to certain characteristic feelings, possibly even to certain documents, and so on. It does not follow that the behavior cannot be considered in and of itself, as it were, including its causal relations to certain dispositions to act in that way, that is, the conditions under which people tend more or less to act according to their values. A certain kind of object may properly be called a satellite only if it stands in a certain relation to another such body; it does not follow *either* that it cannot be considered under a description which makes no mention of that fact *or* that it cannot be considered in its *causal* relations to the body to which, under a certain description, it is definitionally "connected." But if this is so, there would seem to be no reason why one cannot consider in a person his values and each mode of behavior as distinct variables, so that one could ask about their relative importance to each other, causally speaking. Or rather, since we are concerned with social theories, even granted that the way people cooperate to produce the means necessary for their material satisfaction "involves" morality, one can still ask whether among the different modes of behavior, there is one or a few which, considered under the appropriate descriptions, have the lawful relations to the others that would make them a *D*-variable with respect to them. There may well be laws which, given how people satisfy their biological needs, would enable one to calculate specifically or within a certain range what other kinds of behavior will be characteristic of each mode, that is, what values the variables that are the modes of human behavior will have. The fact, if it is a fact, that under the description which makes each mode a properly social relation there must be mentioned the values of those so acting does *not* render this supposition impossible.

But does it make it impossible to consider morality as one of the social variables alongside the others which are modes of behavior? We not only *have* values; we obtain them, we construct value systems, and so on. Since this is so, we may, after all, speak of certain modes of behavior as being *specially* concerned with morality. But even so, we can always ask if certain ways of acting are apt to give rise causally to certain characteristic feelings, thoughts, and so on. To this extent there is, so far as I can see, no reason why it could not be the case that in a significant sense the way people satisfy their material needs is causally related to, even, as we speak, *produces* the morality typically associated with it, even if there must have been some values before people would start acting that way. We might come at this from a slightly different direction. It must be possible to characterize the behavior in question apart from the values which make it only properly called social or else one couldn't characterize it at all. Whether this means characterizing it only in physical terms or in terms of skills, certain dispositions, desires, and so on, it must have ''distinguishable'' features; otherwise the behavior which to be properly called social ''cannot be adequately defined unless we bring normative concepts into the definitions'' can't be defined at all or else *only* in terms of those ''normative'' concepts which is absurd.

I conclude then that Plamenatz, interesting as his argument is, has not made his case against the possibility of there being a true monistic theory of society.

Summary and Conclusion

What are we to make of all this? We certainly are not in a position to say that any monistic theory of society is true even within the limitations imposed by the known empirical facts. These facts are that the social variables interact with variables entirely outside the social realm and that some of the latter are more important than the social ones themselves in determining what goes on in the sense that if and when these variables take on certain values, their effects on society are dramatic. For as Hook rightly remarked, no one has gathered the kind of evidence one would need to show that any monistic theory of society is certainly true. On the other hand, it is not true that there is no evidence at all. Plamenatz (and possibly Hook) to the contrary notwithstanding, it would seem that there is some evidence that *how* human beings choose or are required to satisfy their material and biological needs is more of a determining factor in human affairs than *how* they choose or are required to practice their religions. Or perhaps one should only say that the knowledge of the one is a more reliable guide than the other to guessing the other features of a culture and its subsequent nature.

One must, I think, be sympathetic to the claim that, at least in the social realm, everything interacts with everything else. This doctrine, which I have elsewhere called "total social interactionism,"[13] must not be confused with a view according to which everything has the "same" importance in the social process, whatever exactly that would mean. I have already argued that a view according to which some one (or even a group of) variable(s) determines everything else and there is no determination on the part of the latter is logically incoherent. It derives, I suspect, in part from active/passive notions of causation and thus ultimately from a substance metaphysics (and this in spite of my earlier observations about the relation of monism and substantialism). Thus every system has some mutual interaction or else no lawful connections at all among its variables making it hardly deserving of being called a system. It is quite consistent with "total social interactionism" that some of the social variables should be, causally speaking, more important than others.

One must also be sympathetic to the claim, I think, that no social variable completely determines any other social variable either by way of laws of succession or even by way of laws of coexistence. If there were any such laws, I think we would have discovered them by now, and the attempts to show a direct causal connection between this or that aspect of the social realm and everything else not only usually fail to be persuasive but almost always have patent ideological motivations. Ideologically motivated theories of society are not necessarily false (or true) for that reason whatever Mannheim and others may think, but those who put them forward for such reasons or under such motivations are often blinded to the need for good evidence.

I have indicated earlier that monistic theories of society which limit themselves to laws of coexistence are more likely to be true than those which limit themselves to laws of succession, the main reason being the obvious one that in general laws of coexistence are less open to "interfering" conditions. Plamenatz described the theories he was attacking as theories of social change, that is, as consisting primarily of laws of succession, but his objections, if they are valid ones at all, would apply equally well to monistic theories of social "cross sections."

There is little doubt that our general lawful knowledge of society is mostly of the coexistence type. We feel far more confident in asserting things of the sort that if some society has such and such features at a certain time, then it also has such and such other features at the same time, than we do in affirming that if a society is in such and such a state at this moment, then it will be in such and such a state tomorrow. I don't think this is *primarily* for the sorts of reasons which intrigue Popper and which I have discussed elsewhere,[14] that is, that we can't possibly calculate the future values of the variable which are human knowledge, so much as it is that the nonhuman variables interact with the social ones, including those nonhuman factors which are relevant to the acquisition of knowledge. It is always useful to remember that the social history of the human race is but a part of the history of life on earth and the latter but a part of a yet larger natural process.

IX Ideas and Society

To a certain extent both this and the next chapter are concerned with the relation of a person to society. But whereas the next chapter takes up the issue of the specific and possibly unique influence a single person might have on history, this chapter is concerned with the somewhat narrower issue of the relation of ideas to society. Even so there will be some overlap. For the points I wish to make, I have found it most useful, though admittedly a bit strange, to organize the sections of this chapter under the following headings: *ideas as reflections*; *ideas and idealism*; *intentions and society*; and a *summary and conclusion*.

Ideas as Reflections

Before we can consider how ideas affect or fail to affect society or to "reflect" this or that aspect of material or social reality, we must first ask what we are to understand by an idea. We could take the notion to include anything mental whatsoever: desires, rememberings, and perceptions as well as beliefs, knowledge, and memories — that is, conscious mental states as well as dispositional "mental states." Those philosophers and social thinkers who spoke of ideas as "reflections" of some aspect of the world usually included in ideas what are in fact both dispositional "mental states" and mental contents proper, even though a given theory of reflection might properly apply only to one kind or the other. In fact, it doesn't matter very much for most of what I want to say what exactly we include in the realm of "ideas"; but for some of it, I must limit myself to those "ideas" which are intentions, that is, ideas which people try to "realize," and for another part to those "ideas" which can be true or false, that is, beliefs. Both intentions and beliefs are no doubt some combination of dispositional and conscious mental states.

In this section I want to consider some of the theses to the effect that ideas or some among them are (only) a ''reflection'' of certain aspects of the material or social world as well as some of the real and alleged consequences of those theses. The typical intention of such theories is either (a) to denigrate the role of ideas in the social process, or (b) to cast doubt on the possibility of a truth independent of, say, social class or historical circumstance, that is, any real truth at all, or (c) to affirm one's ''materialism''; and although the consequences that were thought to follow from these theses in many cases don't follow and are in themselves dubious, the theses themselves are sometimes almost certainly true.

There are five senses in which singly or in some combination an idea might possibly be said to ''reflect'' some aspect of material or social reality. In the first place, the idea may *intend* some part of the material or social world. My thought that the Eiffel Tower is in Paris intends or is about the fact that the Eiffel Tower is in Paris. Secondly, an idea may be said to *resemble* some aspect of material or social reality. Thus when I think about the Eiffel Tower in Paris, I may have an image of the Tower which is a more or less accurate ''picture'' of it. In the third place, an idea may be *lawfully parallel* to or simply a *lawful consequence* of some part of the material or social world. Thus my thought that the Eiffel Tower is in Paris is, as it happens, partly caused by the fact that the Eiffel Tower is in Paris, and is lawfully parallel, we may assume, to a certain state of my brain. Fourth, the point of some theories of the reflection of our ideas of material or social reality may be to emphasize a *total empiricism* according to which all our (relevant) ideas come from (are caused by) experience of the material or social world and none come from our genes or pure reflection or revelation or anything else. And fifth, one's ideas may be said to reflect in the sense of being a *rationalization* or *justification* of some aspect of the material but in this case especially of the social world. Thus a political theory as held by some particular person or group of persons might be said to be ''only'' a mask for defending a certain social arrangement which that person considers advantageous to himself or his class or nation.

I don't know whether any *social* theorist was ever really interested in the first of these for its own sake though the fact of the intentionality of thought may have played a role in their theories. That theorists have considered ideas as reflections in the other four senses is well-known historical fact, although it is usually the consequences they drew, whether legitimately or not, rather than the supposition of reflection itself which is more interesting. So let us look at each of the conceptions of reflection in the order listed above.

The intentionality of thought is its "essence" in the sense that it is the aboutness of thought which is crucial to its characterization as thought. This does not imply that everything that might reasonably be called mental, even prior to any philosophical analysis, is a thought even if we ignore so-called dispositional mental states. Be that as it may, if anyone were to maintain that a thought "reflects" something simply by intending it, that would be only to say, without further ontological analysis, that it *is* a thought and one which happens to be of a certain (possibly nonexistent) state of affairs. Since the intentional connection is not a causal one (this is shown by the fact that we can think of what does not exist or obtain), nothing follows with respect to the role of ideas in human or any other affairs since nothing has been asserted about the *lawful* connections of thoughts to anything else to begin with. The facts that we have thoughts and that they intend are compatible with any theory whatsoever about the causal role of ideas in the world (and, incidentally, with both philosophical idealism and philosophical materialism as we shall characterize those doctrines in the next section).

The idea of reflection by resemblance is, no doubt, the most literal sense of the term. Just as the mirror reflects the reality in front of it (though in reverse) so, it has been maintained, our mental images are more or less accurate reflections of aspects of material or social reality. One may wonder, quite apart from other difficulties, how one literally pictures a social reality at least so far as, in any given case, a social fact properly so-called is more than can be "pictured" in a temporal cross section of the physical world. But in any case, whether this is the model some thinkers had in mind or not, I should say that ideas considered as images are of little significance either in the philosophical or in the sociological treatment of mind. They ought to be of only peripheral interest to the philosopher at least in the general analysis of mind because they are not the "essence" of thought and a thought not only can exist but can also, where appropriate, be true or false without them. If there are images at all — it has been doubted by many philosophers — one could, I suppose, say that they are more or less accurate pictures of what one intends in the thought. Thus an image is an *image* only if there is also a thought which intends; otherwise, it is, if it is an object at all, just an object among objects, though like any object it might more or less happen to resemble some other object(s).

The reason the sociologist is not properly interested in ideas as images except in a quite different sense altogether is that the sociologist as such is not concerned with the analysis of mind at all. He studies the mind by studying behavior including linguistic behavior, and while of course he is properly interested in what people believe and value and remember and fantasize, this does not mean that he is interested in the nature of mind itself. It does not matter to him for it in no way affects his research which, if any, of the many philosophical theories of mind is true. This is only another way of saying that in a sense all the scientific student of human behavior studies is *behavior* and not what, according to common sense no less than to some philosophical theories, is ''behind'' much of our behavior. But, finally, and most important, even if some image theory of mind were true, nothing follows with respect to the role of ideas in the social process. Such theories or their denials leave completely open how much difference it makes to our behavior and hence to the behavior of others what we think or value or believe and so on.

Neither the intentional relation nor the resemblance relation is a causal one. The third and fourth conceptions of ''reflection'' of ideas both in their different ways emphasize the fact that our ideas are caused. In the first of them the stress is on the supposition that our ideas or certain ones among them are lawfully parallel or the lawful consequences of certain aspects of material or social reality. Here the emphasis is not on *perception* in the narrow sense in which the British empiricists were concerned with it, but rather on our beliefs and values. That is, it is not a question of the perceptual origin of our ''simple'' ideas but of the social origin of those complex patterns of actual and potential behaviors and conscious mental states which are our beliefs and values. Hence also it is not a question of the lawfully parallel bodily state which presumably accompanies every mental state, conscious or dispositional, but of a more general lawful connection between the contents of our ideas and particular social circumstances. The name of Mannheim is, of course, the first that comes to mind. The consequence he drew, or at least the assumption he was working with, was that there is some kind of logical or ''automatic'' connection between the causal origins of our beliefs and values on the one hand and their truth-values on the other.[1] A brief examination of this belief of Mannheim's may serve to open a longish digression on the philosophy of the sociology of knowledge.

While not all sociologists of knowledge make the assumption that the social causation of ideas has any logical connection with their truth-values,[2] Mannheim and his followers would have it that by showing that our beliefs about society, even those arrived at by systematic methods, are causally connected with our social positions, mainly our class identifications, one has thereby shown that those beliefs are false or distorted.[3] To be sure, Mannheim also claims that the ''free intelligentsia,'' being connected with a class by choice rather than birth or other circumstances beyond one's control, are in a position to come up with theories which are relatively free of ideological distortion, but even they can only approximate the truth. Of the many criticisms, internal and external, that can be made of Mannheim's position, I wish to rehearse only a couple.

The question of the truth or falsity of a thought — a belief to be precise — is logically utterly independent of its causation. By 'logically' I mean that in no case can one deduce a statement of the truth-value of a belief from the statement of its causation. It is indeed of sociological interest to discover the social elements in the causation of some or all of our ideas as the case may be, and it is of political, social, and moral interest to show the self-serving nature of social theories as held by some people, to "unmask" the oppressors by showing how, when they do, they control the production and distribution of ideas, and so on. But the simple logical point remains: a belief or its advocacy or perpetuation may be self-serving, one may be ignorant of its real source, it may be held for totally irrational reasons — and yet the belief may be true. Is it sufficient proof of this point just to express it? If someone is caused to believe that two plus two make four by chemical means, what he believes is true even though he does not have rational grounds for believing it, even though he may not know or remember how he came to believe it, and whatever good or injury it does him to believe it.

Idéologie was, in the hands of the *idéologues,* originally to be simply a study of the "natural history" of ideas with an eye, to be sure, on the improvement of society. In the nineteenth century, mainly through the influence of Marx, the belief emerged that there is a kind of internal or logical connection between the causation and the truth-values of beliefs. With Mannheim this confusion becomes total as his conception of the problem of ideology becomes, in his own words, "totalistic."[4] In part, too, the confusion arises from the assumptions that, to put it succinctly, (a) values are relative (with which, of course, I agree) and (b) there is no sharp distinction between factual and value "claims" (with which I strongly disagree). Hence, it was concluded, facts are "relative." We are able to see at this point that Mannheim shuttles between two quite different positions each of which, however, has the implication that objective social knowledge is impossible: (a) there is no objective knowledge to be had because there are no objective social facts to be known; and (b) though there are or may be objective social facts, we, biased and fallible beings that we are, cannot ever know them, at least in their purity. The first of these is, broadly, an ontological position; the second an epistemological one.

It goes without saying, of course, that people, including social theorists, are often biased and that the content of their theories, as believed and advocated by them, sometimes is partly determined by those biases. Or better said, since we need not use the loaded notion of bias, many people, including social theorists, wouldn't have the (factual) beliefs about society they do have unless they had the values concerning society they do have. If the argument for universal ideological distortion were a purely inductive one, it could on the one hand show only that there is some statistical correlation between certain kinds of values and certain social theories as actually held by people and on the other by establishing the correlation show the way to escape possible ideological distortion in practice. But, most importantly, to show a correlation between the fact that we have certain values on the one hand and the alleged fact of universal distortion in our social theories on the other, it would have to be shown, one by one and using the usual scientific methods, that each of those theories is not true. And that procedure would presuppose the possibility of a nondistorted grasp of objective social facts to begin with. Mannheim's philosophical attempts at proof of total ideological distortion are based on a logical fallacy and have nothing else to recommend them.[5]

The fact that there is no *logical* connection between the causation and the truth-value of an idea is no basis for denying the possibility of a sociology of truth and falsehood, that is, a sociological study of the conditions under which people are more likely to arrive at the truth concerning whatever their beliefs are about rather than falsehood. Indeed the fact that the connection is only lawful (statistically) precisely invites such an investigation. It may be objected at this point that such an investigation presupposes that the sociologist already knows what is true and what is false, thus making such an undertaking absurd. But is this really so? It is not presupposed that the sociologist of knowledge is infallible or knows any more than any other educated person. It is not even presupposed that he understands what he assumes to be true. Hence the sociologist may inquire what social conditions — educational, industrial, political, and so on — are likely to produce the truth in physics, say, without supposing that he understands a whit about physics himself. His presupposition is in a sense a philosophical one, that rational and systematic methods are more likely to produce truth than are other methods (though this, too, is something we know by induction very broadly speaking, those of us who do know it). Thus his question becomes the somewhat narrower one: under what conditions are people able and disposed to apply rational and systematic methods to confirm or to falsify their beliefs and theories? Of course, extra-rational factors enter into every human activity and there is no method which if only carefully followed leads automatically to the truth. Thus the sociologist's undertaking is fraught with the same inevitable limitations as those activities he studies. But all that remains is the misplaced philosophical concern for absolute certainty — something which, except in the purely psychological sense, is never to be.

Still in the context of the philosophy of the sociology of knowledge, it will be appropriate, finally, to examine briefly a view of MacIntyre's on the notion of a sociology of truth or of discovery. The reasons are that he draws from his argument a conclusion which not only contradicts one of the central assumptions of this book, but is also important in itself.

> Two final morals: the first is that, if I am correct in supposing rationality to be an inescapable sociological category, then once again the positivist account of sociology in terms of a logical dichotomy between facts and values must break down. For to characterize actions and institutionalized practices as rational or irrational is to evaluate them. Nor is it the case that this evaluation is an element superadded to an original merely descriptive element. To call an argument fallacious is always at once to describe and to evaluate it. It is highly paradoxical that the impossibility of deducing evaluative conclusions from factual premises should have been advanced as a truth of logic, when logic is itself the science in which the coincidence of description and evaluation is most obvious. The social scientist is, if I am right, committed to the values of rationality in virtue of his explanatory projects in a stronger sense than the natural scientist is. For it is not only the case that his own procedures must be rational; but he cannot escape the use of the concept of rationality in his inquiries.[6]

The assumption of mine which is here challenged is of course that "positivist" view that there is a "logical dichotomy" between facts and values. MacIntyre's argument rests on two claims: that the sociologist cannot escape the use of the notion of rationality in a complete account of human action; and that such a notion is both descriptive and evaluative and in a way that one cannot analytically separate the two elements. The second claim is supported by way of an analogy to logic, the first by way of several considerations which occur earlier in his paper. Both of these claims are, I believe, false, though if the first only can be shown to be so, the truth-value of the second will be irrevelant to the conclusion — that at least some parts of sociology cannot be purely descriptive. I propose therefore to allow the second premise to go unchallenged. (In any case, I agree that in a given context the uses of 'rational' and 'irrational' will almost invariably involve positive or negative attitudes on the parts of their users and hence are "evaluative." What I dispute is that there is no isolable descriptive content and this will emerge in my challenge to the first premise.)

Let us turn then to the premise that rationality is an "inescapable sociological category." There is no way I can adequately summarize the observations and remarks that led MacIntyre to this conclusion; I shall have to ask the reader to examine MacIntyre's paper for himself and judge if what I shall say against it is not correct.

MacIntyre is anxious to establish, contrary to Trevor-Roper and others, that the Victorian historians and social thinkers were not wholly mistaken in distinguishing for explanatory purposes between rational and irrational beliefs. Unfortunately they tended to identify rationality with truth, irrationality with falsehood, and hence to see any who did not hold to the beliefs they had as irrational. MacIntyre of course knows that rationality has to do not so much with the truth of what is believed as the way in which one comes to believe it or at least the grounds one presently has for believing it and also in the coherence of the given belief with one's other beliefs. Thus he is at pains to show that beliefs which are irrational and for which, as actually held by someone, reasoning and appeals to logic and evidence are not relevant will require a fundamentally different kind of explanation from those beliefs which are arrived at in part at least in virtue of such reasonings and appeals. And I think it is easy to agree with MacIntyre that different kinds of explanation are relevant to beliefs we characterize as rational and to those we characterize as irrational. Even so, in the context of scientific explanation it is, from where I stand, only a matter of different variables in differing causal sequences.

But what is needed beyond this? Having shown that someone holds a given belief because he is predisposed to ground his beliefs on evidence, because he actually has such-and-such evidence, and so on, why must the sociologist go on to say that his subject's belief is rational? What is added by way of scientific explanation in so doing? Why is it not enough simply to describe the sequence of events which led to the belief without any further "judgment" of its overall "nature" or "value"? And so for the irrational beliefs as well. If the full, relevant causal explanation of someone's belief involves some aspects of the general social situation, the subject's emotions, and the need to "ground" the emotion in a belief, then again nothing is added by way of scientific explanation in going on to say that the belief is irrational. Of course the sociologist may for shorthand purposes actually use the words 'rational' and 'irrational' for he does indeed need to distinguish beliefs not only in terms of their causation as has just been agreed but also in terms of their effects, for his predictions about a person's subsequent behavior vis-à-vis the belief in question may well differ according to how the person came to hold the belief. Still his use of these words is so far only a matter of convenience and not a requirement of logic, language, or explanatory completeness. Thus it does not follow from the necessity of making such distinctions nor is it true, so far as I can perceive, that rationality and irrationality are basic sociological notions, systematically speaking. Hence, too, MacIntyre's conclusion to the effect that in the sociology of knowledge there is a collapse of the positivist distinction of facts and values must be regarded as unproved.

Anyone who has read this far will know that I am quite prepared to believe that our ideas — whatever one takes them exactly to be — are completely lawfully explainable both in their existence and in their particular contents. Earlier in this section I sketchily argued two points: (a) that as a matter of pure logic the truth-value of an idea (in this case as belief) is logically independent of its causal origin; and (b) while there may be inductive grounds for making some broad correlations between the methods used in arriving at certain beliefs on the one hand and the truth-values of those beliefs on the other, neither this nor any other argument establishes or can establish that *all* thought or even *all* social thought is ideological in virtue of whatever causal connections there may be between, say, social thought and actual or perceived social conditions. But what, if anything, do such causal theories of the origin of ideas show about their role in history? Do they show, for example, that it is relatively unimportant or not important at all what we believe, value, and feel? To this I intend to give a fuller answer in the third section of this chapter and most of the rest of it is at least implicit in what was said in the third chapter. Suffice it here to observe the following.

(1) It might be maintained that human history just *is* in large measure the sequences in time of what humans believe and value. In this sense obviously what we believe and value makes a difference to history whatever the causal origin of those beliefs and values, although there would still be the question of how the beliefs and values of a given person or group affect those of other persons and groups. (2) On the other hand if the question is to what extent it matters in our behavior what in particular we value and believe, the question is a purely empirical one of extreme complexity. The question may be put differently as: To what extent do differences in beliefs and values show themselves in behavior? *And* to what extent are differences in behavior the

result of differences in values and beliefs? So put, it may be seen that the question of the causal origins of those values and beliefs need not be especially relevant; it will depend on what those origins are. If they are themselves the behaviors, then their relevance is obvious. But if, to make the logical point clear, our beliefs and values (and all our ''ideas'') were purely genetically determined, it would leave completely open how ideas affect behavior and so the rest of the world, social and natural. In this, the mere fact that our ideas are caused is quite compatible with the most extravagant theses about the role of ideas in history. (3) To refer to a point of the third chapter, it may be said that whatever phenomena can be explained in terms of ideas — their existence and their specific contents — can be explained without them. This would *not* show that ideas are not causally important, much less that they do not exist. For the laws of coexistence that would make such a possibility a reality would also imply that if there were no ideas and their contents were not what they are, then those phenomena going proxy for those ideas in explanation would themselves also not be there or not be just what they are.

We return, finally, to the fifth meaning that might be assigned to the notion that our ideas ''reflect'' our social environment. This is the thesis that on the whole social theories, religious beliefs, philosophical systems, and political ideologies justify and idealize some, usually the existing, social arrangements, and this whether their advocates are aware of it or not. This might be taken to be a part of a more general view to the effect that human beings tend to rationalize their behavior generally, first and foremost to themselves, and, to a lesser extent, to others. However it is formulated, one who maintains this thesis is likely to go on to tell us about the ''function'' of such beliefs in the stability and continuity of societies or certain of their institutions. We need not accept this pointing to their ''function'' as any explanation of why they are there in order to acknowledge that at least some of our relevant ideas do ''reflect'' social reality in this sense. But does this fact have any significance beyond itself?

The relation of an idea as rationalization to the state of affairs of which it is the rationalization is essentially logical, although presumably there would ordinarily be a causal relation as well. (It could not be causal in a case where the state of affairs rationalized was nonexistent but only believed or perceived to be existent by the rationalizer.) Hence nothing really needs to be added about the implications of such theses for the role of ideas in history. Ideas are never ''only'' rationalizations if that were meant to imply that that is the only relation some ideas have to anything else. But it is a little more complicated than this. Presumably an "idea," that is, a belief or a theory as actually held by someone ("existentially considered" in Mannheim's terminology) is not a rationalization just because it happens directly or indirectly to justify some state of affairs. Engels characterizes "false consciousness" as that in which the bearer of it is ignorant of his real motives in believing what he believes.[7] Here Engels seems to imply that the person may employ rational, scientific methods to figure out the truth and with respect to his results still suffer from "false consciousness." Does not the "ideal" bourgeois scientist at one and the same time make a fetish of his rational methods and labor under a delusion about the ultimate social origins of his beliefs as well as his fetish, according to one extreme strand of Marxist thought?[8] But such an argument would be relevant only if one had already established on independent grounds that the conclusions of such persons in such circumstances are always false or "distorted." Indeed we are all ignorant, I believe, of some of the causes of our beliefs. Not that there are any occult or entirely unsuspected factors operating in us or in "history" but only that in each particular case we can rarely, if ever, isolate analytically all the relevant factors. Since there are no such independent grounds, one must simply fall back on the question whether or not the person used rational and scientific methods to arrive at his social theories. If he did, then even if they do justify some social arrangements or other, they are not usefully referred to as "mere" or "only" rationalizations. And if he did not, the beliefs in question may still be true.

The argument of this section has been that none of the theories of "reflection" implies anything very specific about the importance of ideas in history or in nature, or that the truth-value of any idea is a function of its origin (except in the broad sense that truth is more apt to be the result of the employment of certain methods of discovery than others). All these theories of reflection may be true or "partly" true. No doubt ideas do have causal origins, even "total" ones, some of them intend states of affairs, some are accompanied by images, some are rationalizations, even "mere" rationalizations, for existing or desired social arrangements. In the section after next, I shall examine positively the question of ideas and their effect on and realization in history. But theories of reflection and some other views about the question of ideas and society have also been believed to have some relation to the more abstract, philosophical issue of idealism and materialism, and it is to the question of those alleged relations I turn first.

Ideas and Idealism

Philosophical idealism is the theory that everything is mental or depends on the mental for its existence. What distinguishes its many varieties from one another we can safely ignore, except to say that for our purposes we need consider only those forms of idealism according to which it is *human* minds in which what we ordinarily call physical objects reside (for example, Berkeley) or crucial features of which depend on human minds for their existence (for example, Kant). Now some thinkers, perhaps most prominently certain Marxists, have thought that there is a basic connection between philosophical idealism and its opposite (materialism or realism) on the one hand and certain apparently purely social theories on the other. More specifically some appear to have believed one or more of the following propositions: (a) that ideas are only a "reflection" of the material or social world, for otherwise philosophical idealism is true and philosophical materialism false; (b) that "social being determines social consciousness" and not vice versa, for otherwise philosophical idealism is true and philosophical materialism false; and (c) that ideas have no basic role in social processes, for otherwise philosophical idealism is true and philosophical materialism false.[9] Broadly speaking, we may say that the first two of these propositions have to do with the causation of ideas, the last with their effects.

My thesis is simple and, I believe, clear. Supposing that philosophical idealism is, or can be made to be, internally consistent, there would seem to be no logical contradiction in maintaining that everything is or depends on the mental in the sense required for a nontrivial idealism on the one hand and that social beliefs have a purely socially conditioned nature on the other; and conversely, one could grant whatever importance one wants to ideas in history and yet maintain that each of them, so far as it is or can be reduced to particular conscious and dispositional mental states, exists only in virtue of a certain specific organization of matter. The point is worth stating another way: Classical idealism and materialism (more frequently called realism except by Marxists, though here the use of 'materialism' calls attention not only to the independence of matter from mind but also to the dependence of mind on matter) are philosophical doctrines even though, or so I believe, the evidence for the truth of materialism is, broadly speaking, based on experience. The questions of the specific lawful connections between ideas and the material world are scientific ones and their answers, so far as I can see, have little if anything to do with philosophical idealism and philosophical materialism.

Thus one does *not* prove one's philosophical materialism by showing that ideas are a causal ''reflection'' of a person's social position or other features of his environment. Nor, on the other side, does one prove, or unintentionally exhibit, one's philosophical idealism by asserting that beliefs or values have an important role in human affairs. In short, *it is necessary to distinguish the question of the general dependence of the mental on the physical or the physical on the mental or their mutual dependence from the questions of the specific lawful connections that may hold between the contents of certain or even all ideas and this or that aspect of material or social reality.*

Let us examine this thesis a little further with respect to the three propositions listed above, each one of which it contradicts.

In the first place the question whether we get our ideas from social conditions, from sense experience, from our genes, from the gods, or from anywhere else has nothing special to do with the issue of materialism and idealism. For if materialism only means that there cannot be minds, that is, states of consciousness, without certain configurations of matter to ''support'' them, it is still quite possible in logic for the specific content of those states of consciousness to have their source in anything whatsoever. And even if it were granted that the source must also be ''material,'' one still is not committed to empiricism; for it is not logically but only causally impossible for ''ideas'' of any specific content to be carried by the genes. Nor does idealism imply that there is knowledge a priori either except possibly for the sorts of logical and mathematical knowledge almost all philosophers would agree in identifying as accessible ''prior'' to experience. In short, empiricism does not imply materialism nor materialism empiricism.

We are now in a position to see that the more specific proposition that social being determines social consciousness and not the other way around, since it is a thesis about the particular causal connections between aspects of mind and aspects of material and social reality, has no intrinsic relation to the issue of classical idealism and classical materialism. If the theory that social being determines social consciousness can be restated as the theory that how we go about satisfying our material needs determines the contents of our beliefs about and values concerning society, we may say that an idealist — one who holds that nothing at all can exist without minds, for example — can consistently hold this theory however temperamentally unlikely he is to do so. One is tempted to say, as a matter of observation and not of argument for it cuts both ways in any case, that philosophers and social thinkers have often been pushed to philosophical idealism or philosophical materialism as a result of an inclination to accent or to denigrate respectively the importance of ideas or of thought in the world, especially in the social world. Thus one would be hard pressed to find a philosophical idealist who is also a historical materialist even though if I am right in my analysis there is no logical or philosophical reason why there should not be such theorists.

It is more widely appreciated that philosophical materialism is compatible with virtually any theory about the role of ideas in society. Or perhaps I should say that, contrary to the thrust of my analysis but not in any way disproving it, the more conscious or self-conscious social thinkers are of their "materialism," the more inclined they are to discount the role of ideas in the world, while the relatively unexamined "materialism" of many philosophers and social thinkers lives quite comfortably in the same mind with the most extravagant theses about the role of ideas, especially of intellectuals, in society. Curious. For if my analysis is correct, it is the self-conscious materialists who are on logically unsound ground and not the more or less commonsensical materialists that most people are. Be all that as it may, however, we may now put idealism behind us and look at the matter of the connection between ideas and society directly and for its own sake from a somewhat different direction.

Intentions and Society

The question of the "role" of ideas in society really has two sides. There is, in the first place, the question of the *causal* part ideas play in the social process. And in the second place, there is the matter of the extent to which intentions are *realized* in society. That these are somewhat distinct matters is easily seen. The desires to end war or to build a society with no injustice or to go to Jupiter may never be realized, but the attempt to do any of them may have great consequences, some of them unintended, for what actually does happen. But they are also connected insofar as one may always ask with respect to the realization of some desire or intention the extent to which it was a causal result of the intention or desire.

The philosophical issue is not whether people ever realize their desires — obviously they do — or even really the extent to which ideas causally affect other things, or finally the extent to which in particular cases the result was because of someone's desire for it. The problem is rather to explain how, within a certain framework or conception of mind and its relation to body, any of this is possible at all. The framework, of course, is psychophysiological parallelism, according to which the mental when it consists of genuine states of consciousness and not just dispositions is connected to the physical by means of laws of coexistence. Thus we may treat the whole issue schematically in terms of the following situation. Assume that Jones has a conscious desire and intention to change a certain local ordinance. This he can do by getting himself elected to a certain office. This in turn at least ultimately entails a number of "direct" actions on his part, that is, moving his body in certain ways, mostly his vocal chords presumably. We may ignore the fact that the way in which he performs these actions as well as the effect they will have is a matter largely of cultural conditioning, and concern ourselves only with certain sequences which of course can and will occur only under certain conditions. We may also ignore anything else that Jones hopes to achieve by being elected to office. Thus in the "total" situation, putting aside what has just been put aside, we may analytically isolate the following elements: first, the desire or intention on Jones's part (which may actually be a series of more or less distinct mental states); second, the brain or neurophysiological state to which this mental state is parallelistically connected by laws of coexistence; third, the behavioral state(s), if any, which more loosely parallel(s) the mental and neurophysiological state(s); fourth, the "direct" actions of Jones which are intended to realize the desire; fifth, the other conditions which are necessary for the desire actually to be realized; sixth, the instrumental conditions — in this case, being elected to office — perceived as the way to achieve the "final" goal — in this case, having a certain ordinance changed; seventh, the "final" goal itself; eighth, the actual consequences of the "direct" actions, including both the unintended consequences and the intended ones, if any.

In one sense, the answer to the question how ideas or mental states of any sort "operate" in history and society is that they are connected by laws of coexistence to certain bodily states which in turn are interacting variables with those one identifies as constituting the historical process. In a somewhat different sense one may say that ideas causally affect history by "issuing" in certain kinds of behavior, which behavior is constituted by variables which interact with the bodily states parallelistically connected to the ideas as well as, again, those other variables which constitute the social process. In these ways of speaking, the content of an idea is completely ignored so far as it intends something; *one is simply treating the idea (or its parallelistically connected bodily state) as a variable or the value of a variable in a process.* The inability or unwillingness so to treat minds is simply the concrete result of the failure to look at the mind from the causal point of view in the first place or to distinguish that context from the intentional one. If there is no mystery in the thesis of psychophysiological parallelism itself and if it is a plausible solution to the mind/body problem, then there is no particular mystery how, causally speaking, ideas or mental states in general affect the historical or social process.

This might be a proper place to repeat a point made in the third chapter. It may be objected that one's choices and desires really "make no difference" on psychophysiological parallelism because the "real" explanation of one's behavior and its consequences is to be found in the brain or neurophysiological state which, according to the theory, is connected to the mental states by laws of coexistence. It makes no difference whether the mental state is there or not, really, provided the proper bodily state is there; hence our choices make no real difference to what happens, so the argument concludes. This argument is fallacious and in fact leads to a conclusion directly contradictory to what the theory of parallelism implies if supplemented with the additional premise that the parallelistically connected bodily states are interacting variables in the physical world, which is of course true. Choices *do* make a difference on the very thesis itself; for by it, if the mental state were other than what it is in a given situation, then the corresponding bodily state would be different and so would the behavior, if any, in which it "issues," and so on.

The objector gives plausibility to his argument only by implicitly assuming that the world were quite different in that although the same bodily states obtained, there were no, or at least no lawfully connected, mental states. Then they would make no difference. This is certainly true, but this is not the thesis of psychophysiological parallelism. The laws being what they are, certain bodily states can no more exist without certain mental states than the other way around. And if someone now asks why the world should be that way, he asks either for an evolutionary account of how such beings came to exist or else a question which can only be answered by saying that that is just the way the world is. At least some of the laws of coexistence affirming the connections between mental states and brain states are ultimate in that they cannot be deduced from any other, more general laws. This is not an empirical prediction, but a logical or philosophical matter. Obviously no development in physics could produce such general laws, for they would never contain (the names of) the mental variables and so could never yield the deduction. For the same kind of reason no law mentioning only mental variables could produce such a deduction. At most, some of the laws of coexistence could be deduced from some other laws of coexistence. If all of this is true, I may justifiably repeat my belief that *only* some version of psychophysiological parallelism is consistent with common sense and scientific knowledge of "mind and its place in nature."

Thus, to understand how, causally speaking, ideas or consciousness operate in history, that is, make a difference to the values of whatever set of variables one takes to constitute the historical or social process, is primarily to understand how mind is connected to the physical world at all. But there is not only the question how and to what extent mental states affect some process of which they or their parallelistically connected bodily states are a part (or of which they are not, for that matter) in the purely causal sense. There is also the somewhat narrower but also more complicated question of the extent to which the social process is *as* it is intended to be by human beings. This is still partly a causal matter because ordinarily things don't turn out the way one intends unless one's intention (or intentional behavior) had some causal role in making them that way. Thus while we may acknowledge the abstract possibility that the world is precisely the way someone would like it to be, though not in the least *because* he wants it that way, we may concern ourselves exclusively with those cases where the intention or choice or desire itself played a causal role in the realization of the intention. If someone objects that intentions considered apart from actions are not causal entities or entities at all, such a person may shift attention to the behavior itself which "expresses" the intention with no damage to my analysis, even though I don't agree with the objection. None of this is supposed to suggest what is obviously false — that an intention is ever by itself a lawfully adequate or sufficient prerequisite for the occurrence of the sorts of things human beings intend; it is not even that for what I called a "direct" action — but only that some states of affairs would not occur were it not for human intentions and choices.

Now the question is sometimes raised whether or not we determine our own destiny. Such a question is sometimes confused with or simply interpreted to be the issue to what extent our choices are not causally determined by earlier states of affairs. But in fact these are sharply separable issues — the extent to which (none, I believe) the occurrences of our choices and intentions are not even in principle capable of lawful explanation on the one hand, and on the other the extent to which our choices and intentions are realized. Roughly speaking, where the causal language has connotations of temporal order, we may say that the one question has to do with the causes of choices and the other with their intended effects. As soon as we approach the latter of these questions, which is the one I am presently interested in, we should appreciate that no *general* answer is possible. Patently a totally fatalistic view of man and history is implausible, that is, the view that no humans ever realize their choices or intentions. We all do sometimes realize our choices, though less often perhaps in what matters to us most. We can only answer the question within specified contexts. What is the time span? Is it the intentions of individuals as private persons we are talking about or the intentions of groups (not to go back on anything said about descriptive emergence) as expressed, say, in party platforms? If the intention and the time span are specified reasonably concisely, then we can answer in each particular case whether it is realized. But we cannot say in general either that history is or that it is not as humans intend it to be. We can say that the world today, at least in those characteristics which make it the modern world, is surely not as anyone five hundred years ago intended it to be (or, for that matter that it is different from what they intended it to be — they probably had no intentions about it). On the other hand we can say that the present-day wealth of this or that country is or well may be the realization of some intentions of government leaders of a half- or quarter-century ago.

Thus both the questions *can* we and *do* we choose our own destiny — individually and collectively — must be answered prosaically to some extent yes, to some extent no. It is the tendency of modern society to make the "choices" of the society as expressed through governments of increasingly wider scope, both in time and in the kinds of behavior and other aspects of physical and social reality which are "intended" or controlled, sometimes at the diminution of such possibilities of control for many individuals, but sometimes also widening the possibility of realizing individual intentions. In this sense, the question to what extent persons and peoples can and do determine their own destinies is a historical question. This is the way historians themselves have usually treated it and rightly so. There is no intelligible metaphysical question whether in general human beings choose their own destinies or not, unless we are being asked to confirm the obvious fact that we sometimes do succeed in what we try to achieve.

It may be instructive to consider briefly some views of Sartre as expressed in his introductory essay to *Critique de la raison dialectique* to illustrate the kinds of confusions that may arise from the failure to observe some of the distinctions I have just made.[10] Sartre wishes to embrace historical materialism. But it, according to Marx, and Sartre agrees, implies that "man makes his own history." And if man makes his own history, then, Sartre claims, it follows that the existentialist conception of humans essentially as "subjectivity" is correct after all. In other words, we must be free to choose and so we have free will in that sense that holds our choices to be at least partly outside the realm of causal determination. Thus Sartre concludes that the existentialist conception of man is, in this way, at the very basis of what he claims is nevertheless *the* philosophy of our epoch, Marxism. We need not be either existentialists or "Marxists" to be able to grasp the confusions in this argument. (Perhaps I should say that we must not be existentialists.)

"Man makes his own history." It should now be clear that this proposition can mean either (a) that the course of history is largely and in the most interesting respects the causal result of human doings, which are, in part, the result of human choices, desires, intentions, values, and so on, or (b) that the course of history is as (some) humans have intended and do intend it to be. The first is surely true and also, by the way, what Marx meant by the phrase. The second, we saw, has no truth-value in general, but only when made about specific persons and contexts. Who intended to bring capitalism to England? No one. Who socialism to Russia? Lenin, Trotsky, and many others. Sartre's first error is to assume, apparently, that historical materialism implies that we make history in the second sense or that, what amounts to the same thing in this context, the first sense of the proposition implies the second sense. And some of the Marxist critics of Sartre do not always make this distinction either (or else deny that the proposition is true in any significant sense). That it is an error should be obvious; from the proposition that human history is causally a consequence of human activities, nothing whatsoever follows about the extent to which humans succeed in realizing their short-run or long-run intentions or even that they have any with respect to many of the characteristics in which the historian or social scientist might be interested.

But it is only because he makes this error that Sartre goes on to make a greater one. Or perhaps it would be fairer to say that rather than having committed a simple logical blunder, his "metaphysics of human being" is at fault. In any case, I see the matter as follows. Sartre moves from the assumption that "men make their own history" to the conclusion that human choices are not lawfully explainable, that is, that we have free will in the radical sense. This move is facilitated by his supposition that the sense in which historical materialism does imply that we make our own history itself implies that history is *as* we choose it to be. Thus Sartre concentrates on choice. It is, so I have already argued, a logical fallacy to suppose that it follows from the fact that we sometimes realize our choices that our choices are uncaused. My argument assumes, as I believe to be true, that choices can and should be so characterized to leave completely open the question of their causal relations or lack of them to other phenomena. Since Sartre disagrees, he does not make a simple logical blunder. His conception or argument is as follows: If we ever realize our choices (or even if our choices have any effect, intended or not, on what happens) then *there are* choices. But a choice, by its very nature (if I may be allowed this expression in this context) is the sort of thing which cannot be caused. For while "there are" choices, they are not entities or existents in the same sense that material objects are. (Ortega y Gasset makes this alleged metaphysical distinction between "subjectivity" and material reality the very basis of his philosophy of history.)[11] Hence the doctrine that our choices are effective, by implying that there are choices, also implies the "philosophical doctrine of free will" in my earlier phrase that I took from Donagan.

This metaphysics is, I believe, completely mistaken assuming that it is even fully intelligible. Here I shall not argue that, but make only one observation on its internal consistency. Sartre's doctrine of human freedom, that our choices are not lawfully explainable by their very nature as "subjectivity," is empty unless such choices can themselves be effective in determining our behavior and, by that, occurrences external to our bodies. In short, Sartre always assumes that choices can be causally efficacious, but not themselves caused. This seems to me to be, in light of the sort of arguments Sartre uses, if not a formal contradiction, at least a somewhat paradoxical circumstance. For if, as Sartre would no doubt disagree, causation is only lawful connection, then the radical *metaphysical* distinction between being caused and being a cause that Sartre's view would seem to require does not exist. And even if causation is something more or something other than lawful connection, I don't think Sartre has appreciated that he already, by assuming the efficacy of choice, puts it to that extent in the causal realm. I conclude that Sartre has not made his case.

Summary and Conclusion

We have seen several things. First, that despite a widespread belief to the contrary, classical idealism has nothing to do with various theories about the importance of ideas in history, either in the causal sense or in the logical sense. In saying this, I am making only a logical point. Historically and perhaps psychologically (temperamentally) it is quite a different matter. But the logical point stands that the question of the primacy of mind or matter is independent of the question of the lawful relations between or among certain properties of each. While the classical and traditional issues of idealism, realism, and materialism often seem to be purely "abstract" ones (and indeed they are, properly understood), it is precisely the false belief that they do have something logically to do with the role of ideas in society that feeds many of the ideological disputes about the latter. To the extent that one can show a scientific or historical question to be just that, and not one of philosophy or of policy, one may hope to succeed in removing a source not only of intellectual confusion but possibly of human conflict as well. As always, this de-ideologizing is not a matter of removing questions of value and metaphysics from discussion, which is neither possible nor desirable in any case — they can only be apparently submerged — but of separating such questions clearly from those which are purely factual, whether the latter be ones of lawful connection or ones of particular fact, and from those which are purely logical.

This familiar distinction between lawful connections and particular facts is one we can put to further use. For the questions about the role of ideas in history are, I believe, sometimes confused by reason of failing to make this distinction. Let us, for the sake of convenience, label the relevant kinds of questions that have to do with general causal connection as lawful, those that have to do with matters of particular fact as historical. We may then observe that there are the following lawful questions which are relevant to the broad question of the role of ideas in history or society: How is mind lawfully connected to body so that it can make any difference to what happens in the material world (and so again in the mental)? What are the lawful connections between those kinds of behavior which "express" our choices, beliefs, values, and so on to each other, to other aspects of ourselves, to the behavior of others, and to anything else in the environment? What are the lawful connections between the kinds of changes wrought at some given time in the environment and in ourselves, either intended or unintended, and states of the future physical environment and of later human beings, both their bodies and their ideas, values, beliefs, and so on? Under what conditions, social and biological and environmental, do people or peoples succeed to this or that extent in realizing their ideas in a distinctly social form? Under what conditions are persons or peoples prone to have intentions and choices of this or that sort?

Among the historical questions which are relevant to the more general one of the role of ideas in history are the following: To what extent has this or that person realized his intentions in the world? What have actually been the effects of this or that idea as expressed in behavior in the social process? When or where, if at all, have those conditions obtained where it was particularly easy for this or that person to realize his ideas in a socially interesting sense?

If one had succeeded in answering both the lawful and the historical questions — these and others similar to them — one would have answered the question of the role of ideas in history. What else is there to add by way of a philosophical theory? It may be noticed that I have for the most part ignored in this recent discussion the matter of the causes of ideas, values, beliefs, and desires themselves. This is not because I believe any or all of them are without causation — quite the contrary — or that the question is unimportant. But we already saw how irrelevant it is for general philosophical purposes. Or rather, perhaps I should once more say that causation of ideas on the one hand and their intentions and, where they have them, truth-values on the other are utterly logically distinct. And furthermore the question of the ''role'' of ideas in society usually has been taken to mean one of their effects rather than their causes, a distinction available to me even with my analysis of causation as mere lawful connection.

The only mystery about the role of ideas in society, if there be one at all, is the ''mystery'' how mind can affect the material world at all, that is, the traditional mind/body problem. My solution to that problem I have made clear. It rests primarily on a correct analysis of causation to begin with. Most try to solve or dissolve the problem without first turning to the question of what causation is, or else in despair of finding any solution retreat to materialism in the sense of denying that there is anything distinctly mental to ask the question about. At the same time, if one *starts* with a behavioristic or materialistic theory of mind (in the metaphysical and not the methodological sense), then there is only the question how the distinguished kinds of behavior affect other variables in the physical world. The real problem is for the dualist with an anthropomorphic conception of causation, for he can't even get the mind to affect the body in the first place. Small wonder then that we should find the metaphysical behaviorists of our day often holding to such anthropomorphic conceptions of causation.[12]

X The Individual, Freedom, and Purpose in History

Whereas the preceding chapter dealt primarily with how ideas considered as something mental and intentional have their effects in history, the present one is concerned for the most part with how in general a person does or can affect society. The most important issue I shall take up in this chapter is an old one — the "role of the individual in history." Actually, as we shall shortly see, it is a set of issues, sometimes confused with one another. But this chapter is also the most appropriate place for me to have my say about the related notions of freedom and of purpose in history. About purpose, although I didn't use the word, I have already had much to say in the ninth chapter. About freedom, it is largely a matter of drawing out some consequences of the results of the discussion of reduction in the fourth and fifth chapters. The parts of this chapter are therefore *the role of the individual in history*; *the freedom of the individual*; and *purpose in history*.

The Role of the Individual in History

I do not propose to trace the history of this issue through Hegel, Carlyle, Nietzsche, Plekhanov, et al., except to observe that for some of them their opinions on it seemed to be crucial to their moral conceptions of the world as well as to their theories of history. In point of fact, there are two quite broad issues, often confused with one another, each one of which itself can be broken into further questions. We may distinguish the two questions that identify the broad distinction by considering the following example. Lenin is said to have had a major role in the Russian Revolution and this is obviously true in some senses. For the issues at hand, we may ask the following two questions: If Lenin had never lived (or died at birth or in childhood) and everything else had been the same at some specified time, say 1875, would the Russian Revolution have occurred? What are the historical consequences (or any causal consequences) of Lenin's having acted as he did? Some seem to have supposed that the first question could be satisfactorily disposed of by answering the second; that is, if we knew what the consequences of Lenin's actions were, we would know what would have happened without him. But even so to state the issue is to reveal the fallacy in such reasoning. For it would entirely presuppose that if there had been no Lenin, nothing he did would have been done by anyone else, and that in large measure is just what the first question asks.

We might now generalize these questions a bit and put them as follows: To what extent are the socially significant actions of anyone such that if that person had not existed and everything else had been the same at some given time they would have been performed by someone else (presumably with essentially the same consequences)? To what extent can or do the actions of any single person affect the course of human history? I propose now to turn to the first and theoretically more interesting question and leave consideration of the second until the end of this section.

It may be wondered initially whether the question really is an intelligible one. It certainly is not the sort of question that the practicing historian normally asks himself. Not that he doesn't ask "What if?" questions at all. Indeed, the historian frequently asks what might have happened if so-and-so had not decided on this action or pursued that policy. In this, the historian does in a more systematic manner what we all do frequently in wondering what would have happened if so-and-so hadn't done this or had done that. But only rarely, if ever, does the historian ask himself what would have happened if a certain person hadn't lived. When he does, it is usually not because he is wondering whether that person's *actions* might not have been performed by someone else. Rather he is considering the person's existence as a biological fact which in a certain cultural setting may have considerable social significance. In a country ruled by a hereditary monarchy, the fact that no child is born to the ruling monarch and spouse may have substantial social implications that wouldn't appear in a republic. What would have happened if no child had been born? Would the emerging bourgeoisie have seized power and declared a republic? Would the house of so-and-so have tried to establish itself as the new monarchal line? But here the historian is not considering the person as an *actor* at all, and while this sort of fact complicates our discussion in some ways, we may for the moment dismiss it and return to the matter of the intelligibility of the question whether the nonexistence of a person considered as someone who *acted* in certain ways would have made any difference to the social process.

We may grant then that historians do not, in the ordinary course of their business, wonder what would have happened if a certain important figure had never existed. But then historians don't ask themselves all the intelligible questions that can be asked even about history. And in any case, the question is one which, as I shall interpret it, is at best only partly a historical one anyway. But it may be and has been objected that the question is unintelligible because there is no way to verify or falsify any of a number of seeming answers to it. I am quite willing to accept the criterion of intelligibility implicit in such an objection and answer it directly. We may, of course, as one always must, grant the immense practical difficulties in calculating what the course of history would have been without Lenin, assuming there is no reason in principle why it can't be done. So let us ask first how in principle it could or would be done.

The assumption is that human society is or is part of a system which has process, that is, a deterministic system. Process laws for a system tell us not only how the system behaves under the conditions that actually obtain at any given moment, but how it would behave under any given set of initial conditions. That is, the laws tell us what the "next" or "last" or any state of the system is from the values of its variables at a given moment as well as what *would* have been the "last" or "next" state of the system if the values of its variables had been something other than what they were at that or any other moment. (The cardinality of the objects in the system is itself one of the variables. Or alternatively, we may speak of a different set of related laws for each different set — in the mathematical sense — of objects.) The system may also have certain laws of coexistence which make certain combinatorial possibilities lawful impossibilities. With this limitation, we may speak of all the possible combinations of values of the variables of a system of x number of objects (unless we treat cardinality itself as a variable). These possibilities may well be, and usually will be, infinite in number, not because the variables are infinite in number but because their values may well be. This provides no difficulty, however; we have such a situation in macro-mechanics itself. Now this means that *in principle*, that is, if one knew all the relevant laws and the values of the relevant variables, one should be able to calculate what the course of history would have been had Lenin not existed and everything else at least of any conceivable causal significance had been the same, say, in 1875.

Someone may jump on the phrase 'if everything else had been the same', objecting either that it has no clear meaning or that it can't be both that Lenin could not have existed and that "everything else be the same." With respect to the first objection, the point is not so much whether it *has* a clear meaning but to *give* it one. With respect to the second, we may agree that within the deterministic framework and given that the laws are what they are, if we are to have a world without Lenin, then it must have been somewhat different earlier as well, though not necessarily different in any socially significant way. Thus we may grant that the world would have had to be slightly different from the "beginning" in order for Lenin not to have been born at all and still insist that we can talk intelligibly about the world's being at the time in question otherwise the same. Now to some all this will sound like complete fantasy in any event, for they do not think in the deterministic frame of reference to begin with. So we can alter our situation a bit as follows. We assumed that, as I believe, human society, while not a deterministic system in itself, is part of a larger one which is. Yet in many contexts we treat systems *as if they were* closed systems provided they aren't tampered with from without. So, for example, we treat a certain chemical process in a test tube as "deterministic" even though we may open it and "interfere." Thus let us imagine that, in the spirit of such "contextual" thinking, during the course of her pregnancy with the future Lenin, his mother had been struck and killed by a meteor (it will help our imaginations if something comes *spatially* from without), thus also killing the fetus that was to become Lenin. So thinking, we need not concern ourselves how the world would have had to be different for that meteor to fall in just that place, the point being that so far as we can imagine, nothing would have had to be different earlier in the history of human life or the history of the earth. Now can we not ask how, if at all, the course of human history to date and in the future would have differed from what it has been? Such a question might even be available to one who believes that some human choices are not fully determined at all, for he may still grant that it was only because of certain characteristics peculiar to Lenin that certain choices could be successfully realized. But I shall continue, as I think one should, to discuss the issue within the deterministic frame of reference.

In order to proceed, it will be useful to refer to an exchange between May Brodbeck and myself on the very issue before us. In her paper on "Methodological Individualisms: Definition and Reduction" Brodbeck argued as follows:

Conceivably, there might be a set of macroscopic laws permitting the prediction of the "state" of society (i.e., the values of the group variables) at all times from its state at any given time. This possibility is to be sure most implausible. It is implausible not only because the discovery of such a complete set of relevant variables seems a formidable task, but also because it is rather more than likely that changes in the social process do not depend only upon group or macroscopic units, Marxism to the contrary notwithstanding. People are not like molecules in a gas. Some are different from others and some have more effect upon society than others. It is still a good question whether without Lenin there would have been the October Revolution. If this variance among individuals makes sufficient difference, then the laws have to take the occurrence of a particular kind of individual into account. In this case, a complete set of variables could not all be macroscopic.[1]

In a paper entitled "Freedom and the Marxist Philosophy of History," I challenged Brodbeck's argument as follows:

She assumes that if social changes in any way "depend" on the varying and perhaps unique characteristics of certain persons, then such changes cannot "depend" solely on the macroscopic variables; and thus there cannot be process among the group variables. But this is a mistake. Consider her own example. Suppose there is process on the social level and accept the framework of methodological individualism. Can we consistently suppose further that Lenin had absolutely unique characteristics and that if no one with those characteristics had lived when Lenin did, the October Revolution would not have occurred (then)? Not if Prof. Brodbeck is right. But we *can* in principle define a particular group variable in terms partly of "containing-a-Lenin-like-figure." That is, the definition of some group variable *can* include the perhaps unique characteristics of some particular person. Now if there is process on the social level, we should in principle be able to predict the occurrence of a group having such a person given only the values of the social variables at an earlier time and the laws which state their connection. This sounds implausible only if it is forgotten that the group variables are to be defined in terms of the properties of (and relations among) individuals; otherwise it is quite plausible. And we have already seen that one can consistently hold both that there is process at the level of the macrovariables and that (all) those variables are definable in terms of the microvariables.[2]

Furthermore, still by way of quoting, Brodbeck in her introduction to a section on "Social Facts, Social Laws, and Reduction" in which she refers to the paper from which the quote immediately above is taken says partly by way of reply to me:

There may be laws linking the occurrence of specific personality types with social phenomena. Such a law might, for instance, assert that given a man like Churchill and the social situation of England in 1940, one kind of consequence rather than another would follow. England fought rather than let Hitler take over Europe. It might not have done so if a man like Churchill had not been there. Soft determinism accepts the methodological assumption that every social concept is definable in terms of individuals interacting with one another. Presumably, we could therefore just add this "personality-type" variable to our definition of the social event. (Addis suggests this is his paper.) However, we would no longer have a purely social law and, therefore, we would not have a comprehensive *social* theory. We would have a mixed psychosociological law which covertly contained the personality element in the definition of the collective term.

And it is worth our while to quote a little further from this same section.

Precisely because the definitions of group concepts in terms of patterns of individuals are not of this sort they are sociological rather than psychological terms. They do not mention unique personalities or personality types, but interchangeable *roles*. They are nonetheless individualistic. For a role is a position occupied by a person in a group relative to other persons in that group. It carries with it certain expected regularities of behavior toward others in the group and by them toward the person in the role. As defined by their roles, any two heads of state are interchangeable. If social laws were sufficient, then it would not matter that Churchill was Prime Minister and Hitler the Fuehrer. If group behavior is only determined by the roles of its members and the environment, then specific personalities need not be mentioned in laws about the social process. But if these personality variables make a difference, then no theory of the social process that omitted them could be complete.[3]

In part the differences between us, such as they are, might be seen to arise from a confusion between, to pick a couple of words, *social* laws and *sociological* laws. These notions in turn may be characterized by whether or not all the properties mentioned in the relevant laws can be defined in terms of certain *kinds* of properties of and relations among individuals. Both Brodbeck and I accept the framework of descriptive individualism (what she calls methodological individualism). Thus it is agreed that all properties of groups must be definable in terms of the properties of individual people and things. The question is, Which properties of individuals and things? More exactly the question becomes, In order to have a set of laws which would enable the prediction and explanation of social phenomena, must one mention either directly or as contained in the definition of (the name of) some property mentioned directly, properties of individuals other than those which either characterize their social roles or are the result of their social roles? If not, we may say that we have or can have a purely *sociological* theory of society (ignoring those interacting variables which are altogether nonhuman). If yes, we may say that our *social* laws (meaning only those containing macro-variables) are not fully sociological. In short, the issue is not one either of the truth of descriptive individualism (the nature of social properties) or of whether a *complete* set of social laws is possible (the influence of nonhuman variables), but only of what sorts of properties of human beings need to be taken into account to explain social phenomena completely.

Having so located the issue, in terms of what properties or what kinds of properties of human beings are essential to the explanation of social phenomena, we may proceed to discuss the issue by considering what the various logical possibilities are.

At the one extreme, there is the possibility, which Brodbeck seems to ascribe to Marxism, that the only properties which matter are those which all human beings have in common to begin with, the only differences which are relevant being those, like "molecules in a gas," of temporal and spatial locations. Thus some humans come to occupy different social roles from others, but the actions taken by a person occupying a certain role are determined by the role and the only actions of human beings relevant for the explanation of social phenomena are those in which a role is being acted upon. The real substance of this view is the assertion than none of the obvious inborn differences in intelligence, imagination, sex, constitution, and so on make any difference to one's performance of a role or perhaps even to its acquisition, at least in ways which would be relevant to the explanation of social phenomena. Thus the "theory" is, on empirical grounds known to all of us, patently absurd. But then I seriously doubt that anyone ever held this possibility to be the true one. Yet to deny it does not commit one to holding that the unique characteristics of certain people must be taken into account in the explanation of social phenomena. Some, possibly including Brodbeck, seem to think these are exclusive and exhaustive views. Exclusive they are, but exhaustive they are not.

The other extreme, then, is precisely the view that, for the explanation of some social phenomena, the inborn characteristics or combinations of characteristics unique to some person or other are essential. I think it is important to emphasize that the characteristics or combinations of characteristics in question be inborn or the result of inborn characteristics; otherwise the thesis becomes much less interesting. For being a prime minister at a certain time may be a unique characteristic; or more generally, occupying a certain role will uniquely identify a person in some cases. For this reason, too, I now think it is better to avoid the notion of "personality-type" in discussing such a theory for it is very much open to question to what extent differences in personality are, if at all, the result of inborn characteristics which may be unique. Thus it may be quite true that the Russian Revolution would have occurred only if there had been a person of Lenin's personality leading it. But if that personality, or what is unique in it, was itself a result of his having been in the position of leadership, nothing much is shown for the issue under discussion. What must be shown to establish the view now under consideration is that some of the unique aspects of Lenin's personality, which aspects were essential to the success of the Revolution, were themselves the result of unique, inborn characteristics of Lenin.

A somewhat less extreme view would hold that the Russian Revolution would not have occurred without Lenin not because of the unique inborn characteristics he had, if any, but because of the unique circumstances of his life combined with his inborn characteristics, be they unique, universal, or somewhere in between. (We must acknowledge the logical point, of course, that the single case of Lenin and the Russian Revolution can, if it goes one way, definitely disprove some theories of the role of the individual in history while it cannot, if it goes another, definitely establish any positive theory to the contrary. In general, the single case can only conclusively falsify certain theories, never conclusively verify any one. But I shall continue to discuss it as if it were representative of all cases where the question arises.) We might call this a "social" property of Lenin in one sense if it were a result of his social environment and thus itself something to be explained by sociological theory even if it were unique to Lenin. This is logically the same circumstance as that of the single-person role, that is, a case where, as it happens as a matter of historical fact, only one person undergoes certain experiences, even though some other person going through those same circumstances would have ended up in essentially the same socially relevant position. But we must remember the issue: It is not whether there have been people with unique characteristics and which characteristics have made a difference to the social process — that is patently true — but rather whether the nonexistence of such a person would have made any substantial difference to what happened, whether another leader would have been "called forth" by the circumstances had the actual one not existed and who would have done essentially the same thing. Granted that the unique characteristics of Churchill led to his refusal to make a peace with Hitler, if he hadn't existed would any other person who might have been (or the person who would have been) prime minister also have done the same?

Now the third possibility encompasses such a range that at one end it will virtually approximate one of the extremes, at the other end the other extreme. It is that the inborn characteristics of certain persons which we may suppose must be taken account of in the explanation of social phenomena neither are unique to anyone nor are they universal. Such general characteristics as high intelligence, stubbornness, inventiveness, and many others are, if left at that general level of description, neither singly nor jointly either unique to anyone or universal. Thus Plekhanov, defending what he takes to be *the* or *a* Marxist conception of the role of the individual in history, does not argue that if Napoleon had not lived, *anyone* could have taken his place or even that most persons could have taken his place. He argues only that there were a small number of men, any one of whom could have assumed essentially the same kind of position and who would have pursued essentially the same policies with essentially the same results as Napoleon had he not lived or not been around to do what he did do of social significance.[4] Now this argument, whether it is historically sound or not (I rather doubt it myself), is at least logically sound. It shows that the following two propositions are quite compatible: first, that if Napoleon had not existed, the course of history and particularly of European history would have been the same in most important respects; and second, that people are not like molecules in a gas even with respect to social phenomena. Perhaps the point of view here expressed by Plekhanov is entirely false but it has a certain analogy in the history of science, where it is much more immediately plausible. Few humans could have made the discoveries that Newton, Darwin, and Freud did. But does anyone seriously doubt that if they, either by their nonexistence or for some other reason, had not made them, someone else would have? It is almost a commonplace in the history of science that certain developments are "in the wind," at least in retrospect, and that it is more or less historical accident, to speak very commonsensically, which person makes the breakthrough. (This is less obvious, however, in the case of Freud than in most others.) In any event, the idea is clear and while the progress of science cannot be directly compared to the "progress" of society, it does perhaps help us to understand what is being claimed with respect to the latter in a theory like Plekhanov's.

But now one may begin to wonder whether any *general* theory about the role of individuals in history is possible after all. Is it not possible that what Napoleon did would have been done in its essentials had he not lived, while what Lenin did would not have been done with the result that the Russian Revolution would not have occurred (to put it most radically)? In short, it may now seem that about each situation or each person in which the question arises about what would have happened had that person not existed, we must ask a whole series of questions the answers to which may give one answer to the question in one case and quite a different one in another case. These questions would include the following: What precisely were the characteristics of the person in question who, as it happened, "produced" the actions in question? Which of those characteristics were inborn, which produced by the circumstances of his life to date, which by the role itself of which the actions are the "expression"? Of those characteristics which were inborn and those produced by the circumstances of his life to date, how widespread throughout the population in question were they jointly or separately? How widespread throughout the population are inborn and environmentally produced characteristics which, while not perhaps the same as those of the person in question, would have produced essentially the same actions had a person with them assumed the role instead? Of those persons, if any, whose combination of characteristics would have produced essentially the same actions in the same role, how many, if any, would have had a reasonable access to the role actually assumed by the person in question? If there were persons whose personal characteristics were such that they would have produced essentially the same actions, had any one of them had the role instead of the person in question, would any of them *actually* have taken that role had the person in question not existed?

It will be observed that these questions are primarily ones of particular, historical fact and not ones of lawful connections, though of course they presume that regular lawful connections do hold for human behavior as for everything else. Since that is so, they will or *may* have different answers in different historical circumstances. Yet their answers would jointly in a particular case seem to provide an exhaustive answer to the general question: What if so-and-so had never existed; would the course of historical events have been essentially the same?[5]

We now see that the theory that the nonexistence of any given person (with all else remaining the same) would have made no substantial difference to the course of history can be understood in various ways (I don't mean to suggest that its advocates always, if ever, clearly had in mind one of these meanings): (a) It could mean that the *laws* of collective human behavior, or better the laws which are relevant to the explanation of collective human behavior, in no case require the mention of characteristics which some people have and others don't, or (b) it could mean that so far as they do require mention of those nonuniversal characteristics, they are so widespread in any given population group that the nonexistence of any given person with those characteristics makes no difference to the lawful explanation of the behavior of the group. (c) It could mean that while it may be lawfully possible for circumstances to arise in which the existence of a given person makes all the difference to the occurrence (or nonoccurrence) of some social phenomenon, in point of historical fact those circumstances have never arisen, or (d) it could mean that those just-mentioned circumstances never have arisen and never will arise. None of these theses seems particularly plausible to me, but since the third is the weakest claim, it is accordingly the most likely to be true.

The contrary thesis, so far as it would be verified by the occurrence of just one person whose nonexistence would have made an essential difference to social phenomena, is not, logically, open to so many possible meanings. For if such a person has existed, then it is true both that particular circumstances produced such a circumstance and, therefore, that it is lawfully possible for it to happen. Of course one who emphasizes the role of the individual in history may want to make the stronger claim that there have been many such individuals or even that every society at a given time has some such person. On the other hand, he may also be making only the weaker claim that it is lawfully possible for such a person to exist, whether there have actually been any or not. In that case, his position is not very different from (c) above, with the one putting emphasis on the lawful *possibility* of such a person and the other on his historical *nonactuality*.

In any event, we are now able to see that the question we began with is, first, a question of what is lawfully possible, and, second, one of what, within the framework of the lawfully possible, is historically actual. Naturally one may examine the latter in order to help decide the former. I daresay that no one is in a position to be rationally certain of the answers yet. The answers, I suspect, will come more from biology and psychology than from history and sociology, but such predictions are often as rash as the premature theories themselves which such investigations are supposed to confirm or refute.

The second broad meaning the question of the role of the individual in history may have is that of the effects of any given person's actions on the course of events. We noted earlier that in no case would the answer to this question answer the one we have just dealt with at some length without begging the question. This second question may nevertheless be of some independent interest, though possibly it is less of theoretical than of practical significance. It is not the question then of the extent to which someone else would have performed a given set of actions had their actual performer not been around to have done so, but the question how the world would have been different had no one performed them. This *is* the kind of question historians and decision-makers do have occasion to ask themselves. Could, for example, the different decision of a single person somewhere along the way have made European society substantially different from what it actually is today, say, Islamic rather than "Christian," agricultural rather than industrial, organized into city-states rather than nation-states, and so on? One is tempted to say "possibly yes" to some of these questions such as those of religious beliefs, "probably no" to others such as being agricultural rather than industrial, and "who knows?" to yet others. Again it would seem to be partly a question of lawfulness, partly one of actual historical circumstances which are only a few of the infinite number of lawful possibilities. Perhaps the most valuable observation to make is that the capacity of one individual to affect society in a major way is a function not only of characteristics and roles which, we may reasonably assume, are more or less to be found in all human societies past and present, but also of technological factors which most assuredly are not the same at present as they were in the past nor in some societies as they are in others. Thus, the president of the United States has the power to affect the course of history as probably no one else has ever had. How he acts today may very well have a major effect on the way the world is five centuries from now, indeed whether there even is a human race or civilized society. By way of contrast we may safely assume that the actions of no one person five centuries past, no matter how different from what they actually were, could have had such an effect given the state of technology that existed at that time. Thus again it would seem to be impossible in this sense to have a general theory of the effects the actions of a single person can have on history, since it is a matter not just of laws but of particular historical circumstances.

Freedom of the Individual

There are many senses of 'freedom', even among those of philosophical significance. In terms of interest, at least as measured by how much is written on the subject, the most important sense would seem to be that in which an individual is said to be free if certain crucial ones of his choices are not fully causally determined. This is perhaps the least interesting sense to me because (a) I don't think freedom in this sense exists, and (b) even if it does exist, I don't think it matters much for anything else except for theoretical limitations on the scientific explanation of human behavior. I have no intention here of developing a "theory" of freedom, whatever that would be, or of arguing that that one sense with which I shall be concerned for a few paragraphs is the "true" or "real" meaning of 'freedom'. That it is historically important in intellectual concerns and that it matters to people is all I claim for it. It is simply that sense in which a person is free insofar as his choices can affect the course of historical events. In point of fact, I discussed this notion at some length in the last chapter without using the word 'freedom'; here I raise the matter again in the broader context of the role of the individual in history.

I wish to approach the question as follows: In the fifth chapter, I distinguished twelve possible (logically consistent) views on the nature of and the relations between sociological variables and individual variables. These twelve positions arose out of four distinctions as follows: *individualist/emergentist* for whether or not there are simple properties of social wholes, the latter being the affirmative; *reductionist/nonreductionist* for whether or not definitional reduction is possible for the individualist and reduction by laws of coexistence for the emergentist; *process/nonprocess* for whether or not there is process among the sociological variables alone; and *monist/pluralist* for whether or not the laws of social behavior can be deduced from the laws of solitary behavior and some composition rule, the former being the affirmative. I may now define the sense of 'freedom' with which I am here concerned more precisely as follows: let particular human choices, desires, intentions, and the like be considered as particular values of what in this context are individual variables (in contrast to sociological variables). Then we may say that a person is free to affect the course of history to the extent that differences in the values of those crucial ones of "his" individual variables make a difference to the values of the sociological variables. (Let us here ignore but keep in mind the question raised earlier of what exactly a sociological variable is or should reasonably be taken to be.) Which of the possible positions allows for such freedom, which do not?

All individualist views entail that (the names of) all sociological variables can be defined exclusively by (the names of) the behaviors of the individuals which "make up" the group in question. If we assume that the definition is nontrivial,[6] then the individual's behavior obviously *can* make a difference to the values of the sociological variables *even if there is process at the social level*. Since the sociological variable (or its values) may be defined in terms of a statistical distribution of some property among individuals, and since it may be defined in terms of a certain *range* of distribution, a change in the value of the property of some individual may or may not affect the value(s) of the relevant sociological variable(s). It depends on the case, that is, on the facts. In any event we can safely say that all individualist views — process or nonprocess, pluralist or monist — allow for freedom in the sense I defined it.

How about emergentist (holistic) views with respect to this notion of freedom? We also saw in the fourth chapter that even on such views one can still give a clear sense to 'reduction' in terms of lawful connections of the coexistence sort between the values of the sociological variables and those of the psychological variables. This is the clue to the answer to our question. If there are some such laws, then even on emergentist views — process or nonprocess, pluralist or monist — at least some variations in the behavior of individuals will be paralleled by variations in the values of the nondefinable sociological variables. If there are no such laws or if they are few and trivial then, with respect to *those* sociological variables, people are not free in our sense, that is, not capable by individual choice or behavior of making any difference in their values. I emphasize *those* sociological variables because, as I remarked earlier, no one, not even the most extreme emergentist, is apt to deny that some of what are usually called sociological variables *can* be defined in terms of individual behavior. What distinguishes the emergentist is the affirmation that there are simple, nondefinable properties of social wholes, not any denial that there are also nonsimple, definable properties. Since this is so even on the view of the emergentist nonreductionist, there may be freedom with respect to some sociological variables though not with respect to those whose existence and nature would make his theory true.

The most interesting result of these observations, since some have obviously believed to the contrary, is that even process views of the sociological variables, provided they are also reductionist either by way of definitions or by way of laws of coexistence, permit the possibility of freedom in the sense we have been discussing. This result may be extended to a view in which the sociological variables do not have process in themselves but are a subset of a larger set which does have process, but not including — except by way of definition or laws of coexistence — the crucial individual variables themselves. Thus even if there is a set of variables which, except by way possibly of the definitions of some of them, make no mention of the values of those variables which characterize individual people, and which, given an initial set of values, permit the complete calculation of earlier and later values of themselves, it still does not follow that individual choices and desires make no difference to the course of history or society.

Since only emergentist, nonreductionist views *entail* that we are not free with respect to the course of history and then only relative to the favored ones among the sociological variables, we may safely conclude that, in the sense of the word I have given to it, we are free.

Purpose in History

History, and less often society, has sometimes been claimed to have a purpose or a meaning independent of the purposes of its creators and participants, ourselves. Such ''purposes'' may be invoked as explanatory entities broadly speaking, or, more often, as the bases for moral evaluation and political action, or, less often, simply as a description of what is there. I propose to approach this issue through the context of a discussion of the notion of purpose in general. Let us begin by distinguishing seven different and, I believe, exhaustive ''contexts'' in which the notion of purpose enters. They are as follows: (a) that of a conscious individual human purpose, (b) that of an unconscious human purpose, (c) that of behavior as purposeful, (d) that of something as serving a purpose, (e) that of goals as purposes, (f) that of the purposes of groups, and (g) that of the purpose of the universe, or of the human race, or of human history.

At the level and in the context of our discussion, the first of these is the only entirely unproblematic notion of purpose. We all know what it is to have a felt intention to do something or to achieve something. What is problematic about it, though we needn't pursue it here and in any case the answer is already fairly explicit in what has been said earlier, is how such purposes enter into lawful explanation of human behavior.[7] Unconscious human purposes should probably be treated as patterns of actual and potential behavior as well as the disposition to have certain conscious purposes under certain, usually unrealized conditions. This makes them a species of the third context, that of behavior as purposeful, which, however, is broader than the sum of the first two and what can be defined in terms of them. The rat, we may suppose, has neither conscious nor unconscious purposes; yet its behavior is sometimes purposeful. The notion is essentially that of modifiable and flexible behavior — behavior which will within certain limits tend toward the same result under various and changing circumstances or what may be called ''goal-directed'' behavior but in the sense in which servomechanisms as well as organisms exhibit such behavior. Although one can talk about such matters entirely without the notion of purpose or of meaningful activity, the manner of speaking derives no doubt from the idea that one can view such behavior *as if* the organism or mechanism in question had a felt intention to behave as it does.

The fourth context we may ignore for a moment, for it is closely related to our main theme. We already know the confusions — such as the Master Argument of Diodorus — that the fifth notion of purpose can engender. Correctly understood, a goal as a purpose is an actual *or nonactual* state of affairs intended by someone. That it may be nonactual, that is, never realized, should be sufficient to show that *states of affairs considered as purposes, goals, or intentions* (not to be confused with purposes and intentions as the mental states themselves) *have no explanatory significance*. The desire is one thing and may be called the purpose, the desi*red* is another and may also be called the purpose or meaning of a piece of behavior. The connection between them is intentional, and, when it is incidentally also causal, it is the desire which is "the" cause of the behavior and perhaps therefore of the state of affairs desired and never the desired (as purpose, goal, or intention) which is the cause of the behavior. This general analysis has, of course, been advanced by many before me. I mention it once more partly for the sake of completeness but also to illustrate once more the possibility of both a "logical" (intentional) and an external (lawful) connection's holding between two states of affairs. What we have here, then, is a sense in which a state of affairs may be said to "be" a purpose if it is intentionally related to a purpose in the first (or possibly the second) sense.

Most of what needs to be said about the sixth context we have discussed earlier. For it is a question of defining group notions in terms of those of individuals, which we discussed at great length in the fourth chapter. All that needs to be added here is that while (the names of) purposes of groups should, if they are to be meaningful, be defined in terms primarily of the (names of) purposes of individuals, it does not follow that what we call the purposes of some given group exactly correspond to the purposes of any given person. Thus we may take the program of a political party as expressing the purposes of the party even though it may not exactly express the purposes of anyone in the party. Though the details are complex, the idea is clear, so I leave it at that. The sense in which a group may be said to have a purpose as a simple property of it, and as possibly unperceived by any of its members, that is, the sense in which an emergentist *might* ascribe purposes to a group, falls under the seventh sense.

To return to the fourth context, we again have a somewhat slippery notion and one which has given rise to confusions. At the one "end" of what may be covered by the idea, we may say that it means that an object always, typically, or when functioning normally can or does have a certain characteristic or behave in a certain way. Thus "the purpose of the nose is to smell" might be taken to express such an idea. At the other "end," what could be meant is that someone *designed* the thing to serve certain human (or animal) needs or purposes. Thus "the purpose of that sign is to show you which way to go to get to the subway" might be so understood. And "in between" we have the idea that a state of affairs or a kind of state of affairs may serve human purposes or needs or interests or hopes, even though no one so intended. Thus "the purpose of the institution of the family is to provide a stable environment for children and a basis for the higher organization of society" might be so understood. It is not always so much a question of one of three distinct meanings that a given such proposition does have in a given context — it means whatever its speaker and hearers take it to mean — but of strands of meaning usually more or less to be found in a given statement of this sort. Even for one who believes that there is no *design* in the literal sense at all in the nose, a statement of its "purpose" seems to go beyond merely what it does or can do and to have something to do with the interests of the organism in question. One does not often hear anyone say that the *purpose* or *function* of cancer is to kill people, though cancer may have the same or an analogous relation to death as the nose has to smelling. One might say, though, that the purpose of cancer is to keep the population within certain limits, suggesting thereby that the result, though perhaps not the means, is something to be desired. In any case, what often happens is that someone goes from the circumstance that something in fact operates in a certain way or that its so operating serves human (or other) needs or interests to the assumption that it must have been *designed* to operate in that way. Merely making the distinctions clearly illustrates the fallacy. This "religious" fallacy is, however, paralleled by the "scientific" fallacy of supposing, as some of the functionalists in the social sciences seem to do, that discovering the "purpose" or "function" of an institution, that is, what human interests or needs it in fact serves though perhaps unknown to those humans, is an explanation of its existence. But the sense and nonsense in functional analysis have already been adequately diagnosed by others.[8]

We are now in a much better position to inquire directly into the matter of purpose in history or what has also been called the "meaning" of history, the "goal" of history, or the "significance" of history. Most of what I shall say would apply equally well to theories of the meaning of evolution, the meaning of the universe, and so on, and a lot of it has been said before. The question then is not, What is the purpose or meaning of history? but rather, What could be meant by saying that history has a purpose or a meaning? Of course, religious theories of the world have a kind of answer. What is meant is that human history is a process which someone started with some end in mind. Human history, then, has a purpose in the sense that a sign with an arrow has a purpose; it was designed to satisfy the interests, needs, or purposes of someone. If someone objects that this doesn't capture the idea of history as involving change through time, we can easily modify our analogy to some *process*, say, growing a garden or building a canoe, in which the purpose or meaning of the process is, say, nutritious vegetables to eat and the pleasure of rowing a canoe, respectively. I think we must grant that this religious conception of meaning or purpose in history, however absurd in other senses and on other grounds, does provide for a reasonably clear and unproblematic sense in which history might be said to have a purpose.

The difficulties of even minimum intelligibility come from those semisecularized views of the world in which it is claimed that there is an *immanent* purpose in or meaning of history, especially when the location of such a purpose or meaning is supposed to be an explanation of some or all of what happens in particular in history. Can any sense at all be given to such notions? I think not, if we take them as they are typically meant. History is not an organism, much less an organism with an intelligent mind. Thus in no literal sense does it intend anything, desire anything, choose anything, and so on. That human history is partly the causal result of individual human purposes we need not deny, but that is a long way from saying what is intended. There are purposes *in* history, but there is no purpose *of* history, to paraphrase a theme in a paper of Baier's.[9]

Sometimes purpose in history is used not in the sense of intention but in the sense of goal. Identifying some state of affairs *as* a goal would seem to presuppose either that it is intended by someone or something, or something else which I shall mention in a moment. Here I will only observe that the future existence of the goal is supposed somehow to *explain* particular events and trends in history, something which makes no more sense here than it does in very ordinary situations where a conscious purpose exists. My behavior in getting up from this desk and going to the kitchen is explained not by the goal which is drinking a glass of water, but by my desire or intention to reach that goal for, to repeat an earlier point, my behavior and its explanation might exist even though the goal is not achieved and nonexistent states of affairs do not, by themselves, explain the occurrence of anything.[10] Teleological conceptions of history, so understood, are literally and completely unintelligible and therefore neither true nor false.

The "something else" I alluded to above is only that nothing I have said contradicts the idea that there may be historical trends, indeed one overall trend, which are (is) of interest to human beings (or would be, if known). It may very well be that there is an overall trend in human history toward greater individual freedom, or greater intellectual development, or certain kinds of social institutions. And if someone wishes to pick out one of any such trends as may exist and call it the purpose of history, we may wonder what point there is in so characterizing it, but have no objection otherwise if he is simply calling attention to the existence and/or desirability of such a trend. What must be remembered is that the existence of a trend, simply as a trend, explains none of the particular occurrences which make it up (unless it does happen to be an instance of a "law of historical development," but that would have to be shown independently) and is itself something to be explained. To take an analogy from biology: there is a tendency, not universal, toward increase in size in the members of successive generations. This can, where it exists, be fairly easily explained by natural selection, that is, by the fact that the larger members of most species have easier access to food and sexual mates. It would be a little odd to say that *the* or even *a* purpose of evolution is larger animals; but be that as it may, there is no *law* of which the trend is an instance and the trend is itself something to be explained, as it can be. In short, we have nothing more than an ordinary purposeless process in which certain trends happen to occur. So too in human history there may be such trends. Need I add that since humans have purposes in the unproblematic sense, such trends as exist may be partly the causal result of them, and short-run trends may even be intended by people? More generally, one *could* speak of the purpose of history as whatever humans decide to do "with" it. Seen from without, however, one can reasonably claim that in the strong sense, human history, like those larger processes of which it is a part, is a purposeless, meaningless process in which, however, purposeful beings happen to appear.

We may conclude then, to summarize this discussion of purpose, that there are four basic "elements" into which any intelligible notion of purpose must be analyzable. They are as follows: (a) the felt intention of an intelligent being, (b) a pattern of behavior which is flexible *as if* the organism or mechanism exhibiting it had a purpose in the first sense, (c) states of affairs that in fact satisfy human needs or desires or interests or whatever, and (d) causal trends or patterns. No given notion need involve all these, but what involves more than these risks the likelihood of unintelligibility.

XI Abstract Marxism

Although providing a very convenient way of summarizing most of the main topics of this book, this final chapter nevertheless takes up some new materials in its own right. I have labeled my topic as *abstract* Marxism, because while it is Marxism I intend to talk about, I shall not discuss the actual empirical content of Marx's social theories in anything like a systematic manner. Broadly speaking, one might say that I shall concentrate on the "formal" or "structural" characteristics of the theory of society called historical materialism. But it will also be useful to my tasks if I first indicate my general attitude toward and conception of Marxism. The several sections of this final chapter are accordingly as follows: some *general comments on Marxism*; a brief outline of the theory of *historical materialism*; and then discussion of this theory under the headings of *monism and economic determinism*, *holism*, *process theory and pluralism*, *historicism*, *determinism and fatalism*, and *materialism and naturalism*.

General Comments on Marxism

I intend to indicate my general "picture" of Marxism not so much as a historical phenomenon as an intellectual edifice.[1] The very heart of Marxism, as I see it, is its social theory. Although this social theory is called historical materialism, it has many aspects which have nothing particularly to do with those which go into its definition. This social theory, to my understanding, stands alone in the logical sense that it neither entails nor is entailed by any very interesting propositions about the universe as a whole — either metaphysical or moral. More precisely, the cosmology or philosophy of nature known as dialectical materialism in none of its major versions either entails or is entailed by historical materialism. Dialectical materialism as a theory about the nature of all things, their interactions, and the "logic" appropriate to their understanding is a metaphysics which is essentially a Soviet development of ideas to be found in Engels, especially in *The Dialectics of Nature*, and hardly at all in Marx himself. Marx, I believe, was not a dialectical materialist and indeed, I suspect, would have been very much opposed to some of its versions, especially those which put the method of dialectics in opposition to and as superior to those of science. Be that as it may, however, the important point is that although the general metaphysics of dialectical materialism may possibly suggest certain theories about society, it is not correct to maintain that historical materialism is merely the "application" of dialectical materialism to society. At most one can say that if dialectical materialism were true, certain social theories would have to be false. But that is a long way from saying that historical materialism would have to be true.[2]

With respect to values, I similarly maintain, and here again without any argument, that historical materialism neither follows from nor entails any proposition whatsoever about what the good society is or what people ought to do. In fact, historical materialism neither follows from nor entails any nontrivial "moral" or evaluative proposition at all. No doubt many people who come to believe or disbelieve in historical materialism may for that reason or from that cause be moved to do this or not to do that from certain motivations of a moral nature. But I am talking about the logical connections of certain propositions and not the psychological connections of ideas. It is also true that Marx's social theory contains theses *about* the nature of morality — its sources, its "function" in class society, and the like; but as we all understand by now, a proposition about morality — whether about "judgments" (the favorite of moral philosophers for reasons I don't fully understand), aspects of behavior, or the causes and effects of certain aspects of behavior — need not itself be a moral evaluation and may be only a description of a certain aspect of the world. I believe too, however, that Marx was a moral philosopher, not just in the sense that his own values are reasonably apparent to anyone who reads nearly anything he wrote, but in the sense that he had a partially explicit *philosophical* theory of morality, or better, of what is of intrinsic value. (His historical and sociological relativism with respect to values being only an account of the causes and "functions" of morality in society is a scientific, not a philosophical, theory. It is quite compatible with any of what I would call genuinely philosophical theories, though it may, if true, make certain philosophical theories less plausible without strictly entailing their falsehood.)[3] His philosophical theory is, I believe, one reasonably and profitably called Aristotelian. By that I mean, briefly, that he thinks of human beings as having a distinctive, common *nature* and *therefore* a good society as being one in which people are able to act according to their (common) nature.[4] Unlike Aristotle, Marx emphasized that this nature, or the perception thereof, can be and hitherto always has been distorted by historical circumstances. Hence while in general we may say that historical or sociological relativism about values makes philosophical absolutism about values (a certain version of which I am ascribing to Marx) rather difficult to maintain, in Marx's case we have as part of the *social* theory an explanation of why people do not perceive and act according to the ''real'' values. Of course the notion of ''real'' values, being itself philosophical, does not enter into the social theory proper, systematically speaking. The main point is, however, that whatever Marx's values were or his philosophical theory of the nature of values was, the social theory stands logically independent.

Finally, I would want to dissociate the question of the truth-value of the social theory from whatever motivations — conscious or unconscious — Marx (or anyone else, for that matter) may have had in putting it forward. It would be foolish to deny that Marx was, after all, a revolutionary, that he both anticipated and desired a radical transformation of society and that he hoped his intellectual work as well as his other activities would contribute toward that transformation. But one must not confuse the intellectual content of a social theory or any other theory with the reasons anyone has for formulating, advocating, trying to confirm or falsify, or any other attitude one may take toward, the theory itself. It is some such confusion that seems to lie at the basis of Tucker's book on Marx,[5] for example, not to mention, at a much lower level, the attempts to refute Marxism by claiming or even proving that Marx didn't like Jews, or ''exploited'' his family, or worked for capitalist organizations. One shouldn't even have to mention this point, but one may seriously doubt whether scientific and other kinds of progress which contribute to the accumulation of knowledge have any tendency to diminish the amount of general intellectual confusion; perhaps the opposite is true.

Historical Materialism

Although Marx's social theory is usually called historical materialism, the full-blown theory, in some of its most important aspects, goes far beyond those characteristics which give it its name. As I understand the purely *social* aspects of the theory (I'll explain my restriction in a moment), it is a theory of human behavior statistically considered according to which certain aspects or certain kinds of behavior are taken to be fundamental in the sense of being causally "primary" to all other or at least some crucial other aspects of behavior. (We include in behavior here, à la Ryle, the construction of theories, for example, so that the many kinds of systematic thinking are to be counted as forms of human behavior.) More specifically, it is the thesis that the ways in which we behave (including the legal, moral, and customary prescriptions of how we should behave) in those activities which are involved in the production and distribution of the goods necessary to our physical existence causally determine the specific forms of other aspects of human behavior, including most importantly the behaviors involved in political activities and theory construction; religious activities, practices, and theorizing; the various activities concerned with the arts including theorizing about them; the practice of philosophy and its practical applications; and so on — all of which Marx sometimes calls the "ideological superstructure."[6] The theory is *materialistic* presumably because the emphasis is on the fundamental character of those activities involved in the satisfaction of our biological in contrast to our intellectual, spiritual, aesthetic, and social needs. The theory is called *historical* presumably because the ways in which people do go about the work necessary to satisfy their biological needs is something which changes through time and changes in a very definite way. Those changes are in fact the reflection of other, yet "deeper" changes that take place virtually independently of what has so far been described.[7]

What Marx calls the "forces of production" are something which, as he sees it, tend to increase throughout history. The increase is not to be found at every point of time nor is its rate constant, but overall one may say that those "things" which constitute the forces of production tend to increase over large periods of time. Those "things" include the sizes and numbers of factories and other units of production, the means and speed of transportation (from raw state to factory, from factory to market), the accessibility of natural resources, human skills, labor power, and, one might add, human population. The tendency toward "increase" (it means not quite the same thing for all the aspects of the forces of production) presumably is the result of two factors — the cumulative nature of human knowledge and skills and the semipermanent and therefore also incremental nature of factories, roads, etc. (For this reason one might want to put the activity of science in the forces of production. Marx was uncomfortable about the place of science in his scheme, treating it almost as outside the major categories and yet in other ways as crucial to the whole theory.)[8] Thus we have, broadly speaking, a linear increase in the forces of production, what has been a gradual expansion throughout most of human history but with an explosive expansion under capitalism, at least in its earlier stages.

Now we are to understand that there are certain "relations of production" (which *are* the ways in which people behave in order to produce and distribute what is necessary for the satisfaction of their biological needs) which broadly correspond to and are caused by certain "segments" in this linear progression, relations which at the earlier end of *their* segment are "progressive" and provide for a new spurt in the expansion in the forces of production, but which at the later end of the segment become "fetters," so that a new system of the relations of production is "needed." Somewhere around this time there begins a more or less rapid changeover in the relations of production — slow and unintended in the changeover from feudalism to capitalism, rapid and conscious in that from capitalism to socialism according to further details of the theory — which in turn produces a more or less rapid change in whatever constitutes the "third" level — religion, philosophy, politics, art, and so on.

Now this part of the theory — that in the main the size and sophistication of the forces of production determine the character of relations of production — already goes beyond what in the theory defines it as historical materialism. For one could consistently maintain that how people go about satisfying their biological needs broadly determines the other important aspects of social behavior, but that those ways — the relations of production — are themselves determined not by the forces of production but by something else, say, climate or the development of language or race. That is what I meant in saying earlier that it goes beyond being a purely *social* theory in this sense: that some of the major factors used in the explanation of social behavior are themselves just (the properties of) nonhuman physical objects. Some of those objects, such as factories, are the products of human behavior to be sure, but others, such as natural resources, are not. None of this is said by way of objection to the theory, but only by way of clarification and of understanding what depends on what.

In what follows I intend to ignore the many more specific aspects of this social theory. I shall not at all consider the theory of classes and class conflict, the theory of the origin and nature of the state, and the theory of the nature and "function" of ideology. I shall rather, in keeping with my description of my task as that of discussing abstract Marxism, consider the theory of Marx outlined under the headings indicated in the introductory paragraph.

Monism and Economic Determinism

Marx's social theory is usually taken to be a version of a monistic theory of society. A monistic theory, we may recall, is one according to which one variable is the single exclusive or most important variable, causally speaking, in the system under consideration. I argued in the eighth chapter that for logical reasons alone, when causation is understood as mere lawful connection, no theory can be true in which one variable is supposed to be the only lawfully determining one in the system (unless it were the sole variable in the system). Marx's social theory is a monistic theory but in a sense weakened in two ways. In the first place, although in Marx's theory certain crucial variables are causally more important than the others in the system of variables which characterizes human society — that's what makes it monistic — he not only does not deny but indeed insists that the social variables make up a set of mutually interacting variables. This is indeed part of the sense there is in the notion of dialectics: the emphasis on the mutual interactions of things.[9] I once described Marx's theory as being that of "total social interactionism" — the thesis that the value of every variable in the system is relevant to calculation of earlier or, usually more important, later values of that same set of variables.[10] But this view, which I think really is Marx's, of total social interactionism is quite compatible with the monistic conception of society. Although it may seem inherently unlikely for one and the same thinker to emphasize both aspects, I think this is exactly what Marx has done. The theory, then, is one in which every variable is a relevant variable to earlier or later values of other variables in the system and in which some one or a few variables have a special causal status thus qualifying the system as monistic. That such a theory is logically coherent we saw in the eighth chapter. This is worth emphasizing because some seem to have supposed that as soon as one grants or even insists that a set of variables is a mutually interacting set, one must further grant, if one wishes to be consistent, that they all have the same importance to the system.[11] This is simply not so.

The second sense in which Marx's social theory is weaker than other possible monistic theories is that in it a number of variables rather than just one constitutes the distinguished set. Broadly speaking, the economic variables are the crucial ones in Marx's theory of society, but they, at least for purposes of any serious scientific analysis, constitute rather a large number of variables themselves. Furthermore, as we know, within the economic variables themselves, Marx makes a further major distinction between the "forces of production" and the "relations of production" and tells us that of these two, the former are, causally, the more important. Within that set of economic variables alone, it is fairly clear, I think, what can be meant by maintaining that the relations of production are more a causal function of the forces of production rather than the other way around. But at the moment I should like to inquire briefly whether Marx's *three*-tiered theory really makes logical sense, the three tiers being those of the forces of production, the relations of production, and the "ideological superstructure." (It doesn't matter exactly what goes where for my purposes.) Possibly Marx thought of these relations primarily in terms of certain temporal relationships: A is first the cause of B and then B is the cause of C. In fact, Marx often suggests a theory which in its temporal aspects at least we might project geometrically as follows:

IDEOLOGICAL SUPERSTRUCTURE
RELATIONS OF PRODUCTION
FORCES OF PRODUCTION

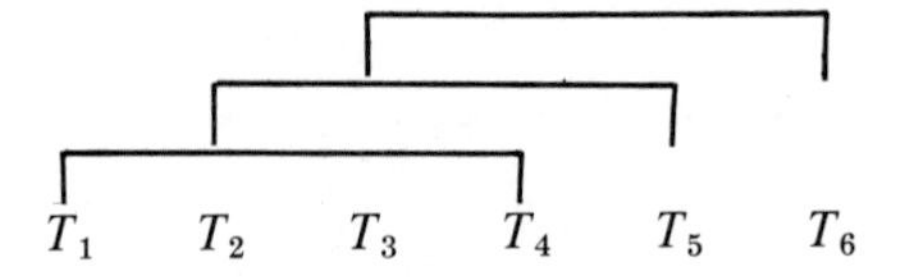

The point is that the relations of production appear later and disappear later than the forces of production that cause them or to which, as Marx says, they "correspond," and the same can be said of the ideological superstructure with respect to the relations of production. At T_1 the forces of production have reached a point at which the old relations of production have become "fetters," thus causing a revolution or change at T_2, at which time the new relations of production "release" the forces of production for a new burst of expansion. At T_3 the ideological superstructure comes into tune with the new society and from then until T_4, the social order is at its most stable, the time when it will most appear to its participants to be permanent and proper. At T_4 the relations of production have once again become "fetters" on the forces of production. At T_5 the revolution or change has occurred, but the old ideas hang on. Perhaps this is the essence of what Marx meant after all, in which case I think we must agree that it is logically unobjectionable, at least as a three-tiered theory. But then its three-tiered nature is more a function of time than of lawful connection. For ideally, and I think Marx shared this *scientific* ideal, what we want is a process theory or a near-process theory which would allow us to predict or postdict states of society from any given time to any other time. And we may assume that Marx would agree that really to calculate the values of all the variables at, say, T_4 we would need to know the values of all the variables at, say, T_3. Within the context of this theory, certain variables may be more important than others and among the important ones some yet more important than the remainder. Thus it may qualify, in one of the senses discussed in the seventh chapter, as a monistic theory of society. What we must not do, for it is both historically false and logically incoherent, is to think of Marx's theory simply as one in which A causes B and B causes C but in which possibly A does not cause C and/or in which there is no mutual interaction.

Since I have already discussed Plamenatz's objections to monistic theories of society, I shall not do so here again. Rather I want, still in this same context, to look at the idea of "economic determinism," for this is often the label given to the particular version of a monistic theory of society which Marx seemed to advocate. I have written elsewhere that Marx was not an economic determinist. The point was not to deny Marx's determinism, of which more later, or the importance which he ascribed to the economic variables, but to deny that he held a certain extreme form of a theory which some have, at least implicitly, ascribed to him. I characterized this extreme view as follows:

> The economic variables constitute a causally closed system, i.e., they may interact with each other but with nothing non-economic. (Interaction is symmetrical of course.) Furthermore, the non-economic variables (including those of group behavior) are connected to the economic variables by parallelistic laws. The laws are not, however, of the one/one and if-and-only-if type. Otherwise there would be no reason to say that the economic determine the non-economic variables, rather than the other way around. Rather, the parallelistic laws are of the simple if-then type going from the economic to the non-economic, whether one/one or many/one. What this means is that given those laws and the values of the economic variables, one can compute the values of the non-economic variables, whereas given the laws and the values of the non-economic variables, one cannot compute the values of the economic variables.[12]

We may first note that simply as a matter of logic this view could be true only if the same ideological superstructure (or whatever is considered to constitute the noneconomic variables) could correspond to different sets of values of the economic variables. Otherwise there would be mutual computability. For this reason alone one may doubt that it is a view Marx would ever have intended to hold.[13] But another matter is somewhat more complicated.

I also wrote in the same context as the quote above that on the view of economic determinism human choices make no difference to what (else) happens, that is, it is a version of fatalism. Looked at in one way this is not strictly true; looked at in another it is completely wrong. We may approach the point by asking what phenomena are to be included among the economic variables. When I wrote that economic determinism implies fatalism, I was assuming that human choices (or purposive behaviors — the difference makes no difference here) were not to be included among the economic variables. Even on this assumption economic determinism does not imply that human choices make absolutely no difference to what (else) happens. For the values of the variables characterizing choice (or purposive behavior) would always determine the values of the economic variables within a certain range though of course not uniquely. The width of the range would naturally depend on the particular theory as well as the initial conditions of the world it was supposed to explain. Unless the range were rather small it would be of little human significance. In any case no version of economic determinism so understood, that is, with the assumption that human choices are excluded from the distinguished set of variables, is empirically true.

But of course the assumption is not true either, except by stipulation, and certainly not as a characterization of Marx's theory. For in fact in the theory the distinction between human and nonhuman variables and even more that between human choice and human nonchoice variables quite cuts across the distinction between noneconomic and economic variables. Indeed one may say that nonhuman variables play a rather small role altogether in Marx's social theory. Put positively nearly all the variables that constitute each of the three levels of the tripartite distinction are themselves human variables. Yet more to the point, the relations of production consist almost exclusively of human variables and the forces of production also in great measure. So that whether the economic variables are supposed to be either or both of the relations of production or (and) the forces of production, human variables some of which will be human choices or purposive behavior will be among the economic variables. Since this is so, even if Marx were an economic determinist in the sense at hand, one could not conclude that he must also, if he wished to be consistent, be a fatalist. But as I have already indicated, I do not believe that Marx was an economic determinist in this extreme sense anyway.

I think therefore that it is better not to call Marx's social theory "economic determinism" at all; it is a deterministic theory (which is or ought to be trivial) according to which the economic variables are the more important ones in the laws that explain both the changes in society and the relations between elements in a cross section of society. But it is certainly not the view discussed above as economic determinism. Even so, if one uses the expression "so-and-so determinism" to mean only a theory according to which a certain variable or set of variables is the most important or the "ultimately determining element" in Engels's phrase, I think Marx's view is better described as "technological determinism" at least as a theory of social *change*. For, to simplify for the purpose of expressing the theory in what I believe nevertheless to be an illuminating way, one could say that Marx's theory is that on the whole social institutions and ideas of people are caused by the state of technology that exists in a given society. Such a way of describing the theory would leave it much less open to the wrongheaded, but unfortunately widespread, interpretations of it that take it as a theory of human *motivation*, especially the interpretation that would have it that all people in all societies are concerned with their selfish economic interests or even class interests and that all "other" human activity and especially theoretical activity is a "cover-up" for the pursuit of those economic interests. So far as, in his analysis of ideologies, Marx may have held some such view with respect to members of *certain* classes in *certain* kinds of societies, it is an addition to the basic social theory of "technological determinism" which is completely open to what conscious or even unconscious *reasons* people may have for acting as they do.

Holism

Marxism is often taken to be a holistic social theory. As we saw earlier, this characterization could be either in the context of description (what there is) or in the context of explanation (what the laws are). The latter context I shall discuss under the heading of *process*. Thus here we take the holistic interpretation of Marx's social theory to be the idea that groups are real, that they are greater than the sums of their parts, and the like. As we also saw, the only clear meaning that can be attached to such ideas and which make them nontrivial is that there are simple properties of social wholes. This is the thesis of descriptive emergentism. We noted that one is not apt to hold such a doctrine unless he also holds that such simple properties interact "back" with the properties that are ordinarily taken to be social, including individual social behavior. But be that as it may, we may first ask whether or not Marx believed there to be any such properties and if it is of any significance for the substance of his social theory.

The answer to the first question is, so far as the texts support an answer,

Marx did not believe in social wholes; Marx, that is, was a descriptive individualist.[14] Furthermore, I daresay there is nothing in what he says that is equivalent to or best analyzed or understood as the doctrine I have called descriptive emergentism. Nor do any of the propositions he did assert that might seem to some to imply emergentism really entail it; for example, that "in the social production which men carry on, they enter into definite relations that are indispensable and independent of their will,"[15] that social phenomena can be explained without reference to the peculiar properties of any individual person, or that the laws of social phenomena cannot be derived from those of individual phenomena, or any of the many propositions about class, class interests, and class consciousness. Nor finally do any of the aspects of Marx's theories of alienation imply the doctrine of descriptive emergentism. The first of these, that some social phenomena are not chosen by any given person, is compatible with any theory about the nature of social phenomena in themselves since all that is required to make it true is that there be some social circumstance which is not *both* as someone chose it to be and the result of that choice. (I ignore the matter of "indispensability" which is patently irrelevant to the question of emergence.) The second proposition does not imply, by affirming that no properties peculiar to any individual (or nonuniversal set of individuals) go into the explanation of social phenomena, that one could not still define all social properties in terms of the properties of individuals. In other words, as we saw in the fifth chapter, process at the level of social phenomena does not imply the doctrine of descriptive emergence. The third proposition, which asserts the doctrine of what I called explanatory pluralism (or what is also called explanatory emergence), does not, as we also saw clearly in the fifth chapter, imply the doctrine of descriptive emergence, so I needn't show it again.

The propositions about classes, by implicitly distinguishing classes or class consciousness or class interests ("real" or felt) from individuals, individual consciousness, and individual interests ("real" or felt) might be thought to imply that the group has a reality over and above that of individual people and their properties and relations. As for class itself, we may surely assume that a given class is simply made up of particular people. Since, as Marx treats them, classes have existence (in a noncommittal sense) and change through time (like a biological species), we may conclude that a class is something more than the individual persons that exist at any given time, but it doesn't follow that it is something more than individual persons (and of course their relations to each other and to other people and things) altogether. The cases of class interest and class consciousness are a little more complicated but for our purposes may be treated together. There are three possibilities: (1) These notions are being used in contrast to those of private, individual, and possibly selfish interests (I don't identify self-interest with selfish interest) in which case the point would be that people may choose to identify with interests larger than their own. Asserting the reality of class interests and class consciousness thus is denying the doctrine of psychological egoism. (2) It is being asserted that people have some private interests in virtue of their membership in a certain class which may therefore be labeled class interests, class consciousness being in part awareness of this fact. (3) The notions are being used normatively as those values and beliefs and thoughts certain members or even all members of a class ought to have or it would be best for them to have (according to someone or other, in this case Marx) and perhaps will have when and if they realize their own situation and what can be done about it. None of these three possibilities implies that in the appropriate and relevant sense there are anything more than individual people and their interests, thoughts, values, and so on.

The unreality of society, that is, as not being something over and above the reality of individual people, their properties and relations, also does not contradict any but the most extreme form of the various theories of alienation in general nor any conceptions of the various aspects of alienation according to Marx in particular. Let us convince ourselves that that is so. In the first place so far as alienation is considered as a so-called "subjective" phenomenon — whether as belief, feeling, emotion, thought, behavior, or any characteristic of a person whatsoever — it is obviously compatible with the unreality of social wholes even if it is precisely the feeling or belief or thought that society is something over and above the "ensemble of social relations." For in general the thought or belief or feeling or even the desire that something is the case does not make it so. In the second place alienation as a so-called "objective" phenomenon as Marx usually considers it is also compatible with descriptive individualism. The "objective" phenomena in question are in fact relations which a person may have to the means of production, to the products of his own labor, to nature, to other people, really to anything whatsoever whether or not they are felt as "alienating" relations or (in some cases) perceived by the person at all. These "objective" phenomena are all describable in the context of descriptive individualism. Marx's theory has it, on the explanatory side, that under certain conditions the "objective" relations of alienation give rise to the "subjective" feelings of alienation whether the subject is aware of the "objective" basis of his feelings or not.

Only a theory (obviously not Marx's) which claimed that one could not have the feeling or thought of the extra reality of society unless one *veridically* perceived it as such would be incompatible with descriptive individualism. Among major thinkers probably Durkheim comes closest to maintaining such a view.[16] The metaphysical or epistemological principle that should be involved in any such view is that one cannot be aware of a simple property unless something actually exemplifies that property. Then the question would become whether anyone actually is aware of simple properties of social wholes.

This last point connects with my final comments about holism or emergentism with respect to Marx's social theory. I have asserted that there is nothing in the theory that would require Marx consistently to hold to emergentism nor does he, so far as I know, ever assert it in its own right. But of course this does not mean that every time he uses social notions he actually gives definitions or refers us to definitions by means of which the social terms could be replaced by expressions which mention only the properties of and relations among individual people and things. In fact he rarely does this. But I take this as no evidence whatsoever that Marx was an emergentist, any more than one would assume the editors of a newspaper to be emergentists who wrote 'the trade union' or 'the government' without giving the appropriate definitions. True, Marx was a social theorist and we rightly demand more of social theorists than of newspaper editors when they talk about society; but unless that is the particular point of his social theory at the moment or unless there is some reason to suppose that his readers will not know what he is talking about unless he actually gives the definitions, there is no particular reason for a social theorist, any more than anyone else, actually to give them. This will be especially true if the theorist believes, as Marx surely did, that there are significant lawful connections to be found among the social properties themselves even if in principle they can be defined in terms of the properties of individuals.

Process Theory and Pluralism

It is sometimes claimed that Marx believed that there is process among the social variables alone.[17] The evidence is not direct, but I agree that this is in the spirit of his work. As we saw in the preceding chapter, this theory could be evaluated for its approximation to the truth only with a clear meaning of the notion of a "social" variable. To be sure, the theory is literally false anyway. Phenomena such as earthquakes, weather, and disease are interacting variables (that is, with the social variables) and no account of the course of human history could be complete without occasional mention of them and Marx knew this as well as anybody else.[18] The more interesting question is, however we define 'social variable', whether the nonrole and sometimes unique characteristics of particular people are ever relevant in the explanation of social phenomena. Some seem to have taken it for granted that Marx, in assuming process or near-process among the social variables, treated all individuals as the same to be differentiated only by their social roles (analogous to differentiating particles in a gas only by their spatial location). I'm not sure the texts support any very definite view on the matter, but I think a much more plausible interpretation of Marx's social theory would be that, although certain characteristics which must go into the definition of the social variables (or into the explanation of social phenomena) are neither universal nor purely role characteristics, they are sufficiently widespread that one may assume that they occur in every reasonably sized human population to an extent that if a person in a significant social role with those characteristics had not existed, another one would have. I think this theory, whether it is Marx's or not, is probably false,[19] but it is certainly much more plausible than the other one sometimes ascribed to him. But now suppose we admit the necessity of such nonuniversal, nonrole characteristics in the explanation of some social phenomena, do we still have a purely "social" explanation of social phenomena? In the last chapter I distinguished a "sociological" from a merely "social" theory of society, depending on whether or not such characteristics need be included, but it now appears that the more interesting question is whether or not the characteristics necessary for the explanation of all social phenomena occur in all relevant populations in the required proportion and less whether they be purely role characteristics or not.

I see no reason to doubt that Marx was aware that there are *inborn* differences in intelligence, imagination, physical constitution, and other characteristics among people and that these differences are *relevant* to explaining both why people end up in the social roles they do end up in and why they act the way they do in those roles. It is characteristic of egalitarian *political* theories (of which Marx's is one form) to emphasize the extent to which inequalities not only of wealth and position but also of intelligence, creativity, and other abilities are themselves determined by social institutions; and rightly so. But does anyone believe that just any person could have done what Einstein did if only that person had had a certain upbringing? But then does anyone doubt, to hark back to an earlier discussion, that if Einstein had never lived, someone else would have come up with essentially the same views about the same time? In any case I see no reason to ascribe to Marx the view that we are as peas in a pod either in fact or even only for the purposes of social explanation.

Finally, we may recall that the assumption of process at the social level does not in and of itself preclude the possibility that individual choices may affect the course of history. For even though, on the assumption of process at the social level, one could, given the values of those variables at a given time, compute by the laws their values at earlier or later times, their values at a given time will depend on the values of the properties of individual things at least on the assumption of descriptive individualism (which Marx *surely* held for most if not all social variables, so to speak, as we saw in the last section) by way of being defined in terms of them. This will sound paradoxical only to those who, like Sartre, confuse a choice's being realized or making a difference with its not being caused or explainable in the first place.

As for explanatory pluralism, I think there is little doubt that Marx's social theory is best interpreted as endorsing it. Explanatory pluralism I explicated to mean that at least some of the laws of behavior in larger groups cannot by way of any composition rule(s) be deduced from the laws of behavior in smaller groups or alone. This issue is sometimes put in terms of psychological in contrast to sociological explanations of this or that aspect of human behavior, but logically explanatory pluralism (also called explanatory emergence or holism) even when specified with respect to human behavior in groups does not presuppose anything in particular about what the various causes of human behavior are. If "psychological" means characteristics which are inborn or peculiar to the life of the person in question and "sociological" means characteristics of social institutions and policies and the like, then no doubt to explain fully a given piece of behavior one would in the typical case need to mention both kinds of factors. Or one might say that it depends on what aspect of the behavior is being explained where "aspect" is used very broadly. To take as an example one of the recent pseudo-issues: the explanation of the behavior of radical students. Is their behavior to be explained by "psychological" or "sociological" factors? The answer can only be that if you want to explain why certain students but not others in the "same" social circumstances become radicals you will probably look for "psychological" factors — factors in their "genes" and their upbringing which the others don't share. But if you want to explain why a larger percentage of students are radicals at one time than at some earlier time, one would look for "sociological" factors, assuming that there has been no great genetic alteration in the meantime, or change in patterns of child-rearing (which would itself need a "sociological" explanation).

But the point of this discussion and its example is to make clear that it is not to be confused with the issue of explanatory monism and explanatory pluralism, for the pluralist can admit, may even insist, that sociological factors enter into every human situation, including the "simplest," and that psychological factors also enter into even the most complex human situations without denying his pluralism. The explanatory monist must of course admit that the same basic factors are operative in every human situation for his reductions to be logically possible, but this still leaves it completely open what those factors are.

Again I don't think the texts of Marx are specific enough to make a judgment of these issues with respect to what Marx himself believed.[20] I think some Marx*ists* have supposed that being explanatory pluralists somehow guaranteed their commitment to purely "sociological" explanations of human behavior (or vice versa) which is logically fallacious, as I have just shown. Thus although Marx's social theory is certainly in general a "sociological" theory of society and of human behavior, he need not have been an explanatory pluralist to hold it. Still he almost certainly was an explanatory pluralist anyway.

Historicism

It would be hard to deny that Marx believed in laws of historical development, a belief based in turn on the idea of the similar linear development of all societies. But was he a historicist in the sense I gave to the term in the seventh chapter? Did he believe that there are laws by which one could predict future stages of society and which are not deducible from what I called the "laws of the interaction of the elements"? I think we must say in light of his detailed analysis of capitalism that he based *his* predictions of the future course of capitalism and of its ultimate downfall in favor of communism not on some alleged law which would mention only a few characteristics of each kind of society and which is not deducible from the laws that would explain the more detailed workings of society but only from those last-mentioned laws (or putative laws) themselves. Thus Marx himself, unlike some of his "Marxist" successors, was not a historicist. Yet he certainly shared some of the historicists' inclinations and presuppositions. And it is worth while considering one of these briefly in the context of this discussion.

Most important of these, as I already indicated, is Marx's belief that every society goes through essentially the same "development" much as the "normal" members of an organic species share a certain common "development."[21] This proposition, whether asserted of members of species, of the species themselves, or of societies, in fact neither entails nor is entailed by the proposition that there are nondeducible laws of historical (or individual or evolutionary) development. But if one believes, for whatever reason, that all specimens of the sort of thing in question in fact do undergo the same sequence of "states" or "stages," then it is easy also to believe that there are laws of historical development. Marx arrived at that conclusion and partly by this presupposition which he never seriously questioned in his own mind, but I do not believe he arrived at the stronger claim, still "suggested" by the presupposition, that there are *autonomous* laws of historical development, that is, at historicism as I have defined it.[22]

In fact, the alleged identity of sequences in all societies does not entail that there are either deducible or nondeducible laws of historical development, nor does it entail that the sequences have any lawful explanation at all in terms only of properties usually called social or behavioral or historical. (I suppose we could say that it doesn't entail that there are any laws whatsoever, since the mere description of particular events even combined with the proposition that one has now described all the events of the kind in question never logically entails any laws of nature.) Furthermore the description is wrong to begin with; societies do not all undergo the same sequences of stages, except possibly in the broadest possible sense of nonindustrial to industrial. Some societies never were feudal and are now capitalist; some are now socialist without ever having been capitalist. It is often said that Marx's social theory assumes wrongly that societies have relatively little impact on each other, at least not enough to "alter" their "normal" course of "development," and this is, I believe, a just and accurate criticism. But on the theoretical level, Marx's social theory is more open to the criticism of failing to appreciate the extent to which nonsocial variables interact with social variables. Or, depending on how you label them, he failed sufficiently to take into account the impact of certain social variables. For example, the relation of population in numbers and in density to living space and natural resources varies widely from society to society and is a factor which has a lot to do with the "development" of societies. In general I should say that the major theoretical criticism to be made of Marx's social theory (as of many other theories of society) is its assumption that all differences among societies can be explained by factors which are themselves social. It is theoretical not in the sense of being a philosophical rather than an empirical question, but in the sense of the unquestioned role the assumption actually has in the thought of Marx and many other social thinkers. It is perhaps an occupational hazard of sociologists to suppose that the phenomena they are studying always have their explanation in other phenomena of the same sort. But this is my old point: sociological theory will never have the status of physical theory, not because we are "free," but because the kinds of variables sociologists study do not form, except in certain special contexts, even relatively closed sets. Marx in his social theory is in part the victim of this same illusion or false ideal: that social theory can have the same theoretical status as physics.

When all is said and done, however, Marx's predictions about the future of societies may be essentially correct after all and essentially from the causes that he claims will effect the changes, at least in societies which are or will be industrial, capitalist societies. Or his predictions may turn out to be largely correct but not for the reasons he thought. But should any of this happen, it would not show that there are laws of historical development after all. Indeed, nothing in the basic premises of Marx's social theory in logic requires belief in laws of historical development, deducible or nondeducible. It does require that there be laws from which one can deduce what later states of a society will be like from a description of its earlier states,[23] but, as we saw in the seventh chapter, one trivializes the notion of a law of historical development when it becomes identical with the process laws by which some sequence can be calculated, not because the notion of process is itself trivial, but because such an identification removes the very heart of the notion of a law of historical development. And this heart is, whether the law be deducible or not from the "ordinary" laws, that only a very few characteristics of a society be mentioned in the law of historical development.

Determinism and Fatalism

Marx was a determinist. Of that there is little doubt. He always presumed that everything that occurs has a scientific explanation, including human choices and human behavior. Yet he is often also taken to be a fatalist as well, where that theory is understood as holding that human choices make no difference to anything else that happens. I have argued elsewhere[24] in more detail that there is nothing in Marx's social theory (there I called it his philosophy of history) that entails either that we don't make choices or that choices are not causally efficacious. Certainly determinism does not entail fatalism, for determinism entails nothing whatsoever either about what kinds of events occur (where by a kind I mean an event described "in and of itself" and not as caused or causeless) or of the particular lawful relations of events to each other. Thus one cannot prove that Marx or anyone else is a fatalist just because he is a determinist.[25]

Fatalism as a general theory of the efficacy of choice is absurd. Its absurdity is empirical, not logical. If anything is certain in our experience, it is that our choices sometimes make a difference to what (else) happens. Thus if one could show that someone's social (or any other kind of) theory entails the general theory of fatalism, he would have shown that the original theory is itself absurd in the same sense. But we need not take fatalism as a completely general theory: we can rather speak of the efficacy of choice with respect to a certain limited class or kind of events. Thus a person may be a fatalist in relation to large-scale social phenomena or the course of history, but not with respect to his personal life. It sounds a little odd to describe a view as fatalist in connection with a class of events or phenomena where there is no reasonable doubt of the inability of humans to affect them. Thus to be a fatalist with respect to the future evolution of the great galaxy in Andromeda guarantees both the truth and the noncontroversial nature of one's limited fatalism. In this sense we all know that at least some events or kinds of events are entirely beyond the control or manipulation or effect of human choice.

There is no reason to suppose that Marx would not agree that at the personal level, in any case, we often succeed in realizing our choices and hence affecting the course of events by our choices. Certainly there is nothing in his social theory to deny this. It is with respect to the course of history and large-scale social phenomena that the question is to be significantly asked. And here we must remember our distinction between something's being causally dependent on or affected by a choice on the one hand and something's being *as* it was intended to be on the other. In order for us to realize our choices, except by pure coincidence, it is of course necessary that our choices by causally efficacious. We have already seen that although Marx's social theory holds that there is process at the social level, that there are (deducible) laws of historical development, and that explanatory pluralism is true, there is nothing in any of this that entails that our choices are not causally efficacious. Thus I think we must agree that there is nothing in Marx's social theory that entails that choices are not causally efficacious. When Marx tells us that "man makes his own history"[26] he means that human history is the causal consequence of many human choices, interests, passions, and so on, although coming out perhaps as no one desires or intends. Engels expressed this point of view in a letter written after Marx died:

> . . . history is made in such a way that the final result always arises from conflicts between many individual wills, of which each in turn has been made what it is by a host of particular conditions of life. Thus there are innumerable intersecting forces, an infinite series of parallelograms of forces which give rise to one resultant — the historical event. This may again itself be viewed as the product of a power which works as a whole *unconsciously* and without volition. For what each individual wills is obstructed by everyone else, and what emerges is something that no one willed. Thus history has proceeded hitherto in the manner of a natural process and is essentially subject to the same laws of motion. But from the fact that the wills of individuals — each of whom desires what he is impelled to by his physical constitution and external, in the last resort economic, circumstances (either by his own personal circumstances or those of society in general) — do not obtain what they want, but are merged into an aggregate mean, a common resultant, it must not be concluded that they are equal to zero. On the contrary, each contributes to the resultant and is to this extent included in it.[27]

It is part of the peculiarly *historical* part of Marx's social theory (alluded to by the word 'hitherto' in the passage just quoted if we may take Engels's words as expressing Marx's view here) that the advance of scientific knowledge and the scientific attitude combined with certain kinds of social arrangements make increasingly possible the conscious control of society — that is, a situation in which history is not merely the causal result of human willing, but *as* it is intended to be by at least some people (presumably acting in the interests and would-be intentions of the vast majority of people). This, no doubt, is what Engels means in part in another place when he refers to the coming of communism as "the ascent of man from the kingdom of necessity to the kingdom of freedom."[28]

Thus when Marx speaks of the revolution as "inevitable," a word that suggests to some a fatalistic conception of history, I should say that what is meant is that the revolution will occur not in spite of any choices humans *might* make but because of the choices they will make. Marx was a determinist. Thus for him the choices people will make in the future are in principle calculable. He thought he had within certain limits calculated what people would choose to do, choices some of which without so intending would help bring revolution and others of which were consciously directed toward bringing about revolution. It is, after all, essential to his account of the final days of capitalism that a sizable number of people come to realize the causes of their own conditions and *choose* to change them. Marx surely does not mean that if we all choose to go out and hang ourselves or to enter monasteries and nunneries there will nevertheless be a socialist revolution. 'Inevitable' in a deterministic frame of reference often means only that it *will* happen, leaving open merely by saying that it is inevitable the answer to the questions whether it will happen in accordance with, contrary to, or completely independent of human intention and desire, and whether the relation of the "inevitable" event to human choice is intentional or merely causal. But in the case at hand, what is "inevitable" in Marx's social theory partly is and partly is not in accordance with human intention and is almost entirely causally dependent on human choice. Of course humans make human history in large measure, but until we harmonize our intentions and have institutions by which they can be expressed, we cannot expect things to work out *as* we choose them to be, and even then only within certain limits.

Materialism and Naturalism

There are at least four senses of 'materialism' relevant to Marxism in general, although only one of them, so far as I can see, is directly relevant to its social theories. The four senses are as follows: *absolute materialism* — only matter exists and mind is but a certain organization or propensity of matter; *philosophical materialism* — matter is primary in that it can exist without mind but not vice versa; *scientific materialism* — what happens in the material world can be causally explained solely in terms of other material events; *historical materialism* — the forms of behavior humans adopt to satisfy their material needs are basically causally determinative of the specific natures of all other major human social activities. Since I discussed some of these matters in the ninth chapter, I needn't rehearse very much. Suffice it to observe here (a) that there is no reason to suppose that Marx was an absolute materialist at all, (b) that he almost certainly was a philosophical materialist and probably a scientific materialist as well, and (c) that if the foregoing is correct then Marx held the correct views on the matters in question, since absolute materialism is false and philosophical and scientific materialism are true.

But the important point here is that none of these three materialisms entails historical materialism nor does historical materialism in any way presuppose any of the three materialisms, whatever Lenin and many others may have thought.[29] Historical materialism as a theory about what kinds of human behavior are causally fundamental is compatible with any account whatsoever of the existence and nature of mind except perhaps that it is the sole causal "agent" in the universe. But I would emphasize again that some forms of philosophical idealism in fact are logically compatible with historical materialism. One thinks of Croce (which, to be sure, only proves that they are temporarily psychologically compatible) as one who seemed to try to hold to both.[30] Hence Marx's social theory, as far as its "materialism" goes, is not very interesting philosophically. I have already demonstrated, I hope, what is philosophically interesting about the theory.

The work of Marx is sometimes criticized as being "unscientific" in the sense that he was too anxious to prove conclusions which would support his moral views, his desires for the future, and so on, with the result that he could not be objective and as dispassionate as science requires. Though it is always important to separate the intellectual content of what a person writes or says from the motives that person may have for saying it, at least analytically, there may or may not be justice in this criticism. On the whole I find it rather uninteresting. In any case the "nonobjectivity" or falsity or distortion would have to be shown independently before the correlation could be reasonably asserted. What is more important is to emphasize the naturalism of Marx's social theory.[31] By the naturalism of the theory I mean several things: the belief that the social world is but a part of nature and that one need not appeal to anything outside of the natural world before us to explain events in it (we might call this the principle of methodological atheism); the belief that there are no "final goals" of history in the sense of the teleologist's purposes which somehow both effect and explain the actual course of events; the belief that within the natural world everything is lawfully explainable and nothing has miraculously escaped from it (many otherwise scientifically minded people would balk at this scientific determinism); and the belief that to the extent that the world can be understood, it is human *reason* and intelligence in its disciplined approach to the world that will bring that understanding.

This naturalism of Marx led him to formulate a certain *kind* of theory of society — one which had room neither for gods nor "final" purposes nor philosophically "free" wills. I have not undertaken to ask, and in any case am not competent to do so, the precise extent to which Marx's social theory may be empirically true. When it is said that we are all "Marxists" now, I presume that means that we all agree that Marx got on to something very important in his emphasis on the economic variables in society, or perhaps that by and large he succeeded in identifying the relevant variables for an adequate theory of society, even if he didn't get their lawful connections quite right. It has been one of the major contentions of this book that the search for even a reasonably closed social theory is futile, not because gods or causeless wills are operating after all, but because of the influence of extra-social natural factors on social phenomena, something which Marx himself knew both only too well and not well enough. Still, the extent to which my belief in the very extensive "imperfection" of society is true or the contrary belief in social determinism is true is to be answered *within* the framework of naturalism.

It is precisely the spirit of naturalism, as I have characterized it above and which in the matter of the study of society we owe to Marx above all, in combination with an obvious positivist inclination, which has been the spirit of this essay.

Notes and Bibliography

Notes

Chapter I

1. Wright (1971), p. 4, Wright's emphasis.
2. Abel (1948).

Chapter II

1. Bergmann (1957), p. 61.
2. Nagel (1961), chapter 4.
3. Here I am concerned only with those laws which are about the world ''directly.'' There are also laws which tells us how to get from one law to another. See the discussion of composition rules in the fifth chapter.
4. See, for example, MacIntyre's claim that Humean causality cannot hold between beliefs and actions *because* they are not uniformly correlated; in MacIntyre (1967), p. 51.
5. Russell (1957), ''On the Notion of Cause.''
6. Most of the terminology as well as some of the ideas of this section come from Bergmann (1957).
7. For more details see Bergmann (1957), the sections entitled ''Process'' and ''Composition Laws.''
8. Quine argues that we must take classes rather than attributes as the values of predicate variables since otherwise we would have the result that ''two'' properties are or could be one. The argument is fallacious. See Quine (1961), pp. 107–108.
9. The sixth chapter has extended discussion of the notion of scientific explanation itself.

Chapter III

1. The analysis of dispositions that I shall propose a few pages hence makes ones of the sort just mentioned consist partly of properties of the body, partly of properties which characterize states of consciousness. For a given disposition, the latter may never be exemplified just as the soluble sugar may never be dissolved. Thus the having of the disposition guarantees only the exemplification of the physical properties. For this reason some may wish to say that the dispositions aren't really part of the mind at all, properly speaking.
2. Addis and Lewis (1965), ''Ryle's Ontology of Mind.''
3. See especially Bergmann (1960).
4. Addis and Lewis (1965), pp. 47–48.
5. Even in the case of conscious states, the connection is almost certainly many/one from body to mind. Thus the relevant laws of coexistence permit the calculation of mental states from brain

states but not the other way around. Some may wish, therefore, to say that brain states are the *cause* of mental states and not the other way around.

6. For further defense on my part see Addis and Lewis (1965), pp. 44–56.

7. Brodbeck (1963).

8. It might even be the thoughts of earlier people, especially in the cases of ritual actions. See the discussion in the next chapter of Ortega's treatment of the handshake.

9. MacIntyre (1967), p. 52.

10. *Ibid.*, p. 49.

11. *Ibid.*, p. 50.

12. This is again the point that the disposition may exist even though "its" conscious states do not and perhaps never will. But in the sense that (the names of) certain conscious states will enter into the definitions of (the names of) these dispositions, those dispositions are partly constituted of conscious states. See the first note of this chapter.

13. One of its virtues would appear to be that it will not be true of a given object that it has just any disposition provided only that it is never put to the test. In other words, this analysis appears to avoid the problem of counterfactuals as applied to dispositions.

14. The "inconsistency" (which is not a contradiction in the world, of course) is ordinarily between the person's linguistic behavior and his other behavior. In such a case we would usually say that he "believes" this but is doing that (something "inconsistent" with the belief). If it is two nonlinguistic behaviors which seem to "cancel" each other out, then we wouldn't ordinarily speak of belief at all except so far as the actor might be able to explain that his actions weren't really "inconsistent" after all or that there was a point to their so being.

Chapter IV

1. The best collection of pieces on the subject is to be found under the heading "Social Facts, Social Laws, and Reduction" in Brodbeck (1968).

2. This way of introducing the idea of reduction comes essentially from Bergmann (1954).

3. From this point on in this chapter I shall stop being so strict and speak of defining properties themselves instead of, as one literally does, the names of the properties.

4. Some also have expressed a view about the *explanation* of social phenomena in words like 'The State is more than the individuals that make it up', for example. Very frequently, too, such persons are confusing the context of description with the context of explanation. In any event, I shall deal separately with the explanatory context in the next chapter.

5. I ignore as not relevant to the issue numbers and their properties and relations which will enter into the definitions of some social properties.

6. It will be easily understood that this is a highly contextual metaphysical claim in that the same words can be and have been used to deny the existence of properties altogether.

7. The idea was in part that metaphysics is that which tries to deal with what is beyond the senses, whereas science deals with what is given to the senses, or can be "hooked up" with what is given to the senses. Then the emergentist's position may seem to be "unscientific" and "metaphysical."

8. There may, of course, be a lawful connection between a property of a social object and a property of an individual person or thing if the latter does not enter into the definition of the former.

9. This does not preclude the possibility of the elimination of those laws, or rather the need for them, by some other or further procedure. See the discussion of the explanatory reduction of sociology to psychology in the next chapter.

10. The extent to which it is not a methodological question has to do with the "psychology" of the scientists. It may very well be easier and even more fruitful scientifically to think about certain lawful connections at the social rather than the individual level.

11. Here it becomes most apparent that the dialectic in operation throughout these arguments tends to equate being causally efficacious with having a simple property with being an existent.

12. There is further discussion of this "postulation" argument in the seventh chapter.

13. Durkheim (1964), p. xlvii.
14. *Ibid.*, p. xlix.
15. *Ibid.*, p. 13, Durkheim's emphases.
16. Ortega y Gasset (1963), pp. 174–175, Ortega's emphases.
17. *Ibid.*, p. 188.
18. *Ibid.*, pp. 179–180, Ortega's emphasis.
19. Goldmann (1969).
20. The temporal order of the environments will also be a relevant factor, of course.

Chapter V

1. Many of the ideas and the terminology in this section come from the section "Composition Laws" in Bergmann (1957).
2. That is, it is assumed with respect to the properties we are talking about. There could still be simple properties of the whole in addition. Hence even the descriptive emergentist can enter into this argument.
3. I put the words 'new' and 'begins' in double quotation marks in my text because they are there stripped of their literal temporal implications.
4. One could possibly speak of absolute emergence in the limiting case of the breakdown of explanation altogether.
5. I made this error myself in Addis (1966).
6. See also along these same lines Bergmann (1944).
7. Weber (1947), p. 88.
8. Skinner (1953), p. 297.
9. Gerwitz (1969), p. 61, Gerwitz's emphases.
10. Staats and Staats (1964), pp. 336–337, taken with slight modification from Sidowski, Wyckoff, and Tabory (1956), p. 115.
11. In this respect the social situation may be thought of as analogous to mass in mechanics.
12. For example, we don't in our minds "put together" a smile out of the constituent properties of shape, size, and so on; nor are we typically even aware of the constituent properties. Of course some of the relevant stimuli from another person may themselves be simple. For example, mating behavior in humans and animals is often triggered by a certain odor emanating from a member of the opposite sex. Is such behavior then possibly a social, unconditioned response and, if so, would that not make the explanatory reduction of sociology to psychology impossible? The answer is that it would not for, call the response what you will, there is nothing peculiarly social about the stimulus. If the odor is really the only relevant external stimulus, then presumably the same response will occur if the odor is produced artificially and introduced as a stimulus even in the absence of the organism that naturally produces it.
13. There will always be some proposition which in conjunction with the several laws of the responses to simple stimuli presented separately will yield deductively the law of the response to the stimuli presented together. But the idea of a composition rule, we may usefully remind ourselves, is that of a proposition which in conjunction with the law(s) of the simple situation(s) allows the deduction of the laws for a number of levels of complexity. A complication to this whole procedure arises from the fact that almost all laws of the stimulus/response type, if they are to be very reliable, must also take into account the physiological state of the organism or, as the psychologist is more apt to put it, the previous conditioning of the organism. But even unconditioned responses vary within the species according to age, size, sex, and many other factors. For the question of reduction, however, these complicating factors can, as it were, be held constant.
14. For a discussion which touches on this issue see Lazarsfeld (1958).
15. Three of the best pieces directed toward that conclusion are Moore (1951), "External and Internal Relations"; Ryle (1935); and Bergmann (1964), "Synthetic *A Priori*."
16. The laws of human behavior, as they would usually be understood, are not process laws. Yet if determinism is true then for every piece of behavior there will be a process law or set of laws which in conjunction with the statement of some antecedent conditions will yield deductively

the statement that that piece of behavior occurs. This is only to say that in practice the psychologists and the social scientists consider only the most important of the "independent" variables in their theorizing.

17. This, as we have seen, breaks down into several possibilities for the emergentist since he has two distinct groups of sociological variables; but I shall conflate these here simply to *process/nonprocess*.

18. I use these expressions here instead of *explanatory reductionism* and *explanatory emergentism* respectively simply to avoid confusion with the issue referred to by *reductionist/nonreductionist* above.

Chapter VI

1. For a useful summary of some of the many kinds see Passmore (1962).

2. So says Ryle, for example, in his introduction to *The Concept of Mind*. But what follows in the remainder of the book is, if I am not mistaken, a defense of one of the traditional theories of what a mind is and not merely an attempt to "rectify the logical geography of the knowledge which we already possess." See Ryle (1949), p. 7.

3. There are, of course, genuine philosophical issues concerning how we think about the world. But here thought is simply being treated as itself *part* of the world and not that through which all reflection on the world must be filtered.

4. See in particular the section entitled "Imperfect Knowledge" in Bergmann (1957); and also Brodbeck (1962).

5. In a private communication Donagan claims that I have not understood him correctly in my interpretation of his text that follows. Although in a sense he is the final judge of what his words mean, I shall leave it to the reader to decide whether my paraphrase of those words is adequate or not.

6. Donagan (1964), pp. 18–19.

7. This formulation comes essentially from Bergmann (1954), p. 65.

8. Another way of saying this is that, contrary to the hopes of some social scientists, behavioral science will never have its Newton. Or, if you like, just by being science at all it has already happened, and the person was — Newton.

9. In the biological cases there will be near-universal laws such as: if anything is an acorn and it doesn't die, then it will become a sapling and then an oak tree.

10. Bergmann so calls them. See the section entitled "Historical Laws" in Bergmann (1957).

11. I don't mean this in the now trivial sense in which every opinion as held by each of us depends in some measure on factors of personality. Views on these issues, and especially that of free will, seem to be so dependent to an unusual degree.

Chapter VII

1. Mandelbaum (1957).

2. For great detail on the historical side of the issue see Mandelbaum (1971).

3. For an analysis of this particular school see Goldstein (1967).

4. It doesn't matter for our purposes what we take to be the "elements" of society, whether, for example, individual persons or institutions.

5. Strictly speaking, there is the possibility that there are some laws of historical development which are and some which are not deducible from the laws of the interaction of the elements. The details of this possibility can be put together, should anyone want to, from the discussion of the next several pages.

6. I ignore here two complications: the possibility of statistical laws of historical development; and the "problem" of counterfactuals. The latter I can safely ignore because, whatever its solution, the distinction between laws and accidental generalities must be maintained. As to the former, the distinction between accidental statistical generalities and genuine statistical laws would allow me to make the same arguments.

7. That is, this is the only possibility if we assume that the world, including human society, is deterministic. Conceivably, there could be nondeducible laws of historical development the subject matter of which does or does not interact back with some of a set of variables which are not either in themselves deterministic or the proper subset of any such set.

8. He seems to suggest that it is up to human beings, who are somehow both inside and outside these laws, to make sure that the laws are instanced in history. See Lukács (1967).

9. Lichtheim (1967), p. 38.

10. That is, these properties (or rather their names) are nondefinable in terms of (the names of) the properties which characterize the elements of society. Some of these properties of social wholes, if there were any, might be definable in terms of some others of the same sort, but at least some would have to be simple.

11. This, as we saw in the fourth chapter, seems to be at least part of Durkheim's reason for his emergentism.

12. Popper (1957), p. 3, Popper's emphasis.

13. Bergmann (1944), p. 219, Bergmann's emphases.

14. *Ibid.*

15. Goldstein (1967).

16. Popper (1957), pp. 108–109, Popper's emphasis.

17. *Ibid.*, pp. ix–x.

18. *Ibid.*, p. x, Popper's emphases.

19. *Ibid.*, p. xi.

20. *Ibid.*, pp. x–xi.

21. *Ibid.*, p. x, Popper's emphases.

22. This point is similar to the one I made earlier about Goldstein's distinction between "developmental" and "causal" laws. Popper almost seems to make the same point in Popper (1963), p. 342.

23. *Ibid.*, p. 341.

24. *Ibid.*, p. 342, Popper's emphases.

25. *Ibid.*

26. *Ibid.*, p. 344.

Chapter VIII

1. My reason, once more, is not that determinism is not true, or that there are nonnatural factors which make a difference, or that lawful (causal) explanation is somehow inappropriate to the social sciences, but rather that what are usually taken to be the social variables do not come close to being a causally closed set.

2. One thinks first, perhaps, of Plekhanov's *On the Development of the Monist View of History*, but this is more a defense of "materialism" in general than of a monistic theory of society; and its title, now often preceded by the original *In Defence of Materialism*, was chosen in order to get it past the censor of the czar anyway. In my opinion, the best defense of what is monistic about the Marxist social theory is Bukharin's *Historical Materialism*. It is surely the most detailed.

3. Hook (1940), pp. 263–264.

4. Plamenatz (1963), p. 285.

5. *Ibid.*, p. 283.

6. *Ibid.*

7. *Ibid.*, pp. 283–284.

8. *Ibid.*, pp. 284–285, Plamenatz's emphasis.

9. *Ibid.*, p. 285.

10. *Ibid.*, pp. 289–290.

11. *Ibid.*, p. 290.

12. *Ibid.*, p. 283.

13. Addis (1966), p. 113.

14. See the last part of the seventh chapter.

Chapter IX

1. Mannheim (1968), especially the second chapter.

2. For example, the questions of truth and causation are clearly separated in Berger and Luckmann (1967).

3. In some measure this claim, at least in Mannheim's own case, derives from the Hegelian context in which the "truth is in the whole" to begin with, so that in no case can any particular belief be "true."

4. For a discussion of the historical development of the notion of ideology see Lichtheim (1967), "The Concept of Ideology."

5. For further analysis along these lines see Bergmann (1951).

6. MacIntyre (1971), p. 258.

7. Marx and Engels (1959), p. 408.

8. I am thinking especially of Lukács in his *History and Class Consciousness*.

9. Lenin and Bukharin were only two of the most prominent who held some such views. I offer the following passages as representative of their views.

Consciousness in general reflects being — this is the general position of *all* materialism. It is impossible not to see its direct and *inseparable* connection with the position of historical materialism, that is, that social consciousness *reflects* social being. (Lenin (1927), p. 278, Lenin's emphases.)

Since materialism in general explains consciousness as the outcome of being, and not conversely, materialism as applied to the social life of mankind had to explain *social* consciousness as the outcome of *social* being. (Lenin (1964), p. 18, Lenin's emphases.)

Everyone will understand that this dispute between materialism and idealism cannot possibly fail to be expressed in the social sciences also. In fact, human society presents a number of phenomena of various kinds. For instance, we find "exalted matters" such as religion, philosophy and morality; we also find innumerable ideas held by men, in various fields; we find an exchange of goods or a distribution of products; we find a struggle between various classes among themselves; there is a production of products, wheat, rye, shoes, machinery, varying with the time and place. How shall we proceed to explain this society? From what angle shall we approach it? What shall we consider its fundamental element, and what its secondary, or resulting element? All these are *obviously the same questions* that have been faced by philosophy and that have necessarily divided the philosophers into two great camps — that of the materialists and that of the idealists. (Bukharin (1969), pp. 58–59, my emphasis.)

10. Sartre (1963).

11. Ortega y Gasset (1961).

12. I have tried to demonstrate that Ryle is such a one in Addis and Lewis (1965), "Ryle's Ontology of Mind."

Chapter X

1. Brodbeck (1958), p. 21.

2. Addis (1966), pp. 111–112.

3. Brodbeck (1968), p. 242, Brodbeck's emphases.

4. Plekhanov (1940).

5. Even that is not quite accurate. There is always the question of whether the "different" actions of the one(s) who would have occupied the social role of the person in question had he not existed would have produced essentially the same results. Partly this is a matter of our second broad meaning of the question of the role of the individual in history, partly one of *deciding* what to mean by "same" and "different" action, whether, for example, to characterize actions in terms of intention, of execution, or of consequences.

6. It will be nontrivial if the values of the sociological variable vary with some variations in the individuals' behavior. The commonsense idea is that we can effect a change in many ways; but

there must be a limit. If the change occurs no matter what we do, then that limit has been far surpassed.

7. I am referring to the discussion of psychophysiological parallelism. Purposes as conscious states are connected by laws of coexistence to brain states which "in turn" are connected to behavioral states.

8. See especially Hempel (1959).

9. Baier (1957).

10. For any given state of affairs to occur, others of course must not.

Chapter XI

1. Furthermore, it is the Marxism of Marx I am concerned with, not the somewhat different Marxism of Engels or the very different Marxism of Lenin and other Russian commentators.

2. For the historical and more or less systematic development of the varieties of dialectical materialism see Jordan (1967). For a point of view similar to mine but with greater detail concerning the relation between dialectical materialism and historical materialism see Plamenatz (1963), pp. 269–273. For the most sophisticated Marxist defense of historical materialism see Bukharin (1969).

3. That is, the facts that people do not all have the same values *and* that there is no agreed upon method of finding out even in principle who is "right" (the latter being unlike the situation in science and everyday disagreement about perceptual facts) seem to call for some kind of special explanation from one who holds that there are moral "facts" of which we can be aware.

4. This theory I call Aristotelian is stated most directly in some of the essays in Marx (1963).

5. Tucker (1961). Tucker "interprets" Marx's theories as the expression of a religious conception of the world.

6. Here the use of 'ideological' is that of its origin; that of ideas being considered with respect to their causal origins and not necessarily as distorted in any way.

7. Marx and Engels found it very important to emphasize the historical side of the theory in order to contrast it with those theories which emphasized the "natural" character or aspects of the existing society, where the notion of the "natural" serves the ideological function of seeming to bridge the logically unbridgeable gap between the idea of what (to someone's mind) shouldn't be changed and that of what can't be changed. Of course Marx's theory is also naturalistic insofar as it is an attempt at a scientific account of the phenomena.

8. For further discussion of this issue see Plamenatz (1963), pp. 290–293.

9. Marx and more particularly Engels systematically overestimate how great the difference is between their general methodology and that of previous scientific practice. It ought not to be a methodological question at all what "things" change and in what respects. If some earlier scientists and philosophers judged certain relatively unchanging aspects of the world to be absolutely so or even as laws of nature (or instances of such laws) they were wrong to be sure. Species change and so do solar systems as well as social systems although many changes may be difficult to "perceive," slow and long-range as they are. Understanding things in their interactions with each other is hardly an innovation of Marx, but simply good scientific practice for centuries preceding him. Newton as much as Marx tried to understand what interacts with what and the laws of the interactions as well as what is relatively or even absolutely permanent in the world.

10. Addis (1966), p. 113.

11. Hook, as we saw in the eighth chapter, seems to maintain this. See Hook (1940), chapter 11.

12. Addis (1966), p. 113. In a well-known passage Engels denied that he and Marx were economic determinists in one sense at least:

> According to the materialist conception of history, the *ultimately* determining element in history is the production and reproduction of real life. More than this neither Marx nor I has ever asserted. Hence if somebody twists this into saying that the economic element is the *only* determining one he transforms that proposition into a meaningless, abstract, senseless phrase.

The economic situation is the basis, but the various elements of the superstructure — political forms of the class struggle and its results, to wit: constitutions established by the victorious class after a successful battle, etc., juridical forms, and even the reflexes of all these actual struggles in the brains of the participants, political, juristic, philosophical theories, religious views, and their further development into systems of dogmas — also exercise their influence upon the course of the historical struggles and in many cases preponderate in determining their *form*. There is an interaction of all these elements in which, amidst all the endless host of accidents (that is, of things and events whose inner interconnection is so remote or so impossible of proof that we can regard it as non-existent, as negligible), the economic movement finally asserts itself as necessary. Otherwise the application of the theory to any period of history would be easier than the solution of a simple equation of the first degree. (Marx and Engels (1959), pp. 397–398, Engels's emphases.)

13. It must be remembered, however, that with a different notion of causation one might hold that while the values of A and B are strictly computable functions of each other, still A is the cause of B and B is not the, or a, cause of A. Can one ascribe any philosophical theory of causation to Marx?

14. Consider the following passages, for instance:

It is not "history" which uses men as a means of achieving — as if it were an individual person — *its* own ends. History is *nothing* but the activity of men in pursuit of their ends. (Marx (1964), p. 63, Marx's emphases.)

It is above all necessary to avoid postulating "society" once more as an abstraction confronting the individual. (Marx (1964), p. 77.)

Society is not merely an aggregate of individuals; it is the sum of the relations in which these individuals stand to each other. (Marx (1964), p. 96.)

15. Marx (1964), p. 51.

16. As we saw in the fourth chapter, Durkheim argues in his *Rules of Sociological Method* that because some of our ways of feeling and acting and especially those of obligation may appear to us as externally imposed we may conclude that there are "social facts," that is, "things" whose properties are not reducible to the properties and relations of individual persons.

17. In general I am thinking of those who ascribe to Marx a "sociological determinism" and not just those relatively few who use the language of "process."

18. Consider the following rather surprising passage, at least with respect to the way Marx is frequently understood:

The form of this relation between masters and producers always necessarily corresponds to a definite stage in the development of the methods of work and consequently of the social productivity of labour. This does not prevent an economic basis which in its principal characteristics is the same, from manifesting infinite variations and gradations, owing to the effect of innumerable external circumstances, climatic and geographical influences, racial peculiarities, historical influences from the outside, etc. These variations can only be discovered by analysing these empirically given circumstances. (Marx (1964), pp. 99–100.)

19. That is, it doesn't apply in absolutely every case though it may be true in most.

20. Popper takes the famous passage in the preface to *A Contribution to the Critique of Political Economy* in which Marx affirms that "it is not the consciousness of men that determines their being, but, on the contrary, their social being that determines their consciousness" as proof of Marx's having rejected the thesis that sociology can be reduced to psychology. (Popper (1962), p. 89.) Popper reasons that if social behavior is determined by environmental and especially cultural factors even in part, then the laws of such behavior cannot be reduced to the laws of psychology. But, as we saw in the fifth chapter, it is not quite that simple. If a "psychological" explanation is only one that explains human behavior in nonsocial contexts, it may be that the same factors are operative in social contexts and the reduction therefore possible. Popper seems to take a "psychological" explanation as one in which environmental and cultural factors would be irrelevant. I think we can grant that the passage of Marx quoted above implies that such explanations are not possible for all human behavior. Indeed one may wonder whether

Marx or anyone else ever seriously believed that such an explanation can be given for *any* human behavior at all, if environmental and cultural factors must be taken to be utterly irrelevant.

21. As, for example, in the well-known passage:

Intrinsically, it is not a question of the higher or lower degree of development of the social antagonisms that result from the natural laws of capitalist production. It is a question of these laws themselves, of these tendencies working with iron necessity towards inevitable results. The country that is more developed industrially only shows, to the less developed, the image of its own future. (Marx (1967), pp. 8–9.)

22. Marx is sometimes also "accused" of "moral historicism," that is, moral relativism. Historicism sometimes also means the idea that there are laws of historical development whether deducible or not. Marx is one of the deducible sort. But most often, and especially as applied to a certain kind of German historiography, it denotes a kind of intellectual hodgepodge that asserts roughly that every historical period is unique and must be "judged" according to the laws or concepts or values peculiarly appropriate to it. Ideologically, this kind of historicism is the expression of the desire to enhance the uniqueness and the status of the German nationalist state (or the Soviet socialist state in its "Marxist" version). Intellectually, it derives from three specific confusions: (1) Facts are not clearly separated from values so that one moves from the idea that values are "relative" or "subjective" or peculiar to their culture to the conclusion that all knowledge or at least all social knowledge is peculiar to the individual society. (2) Uniqueness of historical events is confused with or given as a reason for their nonsubsumability under general laws. In fact, the sense in which a historical event or a culture or a period is unique is the same in which everything is unique and in no way implies the impossibility of explanation by general laws. (3) Laws are confused with their instances or variables with their values. Whether one needs a different set of laws to explain, say, the effects of investment in capitalist societies from the effects of investment in socialist societies may depend only on the generality of the laws one is using. In any case there will always be considerable overlap in the laws which explain social phenomena in all societies even at the lowest level of generality. Otherwise the "law" runs the risk of being so specific as to be trivial.

23. Such laws may, of course, be in whole or in part what I earlier called polychronal laws, that is, laws which mention two or more states of different times in their antecedents.

24. Addis (1966), pp. 115–117.

25. Except in the trivial logical sense of which a few make so much. That is the sense in which whatever will be will be, just as whatever was was, and whatever is is. But then, contrary to what some of those few maintain, this kind of "logical fatalism" is also consistent with causal indeterminism.

26. As for example in this passage: "Men make their own history, but they do not make it just as they please; they do not make it under circumstances chosen by themselves, but under circumstances directly encountered, given, and transmitted from the past." (Marx and Engels (1959), p. 320.)

27. Marx and Engels (1959), p. 399, Engels's emphasis.

28. *Ibid.*, p. 109.

29. For discussion of some of Lenin's philosophical confusions and inadequacies on this area see Jordan (1967).

30. See Croce (1966), for example. One may doubt, however, whether Croce ever really subscribed to historical materialism.

31. Perhaps it would be better here to call it Marx's philosophy of history or even simply his philosophy since as I characterize naturalism its principles are of a rather high level of generality with application beyond the study of society.

Bibliography

Abel, Theodore. "The Operation Called *Verstehen*," *American Journal of Sociology*, 54 (1948), reprinted in Feigl and Brodbeck (1953).
Addis, Laird. "Freedom and the Marxist Philosophy of History," *Philosophy of Science*, 33 (1966), reprinted as "The Individual and the Marxist Philosophy of History" in Brodbeck (1968).
Addis, Laird, and Douglas Lewis. *Moore and Ryle: Two Ontologists*. The Hague: Martinus Nijhoff, 1965.
Baier, Kurt. *The Meaning of Life*. Canberra: Commonwealth Government Printer, 1957.
Berger, Peter L., and Thomas Luckmann. *The Social Construction of Reality*. New York: Doubleday Anchor, 1967.
Bergmann, Gustav. "Holism, Historicism, and Emergence," *Philosophy of Science*, 11 (1944).
Bergmann, Gustav. "Ideology," *Ethics*, 61 (1951), reprinted in Bergmann (1967).
Bergmann, Gustav. "Reduction," in *Current Trends in Psychology and the Behavioral Sciences* (no editor named). Pittsburgh: University of Pittsburgh Press, 1954.
Bergmann, Gustav. *Philosophy of Science*. Madison: University of Wisconsin Press, 1957.
Bergmann, Gustav. "Acts," *Indian Journal of Philosophy*, 2 (1960), reprinted in Bergmann (1964).
Bergmann, Gustav. *Logic and Reality*. Madison: University of Wisconsin Press, 1964.
Bergmann, Gustav. *The Metaphysics of Logical Positivism*. Madison: University of Wisconsin Press, 1967.
Brodbeck, May. "Methodological Individualisms: Definition and Reduction," *Philosophy of Science*, 25 (1958), reprinted in Brodbeck (1968).
Brodbeck, May. "Explanation, Prediction, and 'Imperfect' Knowledge," in Feigl and Maxwell (1962), reprinted in Brodbeck (1968).
Brodbeck, May. "Meaning and Action," *Philosophy of Science*, 30 (1963), reprinted in Brodbeck (1968).
Brodbeck, May (ed.). *Readings in the Philosophy of the Social Sciences*. New York: Macmillan, 1968.
Bukharin, Nikolai. *Historical Materialism* (no translator named). Ann Arbor: University of Michigan Press, 1969.
Croce, Benedetto. *Historical Materialism and the Economics of Karl Marx* (trans. C. M. Meredith). New York: Russell and Russell, 1966.
Donagan, Alan. "The Popper-Hempel Theory Reconsidered," *History and Theory*, 4 (1964), reprinted in Dray (1966).
Dray, William H. (ed.). *Philosophical Analysis and History*. New York: Harper & Row, 1966.
Durkheim, Emile. *The Rules of Sociological Method* (trans. Sarah A. Solovay and John H. Mueller; ed. George E. G. Catlin). New York: Free Press, 1964.

Feigl, Herbert, and May Brodbeck (eds.). *Readings in the Philosophy of Science*. New York: Appleton-Century-Crofts, 1953.
Feigl, Herbert, and Grover Maxwell (eds.). *Minnesota Studies in the Philosophy of Science*, vol. 3. Minneapolis: University of Minnesota Press, 1962.
Gerwitz, Jacob L. "Mechanisms of Social Learning: Some Roles of Stimulation and Behavior in Early Human Development," in Goslin (1969).
Goldmann, Lucien. *The Human Sciences and Philosophy* (trans. Hayden V. White and Robert Anchor). London: Jonathan Cape, 1969.
Goldstein, Leon J. "Theory in Anthropology: Developmental or Causal?" in Gross (1967).
Goslin, David A. (ed.). *Handbook of Socialization Theory and Research*. Chicago: Rand McNally, 1969.
Gross, Llewellyn (ed.). *Symposium on Sociological Theory*. New York: Harper & Row, 1959.
Gross, Llewellyn (ed.). *Sociological Theory: Inquiries and Paradigms*. New York: Harper & Row, 1967.
Hempel, Carl G. "The Logic of Functional Analysis," in Gross (1959), reprinted in Brodbeck (1968).
Hook, Sidney. *Reason, Social Myths and Democracy*. New York: John Ray Company, 1940.
Jordan, Z. A. *The Evolution of Dialectical Materialism*. New York: St. Martin's Press, 1967.
Laslett, Peter, and W. G. Runciman (eds.). *Philosophy, Politics and Society*, 2nd series. Oxford: Basil Blackwell, 1967.
Lazarsfeld, Paul F. "Evidence and Inference in Social Research," *Daedalus*, 87 (1958), reprinted in Brodbeck (1968).
Lenin, Vladimir Il'ich. *Materialism and Empirio-Criticism* (trans. David Kvitko), *Collected Works*, vol. 13. New York: International Publishers, 1927.
Lenin, Vladimir Il'ich. *The Teachings of Karl Marx* (no translator named). New York: International Publishers, 1964.
Lichtheim, George. *The Concept of Ideology and Other Essays*. New York: Vintage Books, 1967.
Lukács, Georg. *History and Class Consciousness* (trans. Rodney Livingstone). Cambridge: MIT Press, 1967.
MacIntyre, Alasdair. "A Mistake about Causality in Social Science," in Laslett and Runciman (1967).
MacIntyre, Alasdair. *Against the Self-Images of the Age*. New York: Schocken Books, 1971.
Mandelbaum, Maurice. "Societal Laws," *British Journal for the Philosophy of Science*, 8 (1957), reprinted in Dray (1966).
Mandelbaum, Maurice. *History, Man, and Reason*. Baltimore: Johns Hopkins University Press, 1971.
Mannheim, Karl. *Ideology and Utopia* (trans. Louis Wirth and Edward Shils). New York: Harcourt, Brace and World, 1968.
Marx, Karl. *Early Writings* (trans. and ed. T. B. Bottomore). London: C. A. Watts, 1963.
Marx, Karl. *Selected Writings in Sociology and Social Philosophy* (trans. T. B. Bottomore; ed. T. B. Bottomore and Maximilien Rubel). New York: McGraw-Hill, 1964.
Marx, Karl. *Capital*, vol. 1 (no translator named; ed. Friedrich Engels). New York: International Publishers, 1967.
Marx, Karl, and Friedrich Engels. *Basic Writings on Politics and Philosophy* (ed. Lewis S. Feuer). New York: Doubleday Anchor, 1959.
Moore, G. E. *Philosophical Studies*. New York: Humanities Press, 1951.
Nadel, George H. (ed.). *Studies in the Philosophy of History*. New York: Harper & Row, 1965.
Nagel, Ernest. *The Structure of Science*. New York: Harcourt, Brace and World, 1961.
Ortega y Gasset, José. *History as a System* (trans. Helene Weyl). New York: W. W. Norton, 1961.
Ortega y Gasset, José. *Man and People* (trans. Willard R. Trask). New York: W. W. Norton, 1963.
Passmore, John. "Explanation in Everyday Life, in Science, and in History," *History and Theory*, 2 (1962), reprinted in Nadel (1965).

Plamenatz, John. *Man and Society*, vol. 2. New York: McGraw-Hill, 1963.
Plekhanov, George. *The Role of the Individual in History* (no translator named). New York: International Publishers, 1940.
Plekhanov, George. *In Defence of Materialism: The Development of the Monist View of History* (trans. Andrew Rothstein). London: Lawrence and Wishart, 1947.
Popper, Karl. *The Poverty of Historicism*. Boston: Beacon Press, 1957.
Popper, Karl. *The Open Society and Its Enemies*, vol. 2. London: Routledge and Kegan Paul, 1962.
Popper, Karl. *Conjectures and Refutations*. London: Routledge and Kegan Paul, 1963.
Quine, Willard Van Orman. *From a Logical Point of View*. Cambridge, Mass.: Harvard University Press, 1961.
Russell, Bertrand. *Mysticism and Logic*. New York: Doubleday Anchor, 1957.
Ryle, Gilbert. "Internal Relations," in *Science, History, and Theology*, Aristotelian Society Supplementary volume 16. London: Harrison and Sons, 1935.
Ryle, Gilbert. *The Concept of Mind*. New York: Barnes and Noble, 1949.
Sartre, Jean-Paul. *Search for a Method* (trans. Hazel F. Barnes). New York: Vintage Books, 1963.
Sidowski, Joseph B., L. Benjamin Wyckoff, and Leon Tabory. "The Influence of Reinforcement and Punishment in a Minimal Social Situation," *Journal of Abnormal Social Psychology*, 52 (1956).
Skinner, B. F. *Science and Human Behavior*. New York: Macmillan, 1953.
Staats, Arthur W., and Carolyn K. Staats. *Complex Human Behavior*. New York: Holt, Rinehart and Winston, 1964.
Tucker, Robert C. *Philosophy and Myth in Karl Marx*. Cambridge: At the University Press, 1961.
Weber, Max. *The Theory of Social and Economic Organization* (trans. A. M. Henderson and Talcott Parsons; ed. Talcott Parsons). New York: Oxford University Press, 1947.
Wright, Georg Henrik von. *Explanation and Understanding*. Ithaca: Cornell University Press, 1971.

Index

Index